Pedagogy, Policy,

and the

Privatized City

*Stories of Dispossession and Defiance
from New Orleans*

Pedagogy, Policy,
and the
Privatized City

*Stories of Dispossession and Defiance
from New Orleans*

KRISTEN L. BURAS
WITH JIM RANDELS, KALAMU YA SALAAM,
AND STUDENTS AT THE CENTER

*Foreword by Robin D. G. Kelley
Afterword by Zeus Leonardo*

Teachers College, Columbia University
New York and London

Published by Teachers College Press, 1234 Amsterdam Avenue, New York, NY 10027

This research was made possible by a grant from Emory University Research Committee.

Chapter 1 is adapted from "We have to tell our story": Neo-Griots, Racial Resistance, and Schooling in the Other South, Kristen L. Buras, *Race Ethnicity and Education*, *12*(4), 2009, Taylor & Francis Ltd., reprinted by permission of Taylor & Francis Ltd.

"Still Here" from *The Collected Poems of Langston Hughes* by Langston Hughes, edited by Arnold Rampersad with David Roessel, Associate Editor, copyright © 1994 by the Estate of Langston Hughes. Used by permission of Alfred A. Knopf, a division of Random House, Inc.

Library of Congress Cataloging-in-Publication Data

Pedagogy, policy, and the privatized city : stories of dispossession and defiance from New Orleans / Kristen L. Buras, Jim Randels, Kalamu ya Salaam, and Students at the Center, foreword by Robin D. G. Kelley.
    p. cm.
  Includes bibliographical references and index.
  ISBN 978-0-8077-5089-6 (pbk.)—ISBN 978-0-8077-5090-2 (hardcover)
1. Hurricane Katrina, 2005—Social aspects—Louisiana—New Orleans. 2. Disaster victims—Louisiana—New Orleans. 3. Community life—Louisiana—New Orleans. 4. Education and state—Louisiana—New Orleans. 5. Educational change—Louisiana—New Orleans. 6. Racism in education—Louisiana—New Orleans. 7. Racism—Political aspects—Louisiana—New Orleans. 8. New Orleans (La.)—Race relations. 9. New Orleans (La.)—Social conditions. I. Buras, Kristen L. II. Randels, Jim. III. Salaam, Kalamu ya, 1947–
  HV6362005.N4 P44 2010
  379.763'35—dc22

                                                                                        2009053257

ISBN 978-0-8077-5089-6 (paper)
ISBN 978-0-8077-5090-2 (hardcover)

Printed on acid-free paper
Manufactured in the United States of America

17   16   15   14   13   12   11   10   8   7   6   5   4   3   2   1

For Z—
May the lessons you taught be learned

Contents

FORWARD!

On the Freedom Dreams of Young Race Rebels

Robin D. G. Kelley

S OMEONE RECENTLY asked me, "So as black parents, how do we raise more
Barack Obamas?"

"You mean future presidents?" I asked.

"No, not necessarily. I mean intelligent, well-spoken, self-confident
people; comfortable around white people and people of different races."

I'd heard this before, many times during the Q&A sessions after talks
I've given or in casual conversation with folks obsessed with the plight of
young black men and women. The question boils down to the choice between prison versus the presidency, and the outcome presumably hinges
on one's behavior, attitude, level of education, mastery of language, and
comfort level with the ruling class.

The question and the intentions behind it rang familiar, but I had just
finished reading *Pedagogy, Policy, and the Privatized City*, and what I learned
from this remarkable book helped me see that the question demanded
an urgent response. Of course we want intelligent, self-confident children, but I want to raise critical thinkers who care about their community
and the world around them, women and men who are *not* comfortable
with neoliberal policies or with men in suits who proclaim themselves
leaders, policy makers, "czars," and the like and decide on the fate of
a people without ever asking what they want. I don't want to prepare
our children to run an empire or get rich at the expense of others. I'd
much rather raise kids who are uncomfortable with injustice, war, displacement, violence, inequality, and an economy built on imprisonment
and privatization, and who can dream and collectively struggle their way
out of our constrictions. We don't need more Obamas; we do need more
young people like Christopher Burton, Deborah Carey, Bruce Coleman,
Tyeasha Green, Maria Hernandez, Jenna Dominique Hill, Ashley Jones,

Vinnessia Shelbia, Damien and Kirsten Theodore, Gabrielle Turner, and Demetria White. And we need more educators like Jim Randels, Kalamu ya Salaam, Katrena Jackson-Ndang, Erica DeCuir, and Kristen Buras. And we need more spaces like Students at the Center (SAC)—free spaces of love, dialogue, consciousness, and community building; spaces devoted to telling and realizing our counterstories.

Pedagogy, Policy, and the Privatized City is more than a compelling, inspiring read. It is one of the most radical works of collaboration I've seen since 1973, when a group of black women welfare rights activists in Mt. Vernon, New York, put together a nearly forgotten text titled *Lessons from the Damned*, authored by "The Damned." Like the present book, it was a collective project; its anonymous essays by adults and children in the neighborhood critique the school system, modes of public assistance, gender relations, racism, and capitalism. Some of the chapter titles include "The Revolt of Poor Black Women" and "The Capitalism System's Family: An Analysis by Four 16-Year-Old Young Women." *Pedagogy, Policy, and the Privatized City* grows out of that radical tradition of cooperative work, and like *Lessons from the Damned*, it was forged in crisis—specifically in the wake of post-Katrina capitalist dreams to expropriate poor black folk, eliminate public housing, privatize public schools and hospitals, and turn New Orleans into neoliberalism's model city. Just consider the fact that in the spring of 2007—nearly two years after Katrina—only 19 out of 117 schools had reportedly opened, 7,500 teachers and staff had been fired, and no money had been allocated for public schools. Yet the federal government under George W. Bush sent $4.8 million to fund private and charter schools (Welfare Warriors, 2007).

Pedagogy, Policy, and the Privatized City beautifully documents the work of SAC—before and after the hurricane—its collective pedagogy of transformation, and the context for its work. As public schools are disappearing at an alarming rate, SAC pushes on, encouraging the freedom dreams of New Orleans youth who were suffering from catastrophic conditions of poverty and racism *before* Katrina. The brilliance of SAC lay in its process: storytelling and careful listening rooted in nonhierarchical, consensus-building practice that focuses on strengthening community. Jim Randels and Kalamu ya Salaam create space to enable young people not only to tell their story but to critique society, to understand why their schools are bad, why developers are pushing them off the land, why opportunities are so elusive, and what is special about New Orleans, its legacy, and the struggle over its future. These very kids—the ones too often dismissed as future inmates or projects to be turned into future Obamas—can invoke the revolutionary legacy of the New Orleans slave revolt of 1811 while recognizing that their precious Crescent City is ground zero for neoliberalism. Indeed, what makes SAC and these young people so special is their attentiveness to place and power. They demand their right to return, to have access to good schools and housing, to live as a community of human beings. They know the enemy and can name it. And they know the exit and can imagine it.

SAC's work grows out of a much older tradition of freedom schools, first organized in neighboring Mississippi by the Student Non-Violent Coordinating Committee (SNCC) nearly half a century ago. Recognizing that the Jim Crow school system was designed to produce subjects, not empowered citizens, freedom school organizers created their own pedagogy of transformation, turning church basements, parish halls, and shady lawns into spaces for young people to tell their counterstories and imagine how they might turn Mississippi and the entire nation into a more caring, democratic place. The teachers asked children to reflect on the difference between "material things" and "soul things," whether they really want what the dominant culture had, and the kinds of resources they possess as a community that sustained them and could possibly sustain a new society. Students and teachers were changed in the process, coming to terms with a vision of society that rejected integration into a burning house in favor of a radical transformation of the entire house.

Of course, just as SAC builds on the legacy of the civil rights movement, the freedom schools had their own antecedents, going back to Reconstruction and the first schools built by post-emancipation black communities, to the Highlander Folk School and South Carolina's Septima Clarke, whose vision of "citizenship education" combined storytelling, political analysis, song, and collaborative readings of arcane voting laws and the UN Declaration of Human Rights. It was dangerous work. White mobs burned school houses to the ground; teachers and students often worked in fear, and some lost their lives; what folks learned was monitored and policed, but the pursuit of freedom education never wavered. And today freedom schooling continues to live, not only in New Orleans but in places such as Bushwick, Brooklyn, where the collective Sista II Sista run their own freedom schools for young women, and Detroit through the wonderful work of Grace Lee Boggs and the Boggs Center. There, teachers and students together have created a community curriculum to "empower" children to become "change agents and decision makers" committed to working "together to change the community." The work continues. The river never ceases to flow. And it is still dangerous.

So, no, we don't need to train more polite, friendly, likeable Obamas. We need more counterstories, more challenges to policies of privatization, privilege, profit, and war (here and abroad), and more spaces like SAC where young people can be active agents in their education and architects of our future—a future we can glimpse in the pages of this book. As long as we support the work, struggle relentlessly for what Kalamu ya Salaam calls "education for liberation, not education for mainstream socialization," future generations might just live the freedom dreams of these young people who refuse to stay on the margins.

Introduction

Counterstories on Pedagogy and Policy Making: Coming of Age in the Privatized City

Kristen L. Buras

REFLECTING ON THE significance of the "freedom dreams" that guided black radical activism in the past, historian Robin D. G. Kelley (2002) warns: "Too often our standards for evaluating social movements pivot around whether or not they 'succeeded' in realizing their visions rather than on the merits or power of the visions themselves" (p. ix). So important are these visions that Kelley seeks to unearth and redeem the critiques, concerns, and desires that inspired liberation movements involving black communists, black feminists, third world resisters, and others. The question that remains, Kelley urges, is "What are today's young activists dreaming about?" (p. 7). Although this question should figure centrally in efforts to "improve" schools and "revitalize" communities, it is scarcely asked. Too rarely do those working in educational policy and reform listen to the voices of racially marginalized groups or the stories of African American, Asian American, Latino, and Native American youth in urban schools. Even in teacher education, which presumably is focused on preparing educators to work effectively with youth, the insights and experiences of students are infrequently sought (Ginwright, Noguera, & Cammarota, 2006). In *The Subaltern Speak* (2006), Michael Apple and I emphasize the long tradition of struggle for voice and cultural recognition that has shaped education, an arena indisputably characterized by unequal relations of power and intense battles over "whose knowledge" matters most. It was precisely this concern over voice that led critical race theorists in the fields of law and education to embrace and defend the necessity of *counterstories*, stories that foreground the experiential knowledge of communities of color in order to counter majoritarian narratives that have been normalized and circulated by dominant groups as the only legitimate view of reality (Delgado, 2000; Solórzano & Yosso, 2002; Yosso, 2006). Perhaps critical race legal scholar Charles Lawrence (1995) put it

1

most eloquently in "The Word and the River: Pedagogy as Scholarship as Struggle":

> Storytelling, the articulation of experience and imagination in narrative, poetry, and song, is an important part of the tradition of African peoples. . . . Litigation is highly formalized storytelling. . . . But the law's tradition of storytelling is very different from the African tradition. Where our tradition values rich contextual detail, the law excludes large parts of the story as irrelevant. . . . Our stories have, for the most part, not been told or recorded in the literature that is law. . . . When we are seen, in stories told by others, our images are severely distorted by the lenses of fear, bias, and misunderstanding. . . . Giving narrative form to [our] experience creates a rich evidentiary record for analysis and assessment of complex social processes. (pp. 343–345)

This is precisely what teachers and students do in *Pedagogy, Policy, and the Privatized City: Stories of Dispossession and Defiance from New Orleans*. Offering accounts of their lives, schools, neighborhoods, and city, educators and youth affiliated with Students at the Center—a critical writing program based in several public high schools in New Orleans over the past decade—challenge teachers, teacher educators, and educational policy makers across the nation to consider how the racial history of New Orleans as well as the destructive and accelerated neoliberal experimentation that has unfolded since Hurricane Katrina represent a window onto larger issues of urban school reform and ongoing struggles for cultural and economic justice. As the teachers and co-directors of Students at the Center, Jim Randels and Kalamu ya Salaam, explain in the second part of this introduction:

> In New Orleans, we do have a new moment. But it is not a moment out of time. And it is not a story that only those in power will tell. This book is about the two sides of the starting point—the new day and the old realities. . . . Without this full picture, our public education, our culture, our souls cannot continue to grow. Without imparting the knowledge of and action in history and struggle, we cannot teach our children well.

Echoing their concerns are numerous critical educators—Michael Apple, Wayne Au, Adrienne Dixson, Maisha Fisher, Joyce King, Zeus Leonardo, Pauline Lipman, and Vanessa Siddle Walker—who bring their own knowledge of history and research as activist scholars to bear on the issues at the center of this book. Each responds to Randels, Salaam, and students, thoughtfully reflecting on the students' experiences with coming of age in a city wrought by neoliberal policies and, most important, examining these experiences in relation to wider contests over pedagogy and policy making. Whether considering the power of language and story as revolutionary forces for African American education and liberation (as do Dixson and Fisher), the effects of strategic class- and race-based disinvestment in urban infrastructure on schools in working-class communities of color (as do Apple and Lipman), the tradition of culturally relevant pedagogy and legacy of educational resistance by black teachers (as does Siddle Walker), or new, more dynamic, democratic forms of curriculum, policy, and grassroots organizing (as do King and Au), these critical scholars join students and teachers in a grounded analysis and critique of neoliberalism. Indeed, such writings collectively provide a rich evidentiary record for thinking through the complex processes of racial formation, class dynamics, and public school reform in New Orleans as well as other urban centers nationally and internationally. Zeus Leonardo provides additional insight in the book's afterword, focusing on the nexus of racial-economic power, whiteness, and the politics of urban space.

WHITENESS AS PROPERTY: RACE, ACCUMULATION BY DISPOSSESSION, AND URBAN POLICY

Arguably, New Orleans stands at the epicenter of neoliberal reform in the United States. But what exactly does that mean? Neoliberalism has been analyzed largely in terms of political economy—and powerfully so. David Harvey (2006), one of the most insightful voices on neoliberalism and urban development, explains that "neoliberalism was from the very beginning a project to achieve the restoration of class power to the richest strata of the population" (p. 13). Central to this project is the neoliberal state, which must "create a 'good business climate' and therefore optimize conditions for capital accumulation no matter what the consequences for . . . social well–being." Doing so has required that "sectors formerly run or regulated by the state . . . are turned over to the private sphere or deregulated" (p. 25). He goes on to clarify:

> The primary aim has been to open up new fields for capital accumulation in domains hitherto regarded as off-limits to the calculus of profitability. Public utilities of all kinds (water, telecommunications, transportation), social welfare provision (social housing, education, health care, pensions), public institutions (such as universities, research laboratories, prisons) and even warfare (as illustrated by the "army" of private contractors operating alongside the armed forces in Iraq) have all been privatized to some degree. (p. 44)

Such deregulation and privatization of public goods, Harvey stresses, has been "redistributive rather than generative," and has necessitated the invention of ways to "transfer assets and redistribute wealth and income either from the mass of the population towards the upper classes or from vulnerable to richer countries." The methods—various as they are—may be understood as processes of "accumulation by dispossession" (p. 43).

The processes that Harvey (2006) moves on to describe have become eerily familiar in New Orleans and other metropolitan areas throughout the United States, as well as in unevenly "developing" urban centers worldwide:

- Commodification and privatization of land and the forceful expulsion of populations
- Conversion of various forms of property rights into exclusive property rights
- Suppression of rights to the commons
- Commodification of labor power and the suppression of alternative (indigenous) forms of production and consumption
- Colonial, neocolonial, and imperial processes of appropriation of assets (including natural resources)
- Slave trade
- Usury, the national debt, and, most devastating of all, use of the credit system as a radical means of accumulation

The state and its apparatus of violence "plays a crucial role in both backing and promoting these processes" (p. 43). Indeed, the counterstories shared by students and teachers in this book expose the aggressive nature of these processes and provide the raw material—the shameful details, wrenching sentiments, profound losses, oppressive experiences, and deadly costs— necessary for a penetrating and humane examination of accumulation by dispossession. Sadly but importantly, testimonies regarding the removal of neighbors and the decimation of neighborhoods, razing of public housing, and the neglect, selective closing, and deregulation of public schools do not just capture the reality of New Orleans alone. Nor do the stories of state-sanctioned abandonment and violence, as student Deborah Carey reminds us in her upcoming story about the "so-called national guards" patrolling the streets of New Orleans (in Chapter 3). The accumulation of some at the expense of the many, along with attendant forms of symbolic violence and brute force, is occurring in Chicago (Lipman, 2004; Stovall & Smith, 2008), New York City (Kinloch, 2007a; Maurrasse, 2006), Los Angeles (Duncan-Andrade, 2006) and elsewhere, as critical scholars squarely point out in the coming chapters. To be sure, Johannesburg, Delhi, Shanghai, Mexico City, São Paulo, and many other places are experiencing truly vulgar levels of resource-transference both within their bounds and from their backyards to imperial centers (Davis, 2006).

The counterstories of students likewise complicate our understandings of neoliberalism and render more transparent a set of cultural and racial dynamics that have not been sufficiently appreciated. The words of New Orleans youth urge us to confront not only the political economy of neo-liberalism, but the devastating cultural and racial components of this proj-ect. We are reminded that neoliberalism was from the very beginning a project to achieve the restoration of *racial* power to the *white* strata of the population. Harvey (2006) partly recognizes this when he writes about the propagation of myths by the dominant class: "If conditions among the lower classes deteriorated, this was because they failed, usually for per-sonal and cultural reasons, to enhance their own human capital (through education, the acquisition of a protestant work ethic, submission to work discipline and flexibility, and the like)" (p. 42). In this respect, neocon-servative ideology weighs heavily: Poor communities must be saved, we are told, from a "culture of poverty" that fosters dependence on the state and only worsens national character and national debt (see Buras, 2007, 2008). It is undeniable, in fact, that this majoritarian narrative is the back-bone of accumulation by dispossession. More to the point, those who accumulate must be entitled without question and those who are dispos-sessed must be responsible for their own dispossession. That the lines are racial, however, is a fundamental issue generally sidestepped in economic critiques. One of the ways to begin thinking seriously and powerfully about the relationship between neoliberalism and race is to weld together the counterstories of urban youth of color, Harvey's Marxist notion of accumulation by dispossession, and critical race theorist Cheryl Harris's conceptualization of "whiteness as property."

Harris (1995) reminds us that "American law has recognized a prop-erty interest in whiteness" (p. 277). By this she means that

> property as conceived in the founding era included not only external objects and people's relationships to them, but also all of those human rights, liber-ties, powers, and immunities that are important for human well-being. . . . White identity conferred tangible and economically valuable benefits, and it was jealously guarded as a valued possession. (pp. 279–280)

Among the property rights of whiteness were and are "the right to use and enjoyment" and "the absolute right to exclude." Simply put, the right to use and enjoyment refers to those benefits and privileges secured as a result of one's ability to stake a claim to whiteness. In a very real sense, then, it might be said that whiteness refers to accumulation by possession: If one possesses "it," one can access and accumulate an array of social goods (see also McIntosh, 1989; Roediger, 1991). Moreover, whiteness translates into the absolute right to exclude or to dispossess others of such benefits and privileges (see also Leonardo, 2009). These racialized and racist processes are all too apparent in the stories that youth of color tell here, as they speak out in uncensored ways about *who* is able to enjoy life in the city they call home, *who* has access to protection, and *who* possesses the right to education, housing, and community. On the flip side, they unearth the exclusionary aspects of neoconservative and neoliberal projects, providing insight into *who* is prohibited from maintaining family, "choosing" a school, and asserting one's place in the history and cultural legacy of the urban landscape or, for that matter, the curriculum in schools.

In her exposition on whiteness as property, Harris (1995) recollects her grandmother's tortured decision in the 1930s to "pass" as white in order to obtain a job at a Chicago department store which neither hired blacks nor served them—all of this in order to economically support her children. "Every day my grandmother rose from her bed in her house in a black enclave on the south side of Chicago," she writes, "sent her children off to black schools, boarded a bus full of black passengers, and rode to work." Yet the white women with whom her grandmother worked presumed that her grandmother was white, remaining unaware of her actual identity. Sharing this counterstory, Harris explains:

> She came to know them, but they did not know her, for my grandmother occupied a completely different place. That place—where white supremacy and economic domination meet—was unknown turf to her white co-workers. They remained oblivious to the worlds within worlds that existed just beyond the edge of their awareness and yet were present in their very midst. (p. 276)

It is precisely the "worlds within worlds" that the writings of Students at the Center seek to render visible. In engaging these stories, we are compelled to link accumulation by possession with accumulation by dispossession—that is, whiteness and white power with capital—and to challenge the classed and raced dimensions of this disastrous, conservative project.

It is significant that one of Harvey's (2006) works on spaces of global capitalism has a cover photo of a city submerged in water: New Orleans. Although Harvey does not mention New Orleans—the book came out shortly after Katrina—he does emphasize that "crisis creation, management, and manipulation" are at the heart of the neoliberal project. With the United States Treasury, Wall Street, and International Monetary Fund in mind, he points out that "one of the primary functions of state interventions and of international institutions is to orchestrate crises and devaluations in ways that permit accumulation by dispossession to occur without sparking a general collapse or popular revolt" (p. 47). Katrina represented such a crisis—or more accurately, an "opportunity"—and conservative modernizers, assisted by neoliberal state policies, were quick to step into the vacuum (see also Saltman, 2007b). Nonetheless, it would be grossly naïve to assume that the crisis in New Orleans was or is an anomaly, even if its scope is indeed more extreme than crises evidenced in some other urban centers. Conditions in New Orleans, such as those described in the forthcoming chapters, are not a local or even a regional matter; they constitute a catastrophe of national proportion and significance. This is precisely what inspired Gloria Ladson-Billings to place New Orleans at the center of her presidential address to the American Educational Research Association in 2006. She emphasized:

> The subaltern can and do speak. They speak from the barrios of Los Angeles and the ghettos of New York. They speak from the reservations of New Mexico and the Chinatown of San Francisco. They speak from the levee breaks of New Orleans where they remind us, as education researchers, that we do not merely have an achievement gap—we have an education debt. (p. 10)

Not only does the education debt remain unpaid—that is, resources continue to be withheld and withdrawn from marginalized communities by the racialized neoliberal state—it only deepens.

The conditions that prevail in New Orleans, while distinct in some ways, clearly reflect the racial inequities and struggles that exist in urban school systems across the nation. In this regard, New Orleans, which has become experimental ground for a host of educational reforms, might provide deeper insight into the crises that characterize schools in other cities and ultimately the legitimacy of the "solutions" being proposed and enacted. This is exactly the argument made by the critical scholars contributing to this collection, as serious questions are raised about who precisely are the beneficiaries of existing policies. The need for asking questions is acute, as the mainstream media has little to say about the effects of targeted austerity on New Orleans and other cities, while the accounts of those who are most affected and continue to struggle against this state campaign of "benign neglect" remain untold (see Buras, 2007). These are the accounts that *Pedagogy, Policy, and the Privatized City* aims to circulate. We believe that doing so is itself a pedagogic act of resistance.

STUDENTS AT THE CENTER
AND CRITICAL RACE COUNTERSTORIES

As mentioned earlier, Students at the Center (SAC) is a high school-based writing program in New Orleans that was founded in 1996 (see Randels & Carriere, 2002; Buras, 2009b). Co-directed by New Orleans veteran public school teacher Jim Randels and New Orleans poet and producer Kalamu ya Salaam, SAC engages youth in historically informed writing initiatives aimed at transforming their schools and communities. Over the past decade, SAC has produced books of student writing, poetry collections, a teen newspaper called *Our Voice*, plays, records, radio broadcasts, and digital videos. The program, in short, has built upon the experiences of the students, as its name implies, and formulated a pedagogy rooted in the voices, cultures, and histories of traditionally marginalized youth, their families, schools, and neighborhoods. For the students and teachers in SAC, voice and critical historical consciousness are instruments of identity formation, means for critical commentary, and levers of community engagement. Continuing their grassroots work in the aftermath of Katrina and amid dramatic educational experimentation in the New Orleans Public Schools, SAC produced a compelling set of writings, part of which constitutes this book.

These writings consist of firsthand accounts and narratives related not only to the immediate aftermath of Hurricane Katrina and its unexplored effects on youth of color and their families, but the profound influence that more recent state disinvestment and educational reform have had on the reconstruction of public schools and neighborhoods across the city. There has not been a substantive space for the articulation of concerns by urban youth and teachers at the center of these crises. Often policy makers focus myopically on the promise of the new, only paying heed to the old when its apparent ugliness or impoverishment substantiates the agenda of neoliberal and neoconservative reformers (Buras, 2005, 2008; Saltman, 2007b). *Pedagogy, Policy, and the Privatized City* is intended to disrupt these silences and distortions by telling the untold stories. Like a magic mirror (Hall & Karsten, 2008), these testimonies reveal the ongoing centrality of race and racial power in a nation portrayed as color blind (Dixson & Rousseau, 2006; Lieberman, 2006). Equally important, they have the capacity to inspire grounded and thoughtful discussions regarding the possibilities of youth engagement, critical educational practice in urban settings, and democratic policy making in an era of neoliberal power. What's more, these pages reveal the deep interconnections between schools and other aspects of urban infrastructure, linkages too often overlooked when schools are studied in a vacuum (Anyon, 2005). The reforms unfolding in New Orleans, which link, as one example, displacement and the destruction of public housing to bigger plans for "rebuilding" schools and "revitalizing" neighborhoods, illuminate an intricate politics of race and urban space occurring in cities nationwide. Allow me to say more about these contributions as reflected in the book's content.

MAPPING THE BOOK

In the second part of this introduction, Randels and Salaam make the case for putting these processes in historical context and challenging the "scorched earth" policy that has prevailed since the 1980s—one that says disinvestment and destruction are actually regenerative and that "benign neglect" fosters the improvement of so-called backward, state-dependent communities (see also Buras, 2007). In Chapter 1, I provide a substantive examination of SAC's work over the past decade and situate this work in relation to struggles over schooling and educational reform in New Orleans. Working from interviews with teachers, classroom observations, and a thorough review of the writings and digital media produced by SAC since its inception, I offer a portrait of liberatory pedagogy that has the capacity to challenge dominant narratives on race and neoliberal policy. As I demonstrate, the contest over neoliberal policy has itself led to a fierce battle over the potential closing of the open access, neighborhood high school in which SAC works. I argue that students' counterstories represent a call to critical consciousness around the meanings of urban revitalization and underscore the need to build alliances globally around issues of racial inequality and capitalism (see also Buras & Motter, 2006).

In Chapters 2, 3, and 4, I provide an opening reflection that begins to weave students' individual stories into a collective one. Each opening reflection is followed by a series of exchanges in which students and teachers "speak out" regarding the issues at hand, while critical scholars "speak back" in commentaries by responding to their stories and relating them to struggles over pedagogy and policy in other urban contexts, both past and present. Along the way, I facilitate the exchanges with a narrative thread of my own. Each of these chapters concludes with a closing reflection in which I draw connections between the stories and lend some thought on the substance and wider significance of the exchanges.

Thus in Chapter 2, "Students at the Center: The Word, the River, and Education for Liberation," the history, philosophy, and pedagogy of Students at the Center is explored through a series of short writings from teachers, students, and graduates of the program who have returned as teachers. These writings provide a vision of education grounded in liberatory practices and an understanding that "the articulation of experience and imagination in narrative . . . is an important part of the tradition of African peoples" (Lawrence, 1995, p. 343; see also Fisher, 2009; Freire & Macedo, 1987; Students at the Center, 2005). In turn, Adrienne Dixson, whose scholarship is at the forefront of critical race theory and is itself partly informed by familial and educational connections to New Orleans, responds to these writings. Maisha Fisher, whose work has explored African American literacy practices across time and space (e.g., black press in the 1960s, contemporary spoken word poetry in the Bronx, and playmaking in Atlanta's school-to-prison pipeline) also provides commentary. Collectively, they reveal how the work of Students at the Center represents a powerful current in a longer tradition, or river, constituted by radical preaching and teaching among racially dominated groups (see Lawrence, 1995). The river, a metaphor with particular significance to New Orleans, thus has the capacity not only to destroy but more importantly to nurture educational communities organized around liberation rather than exploitation.

In Chapter 3, "Race and Reform in the Privatized City," a range of firsthand testimonies, accounts, and stories focus on various aspects of the neoliberal agenda and their relationship to the capitalist dreams and racialized rights described by David Harvey (2006) and Cheryl Harris (1995). Students and teachers speak out on the tragedies that unfolded in the days after Katrina and the racialized abandonment of African American families in the city; experiences of displacement and return; the destruction and reconstruction of schools, homes, cultural traditions, and neighborhoods; and the educational crisis that has ensued amid newly instituted reforms, such as charter schools and choice, the razing of public housing, and teachers union busting. The forms of struggle and defiance—both personal and communal—that have occurred are made transparent as well. Much like Chapter 2, a substantial component of this chapter consists of responses, or critical commentaries, authored by scholars with deep knowledge in areas pertinent to these accounts. Thus Michael Apple examines state disinvestment and school choice in New Orleans as part of a larger set of rightist policies and examines what is at stake if we don't more forcefully challenge privatization across the globe. Pauline Lipman, focusing on the confluence of school reform and housing policy, likewise widens the lens and provides a comparative analysis of New Orleans and Chicago with respect to affordable housing in increasingly gentrified neighborhoods. Finally and importantly, Vanessa Siddle Walker, a noted historian of African American education in the Jim Crow South, places the work of SAC in historical context and reflects on its connection to earlier forms of educational resistance enacted by black teachers and communities, particularly in light of attacks on black veteran teachers in New Orleans. In this way we begin to appreciate the interconnections between New Orleans, its sister cities, and the ways in which struggle in New Orleans is situated within a much longer tradition of subversion and protest (e.g., see Kelley, 1996). All of this, of course, is intimately tied to a complex web of conservative forces and reforms, as I make clear through my critical narration in this chapter and others.

In Chapter 4, "Putting *All* Students at the Center: Charting an Agenda for Urban Educational Transformation," additional narratives from SAC teachers, students, and community activists suggest new directions for reconstructing schools in New Orleans and elsewhere. A range of interventions are advocated, from reconstructing the curriculum to reflect the experiences and histories of dispossessed groups to questioning the legitimacy of selective admissions charter schools that separate and destroy the potential of community, from developing networks of student mentors and teachers who challenge the "one-size-fits-all" agenda of No Child Left Behind to mobilizing community groups and coalitions and making schools centers of strategic organizing, and more. The writings in this chapter thus ensure that *Pedagogy, Policy, and the Privatized City* does more than critique existing conditions: It offers a vision for change. Here again, scholars underscore the necessity of such change, particularly in light of the destructive tendencies of prevailing conservative reforms. Joyce King examines the implications of SAC's work for the reformation of teacher education and the school curriculum, paying special attention to issues of racial identity and historical consciousness. In rather compelling terms, Wayne Au critiques the differential and reproductive effects of curricular policy and schooling, and highlights the vital contributions of educational movements that expand upon the vision of transformation so powerfully articulated by SAC and a coalition of community activists in New Orleans. These analyses provide insight into the importance of the freedom dreams (Kelley, 2002) of New Orleans youth for informing policies and initiatives that put *all* students' interests at the center of urban revitalization, with "revitalization" radically redefined. The ability to first imagine a different world is the bedrock of change—a point driven home by Robin D. G. Kelley in the foreword.

The book concludes with a final set of reflections. Drawing together our cumulative insights, I challenge the politics of disposability at the root of dominant pedagogic and policy formations and explore what might be learned about the power of critical race pedagogy and counter-storytelling for building truly democratic urban schools and communities. I return once more to battles over schooling and housing and explain how the uncertain future of a particular high school in New Orleans—one in which SAC has a long history—is intimately related to wider plans focused on constructing an exclusionary and privatized city. Sadly, I discuss how the racial politics of accumulation by dispossession have been evident not only in the United States, but irrefutably in the neocolonial expeditions of global elites. The example of SAC and related initiatives across the Global South, therefore, assist us in raising fresh questions regarding how pedagogies of voice and struggle might shake neoliberalism. Along these lines, Kalamu ya Salaam provides a final glimpse into the destructive effects of government neglect and disinvestment and reveals that the very instruments we need to alter these circumstances can never be destroyed. Jenna Dominique Hill, a SAC student, demonstrates her agreement by sharing a narrative about the incalculable value of family and community—something often forgotten or, worse, viewed as disposable when policies of urban renewal are based on skewed understandings of families of color. In the afterword Zeus Leonardo furthers the conversation by critically dissecting the neoliberal view that black communities are nothing more than "empty places to be invested in by white profiteers."

COUNTERSTORIES AND THE BUILDING OF MOVEMENTS FOR EDUCATIONAL JUSTICE

Writing about the role of storytelling, Richard Delgado (2000) presses:

> Most who write about storytelling focus on its community-building functions. . . . But stories and counterstories can serve an equally important destructive function. They can show that what we believe is ridiculous, self-serving, or cruel. They can show us the way out of the trap of unjustified exclusion. They can help us understand when it is time to reallocate power. They are the other half—the destructive half—of the creative dialectic. (p. 61)

As I demonstrate in the next chapter, counterstories have been a core part of SAC's pedagogic work. Their function has been both constructive and destructive—in a positive sense—for students and communities in New Orleans. On one hand, the invitation to history and counterstory has enabled Randels and Salaam to build bridges between students and between students and surrounding communities. On the other hand, the stories told have often shattered more widely held beliefs about the nature of the "Big Easy," where life isn't so easy for many working-class African American, Vietnamese American, and, increasingly since Katrina, Latino students. It is the hope of the students, teachers, and scholars contributing to this book that the counterstories shared will have both constructive and destructive effects.

Counterstories are the seeds of social movements. Shared experience and storytelling bond individuals, shape consciousness, and ignite collective action. Reflecting on everyday forms of black working-class resistance, Kelley (1993) makes the point this way:

> An infrapolitical approach requires that we substantially redefine our understanding of politics. Too often politics is defined by *how* people participate rather than *why*; by traditional definition the question of what is political hinges on whether or not groups are involved in elections, political parties, grassroots social movements. . . . By shifting our focus to what motivated disenfranchised black working people to struggle and what strategies they developed, we may discover that their participation in "mainstream" politics . . . grew out of the very circumstances, experiences, and memories that impelled many to steal from an employer, to join a mutual benefit association, or to spit in a bus driver's face. In other words, those actions all reflect, to varying degrees, larger political struggles. (p. 78)

The crucial point here is that the transformation of experience into story—and the sharing of memory through story—is a deeply political and potentially subversive act. To tell counterstories is to begin to reconstruct "common sense" understandings about the way the world works, produce new identities, and stir consciousness (Hoare & Nowell Smith, 1971). The bonds created and the consciousness that emerges may become the basis for larger social movements. This perhaps is what leads Salaam to describe SAC's work as "prerevolutionary" (see Chapter 1). In so many words, stories told are seeds planted. It's from these seeds that movements for educational, urban, and global justice might sprout and spread (Apple & Buras, 2006; Solinger, Fox, & Irani, 2008). This is the "creative philosophy" about which Antonio Gramsci wrote in his *Prison Notebooks* (Hoare & Nowell Smith, 1971): the refinement of spontaneous common sense into a critical and coherent philosophy of the world, one able to guide subaltern action in history.

Yet counterstories for all their constructive dimensions simultaneously constitute an undoing, as Delgado (2000) well knows. This destructive function is one taken very seriously by the book's contributors. The narratives of neoliberal and neoconservative elites must be contested, as they construct and market understandings of race, culture, and political economy that are warped and broken. Harvey (2006) questions why so many have been persuaded that neoliberalism is the "only alternative" (p. 42). We are told time and time again that the free market is the same as freedom. We are told time and again that the poor are poor in character and motivation. We are told and told once more that the oppressors are the newly oppressed—victims of a radical leftist monopoly over culture and economy (see Apple, 2006; Hirsch, 1996; Whitman, 2008; Wilson, 1996). The counterstories voiced by Students at the Center undercut, protest, and defy the legitimacy of these dominant accounts. In speaking out, students reveal that the drudgery of their schools and the disinvestment in their communities are very real and they present us with alternative visions—ones shared in Chapter 4. How these stories and visions might engender movements for educational justice is a question that should be at the forefront of our minds. It is hoped that the dialogue initiated here will move others toward activism within their own communities and inspire solidarity. There should be little doubt that the voices and creativity of youth can have an immense impact on the future well-being of communities across the globe (Dolby & Rizvi, 2007).

There likewise should be little doubt that conditions in New Orleans reflect trends in urban education reform before the storm and underscore the deep connections between schools and other aspects of urban infrastructure presently, such as housing and education (Anyon, 2005; Buras, 2009a; Lipman, 2008). With the entire infrastructure of New Orleans destroyed, the city has become an experimental arena for a variety of policies, including decentralization, charter schools, vouchers, and mixed-income housing. Not long after Katrina, the Bring New Orleans Back Commission (2006) formed by Mayor Ray Nagin generated a report suggesting the development of an all-charter school district (see Buras, 2005). In August 2006 the city's paper urged, "Parents trying to maneuver the maze of public schools in post-Katrina New Orleans would do well to start with a new premise: Think of yourselves as consumers in a brand new marketplace" (Ritea, 2006e). That marketplace, however, is not so new, as deregulation, choice, and state disinvestment in other contexts have led to increasing levels of segregation and inequality (Buras & Apple, 2005; Scott, 2005; Wells, 2002). In this way *Pedagogy, Policy, and the Privatized City* contributes to heated debates regarding the effects of neoliberal policies on urban schools and communities. These testimonies also cast critical light on the persistence of neoconservative ideology and the framing of communities of color as a deprived underclass in need of reformation by white, middle-class culture (Whitman, 2008; for a critique, Buras, 2008).

In the end, policy making in New Orleans represents the most significant episode of racial marginalization, removal, and state disinvestment in recent U.S. history and challenges us to consider what forms a socially just reconstruction of schooling might take. Two human rights experts for the United Nations issued a statement condemning the racially discriminatory impact of federal and local housing initiatives in New Orleans, where the demolition of public housing threatens low-income African American residents' right to return (*Times-Picayune*, 2008). These concerns were echoed by a United Nations committee constituted, in part, to determine whether or not the United States government had violated international conventions on human rights and racial discrimination (Hammer, 2008). It decided that violations had occurred and called for greater consultation of African American communities in New Orleans and fuller participation in formulating plans for rebuilding the city. This book has something crucial to contribute to that conversation and the effort to build movements for more socially just urban spaces.

Scorching the Earth Isn't the Way: New Orleans Before and After

Jim Randels and Kalamu ya Salaam

Before and After. New Orleans has a new time line. A new zero point. However, a natural event is by no means the sole cause for our new era. To understand post-Katrina, you have to understand pre-Katrina. Many folks in post-Katrina New Orleans, particularly in terms of public education, don't follow this simple pre- and post-postulate. They are salivating to start from scratch, to establish a new day and a new order, with nothing but disdain for the prezero.

The writings in this book recommend a different path. Students, teachers, and community supporters certainly want much better public education in New Orleans. We just don't believe scorching the earth is the way to do it. We know it too well from our study of history about other eras in New Orleans. We know from the post-Reconstruction era the moral and practical costs our city incurred when anything run by black folks was deemed worthless and corrupt by the white power structure. We know that the best school buildings were built by people in New Orleans.

So in *Pedagogy, Policy, and the Privatized City: Stories of Dispossession and Defiance from New Orleans*, you won't read only stories of fleeing and being displaced by Katrina. You will also read about a 15-year-old writing program developed and nurtured in the New Orleans Public Schools that many writing programs across the nation look to as a model. And when you read student memoirs, you won't just hear their Katrina moments but also their family and community histories.

New Orleanians live and work and love here for many reasons. Most of them, however, involve knowing what went before us. Enslaved Africans brought with them the knowledge of how to grow rice in this climate, making it possible for New Orleanians of European and African descent to have the sustenance to survive to the next generation. Our culture is born from remembering ancient Bambara rhythms and placing our new experiences within them, from paying respect to Indian tribes who sheltered us and taught us and danced with us. Our sense of justice and freedom comes from revolutionaries displaced from Haiti and France and from Creole New Orleanians building collective strategies to respond to state laws meant to take political power away from them.

Those of us who work in education also know and honor and pass on a history of struggle. Black folk fought in 1917 to open McDonogh 35 High School, providing free, public high school education for black youth for the first time since early in the post-Reconstruction era. The 7th Ward Civic Improvement Association engaged in collective work to build a new public school building, Valena C. Jones Elementary, for black students in 1927. Black teachers formed American Federation of Teachers Local 527, now United Teachers of New Orleans, in 1937 to fight for equal pay for black teachers. And in the aftermath of Katrina, the United Teachers of New Orleans and other civic-democratic groups had to bring great pressure on the state of Louisiana to open schools for children who were on the streets rather than in school.

In New Orleans we do have a new moment. But it is not a moment out of time. And it is not a story that only those in power will tell. This book is about the two sides of the starting point—the new day and the old realities. The before and the after. The respect for elders and ancestors and cultural traditions. Without this full picture, our public education, our culture, our souls cannot continue to grow. Without imparting the knowledge of and action in history and struggle, we cannot teach our children well.

CHAPTER 1

"We Have To Tell Our Story": Neo-Griots, Schooling, and the Legacy of Racial Resistance in the Other South

Kristen L. Buras

THE LATE BRAZILIAN educator and scholar Paulo Freire understood the power of story as a force of oppression as well as an instrument of liberation. Although not commonly viewed as such, Freire's (1970/1993) *Pedagogy of the Oppressed* is a treatise on storytelling. "Education," he wrote, "is suffering from narrative sickness." That is, as traditionally conceived, the teacher-student relationship "involves a narrating Subject (the teacher) and patient, listening objects (the students)." The role of the teacher has been "to 'fill' the students with the contents of his narration—contents which are detached from reality, disconnected from the totality that engendered them and could give them significance" (p. 52). All the while, students are expected to "memorize mechanically the narrated content," even when the stories told do not reflect their knowledge of the world. In opposition, Freire asserted, "Education must begin with the solution of the teacher-student contradiction, by reconciling the poles of the contradiction so that both are simultaneously teachers *and* students" (p. 53; see also Au, 2007).

Put another way, liberatory education is not founded on the narratives embedded in teacher talk or state-mandated curriculum. Rather, it is grounded in teachers and students collectively constructing stories based on critical analyses of the problems before them and the historical context out of which such problems emerged. Indeed, Freire (1970/1993) stresses, "problem-posing theory and practice take the people's history as their starting point." Recognizing that history is unfinished and accepting

17

"neither a 'well-behaved' present nor a predetermined future," such education "becomes revolutionary." Ultimately, he concludes, "looking at the past must only be a means of understanding more clearly what and who [a people] are so that they can more wisely build the future" (p. 65). It is at the intersection of storytelling, historical consciousness, and futurity that Students at the Center—a writing program based in two public high schools in New Orleans, Louisiana—takes form and becomes transformative.

In this chapter I will document and analyze the work of Students at the Center based on original research, including interviews, classroom observations, and student writings. My intent is to underscore the ways this program constitutes a pedagogy of the oppressed by creating a space for the development of neo-griots, or young storytellers of color who use spoken, written, and digitally produced texts to narrate the struggles encountered by African American and Vietnamese American communities in the city. In doing so, I argue that Students at the Center not only honors and extends the legacy of Paulo Freire by connecting his work to histories of racial struggle and resistance, but challenges the unfolding of an immensely destructive set of reforms in post-Hurricane Katrina New Orleans, where neoliberal attacks on the public school system are wedded to the attempted erasure of black culture and memory (see Buras, 2008, 2009a). Under such conditions the stories told by Students at the Center—or more accurately *counterstories*, as critical race theorists call those accounts that challenge white majoritarian narratives (Delgado, 2000; Yosso, 2006)—take on heightened significance locally, nationally, and internationally. After all, the reforms being implemented in New Orleans, while more accelerated and extensive due to the vacuum created by the displacement and destruction following Hurricane Katrina in 2005, are not fully distinct. Thus students' critiques of such experimentation shed light on reforms and racial projects elsewhere and ultimately the legitimacy of the "solutions" being proposed and enacted, including decentralization, charter schools, market-based educational choice, and disinvestment from public infrastructure more generally (Davis, 2006; Omi & Winant, 1994). In sum, the counterstories of these youth are penetrating in their condemnation of the racial state's utter dismissal of the "other South"—one consisting of predominantly working-class African American neighborhoods in low-lying areas of the city. They also serve as a powerful reminder that solidarities between the "Global South" and the "South within the North" are imperative if a wiser future is to be built.

In what follows I briefly introduce and explore the pedagogic foundations of Students at the Center and the context of educational reform in which the program's work is situated in New Orleans. Next, the program's pedagogy is more deeply examined through portraits of the schools and classrooms in which students and teachers develop critical understandings of their lives through the collective process of writing and telling stories. Widening the lens yet more, I move on to consider key illustrations of how these young neo-griots connect counter-storytelling to the racial history of New Orleans and ongoing struggles within the city, including the efforts of neoliberal elites to aggressively implement post-Katrina reforms that serve only to worsen longstanding forms of racial marginalization, disinvestment, and displacement. Finally, I chronicle the state's attempt to close one of the high schools in which Students at the Center has its roots and the resistance that has ensued in this corner of a more expansive Global South.

STUDENTS AT THE CENTER AND
NEW ORLEANS PUBLIC SCHOOLS

Students at the Center (SAC), as its name implies, is a student-centered writing and digital media program consisting of several courses that students attending either Frederick Douglass High School or Eleanor McMain Secondary School in New Orleans may elect to take. Founded in 1996 by veteran public school teacher and teacher unionist Jim Randels and two of his students, Erica DeCuir and Kenyatta Johnson, and now cotaught with poet and producer Kalamu ya Salaam (whose name means "pen of peace"), the program has been in existence for over a decade. It is closely bound to the racial history of New Orleans, a southern city in the United States recognized globally as the birthplace of jazz, but also known for its traditions of both white supremacy and black resistance, neither of which are disconnected from either its musical or literary culture. Indeed, SAC is partly rooted in the tradition of the *griot*, or West African storyteller, and the knowledge that oppressed communities must tell their stories in order to survive as well as challenge racism. Producing books of student writing, a teen newspaper called *Our Voice*, plays, music recordings, radio broadcasts, and digital videos—what is described as "writing with text, sound, and light"—the program has built upon the experiences of students and formulated a pedagogy rooted in the voices, cultures, and histories of traditionally marginalized youth, their families, and neighborhoods. For students and teachers involved with SAC, the word is an instrument of identity formation, a means for critical commentary, and a lever of community engagement. "Naming the world in order to transform it" (Freire, 1970/1993; Freire & Macedo, 1987) provides the impetus for SAC's work, as reflected in the community involvement of

SAC students and networking with local grassroots organizations around issues of racial equity and economic justice.

Those affiliated with SAC follow this guiding principle:

Start with what you know to learn what you don't know;
start with where you're at to get where you want to go.

Keva Carr, a former student, speaks rather profoundly about the program, explaining, "The teachers were different: It wasn't simply always their input but ours as well. . . . We sat in a circle. We told stories and discussed real issues. . . . I love Students at the Center for what it brought to me. And I love myself for what I brought to it" (SAC, 2007a, p. 144). Such sentiments are rarely shared by students, particularly African American students in urban schools throughout the United States, who are generally taught as if they don't know and told where to go. Educator Kalamu ya Salaam echoes Keva's sentiments when he stresses:

We have to model social commitment not by sloganizing or by using clever rhymes to fight oppression, but rather we must do the hard work of helping others without requiring students to look up to us on our teacherly pedestals. . . . We must be serious about keeping students at the center of our work. (SAC, 2007a, p. 143)

Although Students at the Center has been doing serious work since 1996, the challenges faced by the students and teachers involved and the significance of their contributions have only been heightened since Katrina, when the levees broke, submerged parts of the city beneath water, and destroyed existing infrastructure. Ashley Jones, a former student who had gone on to complete a university degree and returned to teach in the program, recollects her thoughts during the process of evacuating New Orleans before the storm:

Riding in the back seat of a packed car, watching the trees and birds and the sky whiz by me like the snapshots one sees before dying, I began to think about life after this storm. . . .

    Before I thought about the place I used to get my chicken sandwiches from on Freret Street or Ms. Sadie the iceberg lady right off of LaSalle Street . . . I saw Maria and Rodneka, Earlnika, Keva, and Daniel. I thought about Douglass High School and the gloomy hallways that always made me feel that I was in a scary movie or something. I wondered what would be next for them, no longer having Students at the Center. I thought about the schools they may be forced to go to, those cold, stiff rooms where the real world never becomes a part of the lesson plan. (SAC, 2007a, pp. 19–20)

Likewise considering what was to come after Katrina, founder and teacher Jim Randels called attention to the long history of unequal power and struggle that has characterized the city, recollecting some well-known song lyrics:

> Randy Newman, in his song about the 1927 floods in New Orleans when the business leaders of the city decided to break the levees and flood the poorer parts of Louisiana in order to save their city, sang, "They're trying to wash us away." Maria and Ashley and all of us are living that in terms of our public schools. (in SAC, 2007a, p. 42)

Here Randels refers to the current neoliberal experiment aimed at reconstructing the city's public education system along class- and race-based lines, which are even starker than those that predated Katrina. In fact, the very concept of a truly "public" education is at stake, as open access neighborhood schools are threatened by the proliferation of selective admissions charter schools supported not only by state policy, but by government funding as well as resources from local and national organizations devoted to educational choice and privatization (see Cowen Institute, 2008; Maxwell, 2007; New Schools for New Orleans, 2008; United Teachers of New Orleans et al., 2006, 2007a). It is especially noteworthy that Frederick Douglass High School—the school with which SAC has been affiliated since the program's founding and one of the only remaining high schools downtown, where low–income black youth are concentrated—has been threatened with closure by the state-run Recovery School District, a concern I will address later in this chapter (fieldnotes, 2008; Save Frederick Douglass, 2008; Vallas, 2008).

More immediately, it is important to understand that even before the storm, the history of slavery, state-sanctioned segregation, ongoing racism, and white flight from the city has translated into strategic state neglect and disinvestment in African American education, as, I will show, the writings of SAC powerfully remind us (see Buras, 2007; DeVore & Logsdon, 1991; SAC, 2005). Already in deplorable condition and long deprived of state resources, 80% of New Orleans Public Schools were further damaged or destroyed by Hurricane Katrina in August 2005 (Ritea, 2006a). When President George W. Bush spoke in the city two weeks after the storm, he called for the nation to "rise above the legacy of inequality" (Bush, 2005). Instead, the federal government rapidly began flooding the city with millions of dollars to support the development of charter schools ($45 million in the ten months following Katrina), while the Louisiana State Legislature passed Act 35, which redefined what constituted a "failing" school so that most of New Orleans Public Schools could be deemed as failing and placed in a state-run Recovery School District (United Teachers of New Orleans et al., 2006). In November 2005, 107 of 128 schools had been folded into the Recovery School District (RSD); only 13 schools could have been assumed before Act 35. During this same period the Orleans Parish School Board (OPSB), which originally governed the schools, placed some 4,000 school teachers on "disaster leave" (a majority of them black, veteran, and unionized), only to terminate all but 61 of its 7,000 employees by January 2006 (Goodman, 2006; United Teachers of New Orleans et al., 2007a). That same month Mayor Ray Nagin's Bring New Orleans Back Commission (2006) issued "a plan for world-class public education" in New Orleans, suggesting the formation of an all-charter school district. Significantly, only a handful of schools had reopened, spurring lawsuits regarding an inadequate number of seats in the schools and the refusal to enroll particular groups of students, including low-income African American students and students with disabilities (Ritea, 2006b, 2006c). One youth in New Orleans explained: "I don't go to school. My mama tried to put us in school and nobody would take us" (Center for Community Change, 2006, p. 29).

One year after the storm New Orleans remained utterly devastated (Buras, 2005; Buras & Vukelich, 2006). Only one third of the city's population actually had been able to return, and much of the 9th Ward, which is home to Douglass High School and had one of the highest rates of black working-class homeownership in the nation before Katrina, was still without potable water and electricity (Common Ground, 2006). Meanwhile, on August 5, 2006, just two weeks before the start of the academic year, parents were invited to the New Orleans Arena where information was provided by schools planning to open in the city, many of them newly chartered. Sorely needed financial resources were wasted as schools spent "thousands of dollars in newspaper and radio ads," with one school expending $30,000 on its "outreach budget" to recruit students. The city paper urged, "Parents trying to maneuver the maze of public schools in post-Katrina New Orleans would do well to start with a new premise: Think of yourself as consumers in a brand new marketplace" (Ritea, 2006d). That marketplace, however, is not so new, as deregulation, choice, and state disinvestment in other contexts, including those outside of the United States, have led to increasing levels of segregation and inequality (e.g., see Buras & Apple, 2005). In this instance a number of public schools in the decentralized, charter school-driven system that now characterizes New Orleans were unable to open at the start of the 2006–07 school year, particularly noncharter schools in the RSD, which are now part of a dual school system. This system largely consists of charter and noncharter schools under the jurisdiction of the RSD and a smaller number of charter and noncharter schools under the jurisdiction of the Orleans Parish School Board, with the charter schools in each given greater status; notably, 32 of 53 schools in 2006–07 were charters, many of them either having selective admissions policies or filling to capacity and thus turning students away (Center for Community Change, 2006). As late as October 2006 many students in the RSD, who were nearly twice as likely to be low-income, were still without teachers, books, buildings, and school buses (Ritea, 2006e; United Teachers of New Orleans et al., 2006). In late January 2007 the American Federation of Teachers released a public statement condemning the refusal of public school officials to enroll at least 300 students and underscored that the Southern Institute for Education and Research had deemed the New Orleans Public Schools "the most balkanized school system in North America" (McElroy, 2007).

The start of the 2007–08 school year was no more promising. By this time, the city had 82 public schools and 42 were charters, most of them with selective admissions criteria, enrollment caps, and other barriers to entry (United Teachers of New Orleans et al., 2007b). A 90-page *Parents' Guide to Public Schools* put out by New Schools for New Orleans (2007)— one of numerous procharter school organizations advocating such reform in the city—suggested that parents seeking to enroll a child determine which documents were required by a given school in order to apply or register, including report cards and test scores, which "can help *properly place* your child" (p. 9; italics added). Parents are also offered guidance on how to "choose" a school: review some 68 pages of information to "identify schools that may meet your family's needs," then arrange visits, tour the schools, observe classes, interview principals and teachers, and possibly apply—that is, if the child qualifies and the application deadline has not passed (pp. 9–15). Clearly, such processes are navigated more easily by parents with surplus time, readily accessible transportation, intact documents, repaired or undamaged homes, monetary resources, and education, thereby advantaging more privileged families as well as families with "able" and "high-achieving" children (see also Ball, 2003).

What is more, while veteran teachers, their hard-won rights, and the collective bargaining agreement negotiated by the union that represented them—United Teachers of New Orleans (American Federation of Teachers Local 527)—no longer had recognition or standing in the Recovery School District of post-Katrina New Orleans, the city simultaneously became the site of the highest concentration of Teach for America teachers in the nation. This organization places graduates from elite universities, who aren't certified as teachers, in public school classrooms. Indeed, TeachNOLA, a Web-based teacher recruitment project organized by the Recovery School District and New Schools for New Orleans, assumed a "no experience necessary" posture, directing certified teachers to charter schools and uncertified teachers to the noncharter schools (Robelen, 2007; United Teachers of New Orleans et al., 2007a). In sum, this means that charter schools received a disproportionate share of post-Katrina funding, returning veteran teachers, and carefully selected students, while noncharter RSD schools were deemed "schools of last resort" for "leftover children" (United Teachers of New Orleans et al., 2007a, 2007b). With such mechanisms in place and the advantages they bestow to charters largely hidden from view, many nonetheless are declaring charter school reform a relative success in comparison to traditional public schooling (Cowen Institute, 2008).

The development of the School Facilities Master Plan for Orleans Parish (RSD & OPSB, 2008) has also been underway; it determines which schools remain open, undergo renovation, or get closed—decisions with clear implications for working-class and middle-class communities of color where flooding was most destructive, resources are scant, and rates of return have been alarmingly low. Alongside the "washing away" of the public schools has been the indefinite closure or razing of numerous public housing developments in a city where escalating rents and the destruction of more than 250,000 houses mean that little affordable housing is available—circumstances criticized by United Nations officials (see *Times-Picayune*, 2007a, 2007b, 2008).

THE STUDENT'S LIFE HISTORY AS STARTING POINT: FORMING A STORY CIRCLE

Students at the Center does not exist apart from this more immediate history nor from the more distant past, which informs and inspires it. "SAC understands that its work is part of a long stream of movements for liberation and social justice," Randels writes in a collection of stories produced by teachers and students after the storm (SAC, 2007a, p. 171). The influences are many and include the historic civil rights movement in New Orleans, black writers and musicians, Free Southern Theater, the NOMMO Literary Society (founded by Kalamu ya Salaam, with *nommo* meaning "power of the word"), local efforts to form a teachers union and improve educational conditions (Randels is a member of the executive council of United Teachers of New Orleans), and liberatory educators such as Paulo Freire (for a related history, see Fisher, 2009).

For instance, SAC adopted the tradition of the story circle from Free Southern Theater, a cultural outgrowth of the civil rights movement that ultimately housed itself in New Orleans (Free Southern Theatre, 1963; see also Breunlin, n.d.). Randels describes a *story circle* as

> a small group forum in which participants sit in a circle and move around the circle . . . reflecting on a theme or concept. . . . The story one tells must be grounded in one's personal experience. . . . All participants are encouraged to listen . . . without interrupting. After the circle has been completed, participants ask questions, summarize lessons learned from the stories, develop visual images and other creative responses . . . and engage in other forms of "cross talk." (SAC, 2007a, p. 158)

Observing SAC's historic debt, Randels underscores, "We didn't learn the story circle technique from colleagues or from our education courses" (p. 159). Instead, one of the founders of Free Southern Theater, John O'Neal, is a partner of SAC, and one of its former members, Salaam, is a teacher with SAC. Just as O'Neal, Salaam, and others in the late 1960s wished "to emphasize story rather than argument, understanding that stories tend to bring people together" (p. 159), SAC likewise embraces the circle as a way of creating community (see also Crossroads Project, 2006; SAC, 2007b).

At the same time, Salaam stresses, "it's not a direct line" between earlier movements and SAC. By this he means, "There's a certain politics to who we are. And that politics informs *how* we do what we do, but we're not trying to teach politics. . . . We use liberatory education as a process, but it's not a project" (interview, 2007). The distinction is subtle, but profound. He continues:

> So we have young people that span the spectrum. We encourage all of them. So like in the writing class at McMain right now, I'm really excited about being able to develop a group of young people that range from [a student] who . . . could be called a pure integrationist both at heart and at mind, and somebody like [a student] who doesn't give a damn about none of that stuff, and they both can see the value in each other's writing and begin to respect each other and develop.

Clarifying the nature of SAC's work, Salaam declares "we're sort of like a catalytic agent," then shares:

> I do not view the work we're doing right now as revolutionary work; I view it as prerevolutionary work. And that, it seems to me, is important. The revolution will come later, but you have to do some level of

preparation and get some understanding and build some trust. What we have with the students right now is something that I don't see in most other classes.

Randels asserts that SAC is based on the recognition that "students need a place that's smaller, so it's providing that setting." Indeed, no more than 15 students are in each class, and no more than four classes are taught per day by the teachers, who coteach classes such as creative writing and English literature. Beyond this, he makes clear that SAC is based on "a decision to stay within an existing system of public schools and to recognize that those were not set up in ways that fully meet the needs of the students or the teachers." Rather than setting up alternative schools, Randels instead chose to ask, "What happens if within [the public system], you create some alternate structures or formations?" As a result, he explains, the program is "this weird reformist, revolutionary blend" (interview, 2007). This commitment to public education is all the more important in post-Katrina New Orleans.

At McMain and Douglass high schools each class with SAC consists of teachers and students sitting in a circle, sharing their stories and writings, carefully listening, and engaging in critical dialogue—practices informed by an appreciation of the dialectic of reflection and action (Freire, 1993). That is, "the best education is a collective and social rather than an individual endeavor" and "students learn when they teach and when they apply to community improvement and liberation what they learn in the classroom" (Randels in SAC, 2007a, p. 166). In the process Randels and Salaam are not only mentoring but also learning from a generation of student writers and storytellers in New Orleans whose work is closely connected to the surrounding community. There is, in fact, a lineage developing: The more experienced students in SAC agree to mentor non-SAC peers in their own high schools, and some even work with elementary-age students at nearby public elementary schools (e.g., see SAC, 2007b). Graduates of SAC also have returned as teachers in the program after completing college degrees. Speaking of returnee Ashley Jones, Salaam asked students presently with SAC: "Why would Ashley identify with the bottom of the ship when she's got a spot on the deck now?" (Crossroads Project, 2006). For most students, the answer is clear—they, like Ashley, recognize the importance of SAC and appreciate that what sets the program apart is "harder work" and "peer critique," "a 'with us' versus 'against us' way of learning," "hearing different opinions" instead of being told "you're wrong," and the fact that class "relates to our lives," which means more than learning "such and such happened in 1895" (fieldnotes, 2007). LaQuita Joseph describes the SAC experience this way:

> SAC is not only a class in a school where we all learn facts and figures, but it's more of a way of life. Because what we learn, we apply to our everyday life. In many classes you are taught about people who make changes, but in SAC we take this to another level. We are taught how to make change through our writings, videos, and jobs that are provided for us where we tutor the young students. This is true praxis, taking what we have learned and putting it into action. (SAC, 2007b)

Since its founding, SAC has produced some 16 books, an array of videos, and a newspaper, and garnered about $1.5 million dollars in grants (SAC, 2007a, p. 166).

I had a chance to join Students at the Center in New Orleans, the city where I was born and raised, and witnessed firsthand its distinct contributions. I briefly want to situate each school contextually and offer a sense of what occurs in classrooms, where each student's life history is the starting point of SAC's work. (Please note that students' identities have been masked in classroom portraits of SAC pedagogy, with details altered to ensure confidentiality.)

Eleanor McMain Secondary School

Before Katrina McMain, an uptown public high school, was a selective admissions school, but in post-Katrina New Orleans it is an open access high school, one of only a handful of nonselective schools operated by the Orleans Parish School Board. Indeed, McMain "went through a major identity shift," according to Randels, as "a group of teachers who were somewhat veteran came from a dozen different high schools and said, 'We'll be here together and take all the kids'" (interview, 2007). Reflecting on these changes, Adriane Frazier—once a student with SAC and now a coordinator of SAC's community partnerships—relates how preexisting tensions rose to the surface as students from an array of pre-Katrina high schools congregated at McMain. "I could tell . . . the discussion [in class] was going to get heated," she observes, "because for so long the city had separated its children into pockets of poverty and privilege, and now the two worlds were colliding before us" (SAC, 2007a, pp. 15–16). Today, the school is largely made up of African American and Asian American (more specifically, Vietnamese American) students, some of whose parents are first generation members of the city's professional-managerial class.

At McMain several creative writing and advanced placement English literature classes are a part of SAC. Before class begins, students and teachers quickly grab the chairs, arranged in rows from the previous period, and form a circle where everyone sits. After a minute or two of informal exchanges, the first question is usually "Who wants to start?" Next begins the hard work of sharing one's writing aloud, listening fully to the writer-speaker, choosing two peers to provide comment, and engaging in an overall dialogue around the text. In creative writing, for instance, an African American young woman read a piece she drafted on the racial tensions associated with having a white boyfriend; "Things People Say to Get in Your Way" was its catchy title. It resembled a response to critics, proclaiming that "race shouldn't matter." Writing nothing down but having listened intently, the first student to provide feedback referenced specific lines from "Things People Say" and responded to them. Another student chimed in and suggested that the piece would make an ideal children's book on issues of race. Adding to these remarks, one male student expressed agreement with the author's sentiments, proclaiming, "You fine, you fine. You ugly, you ugly." "Okay," Salaam interjected, "but where do concepts of 'fine' and 'ugly' come from?" (fieldnotes, 2007). All of this led to a conversation on color blindness and some of the complexities surrounding the notion that "race shouldn't matter." Serious and engaging conversations frequently emerged in the process of discussing students' writings, and these conversations then informed the process of rethinking, refining, and rewriting.

On another occasion in this same class, students entered the room commenting on "drug tests" and the fact that classrooms would soon be on "lockdown," meaning that police dogs would be roaming the school's halls in search of drugs. As things quieted down, one young man exclaimed, "I'm tired of pissing in a cup!" Ever encouraging students to connect their innermost thoughts and lived experiences to their compositions, one of the teachers suggested, "You should write something with that title." But not all students' writing addressed such politicized subjects. The would-be author of the above piece went on to read a rather lengthy reflection he had penned on his "first time" with a girl. Whatever the content, rich exchanges generally took shape, leading Salaam to note, "People now want to read and write—that's what collective work does. And like a true collective, we don't seek to imitate one another. Each person offers something distinct" (fieldnotes, 2007).

Although closely tied to particular state-mandated texts and thus a bit more structured, the exchanges in advanced placement English literature at McMain were equally dynamic. In this case, the text was Geoffrey Chaucer's *Canterbury Tales*, and students were focusing on "The Wife of Bath's Prologue," which addresses gender relations in fourteenth-century England. Notably, students didn't read the text in isolation, but were expected to read it against others, including bell hooks' *Black Women: Shaping Feminist Theory* and selections from one of SAC's own books in progress, *Men We Love, Men We Hate*, to which students were invited to contribute.

Engagement with such readings informed essays that students were authoring on issues of gender oppression. One young writer shared a draft essay titled "I Hesitate to Thank You." It focused on the boy's father, who was a drug dealer and only sporadically visited his son. Despite these circumstances, the boy nonetheless "thanked" his father because his father's absence revealed the "strong women" in his life, such as his mother, and also taught him that he could "depend on himself." With all that Katrina brought, he concluded the essay, "my family stayed together," something that again served to show his family's vitality. Many students around the circle were anxious to share their thoughts in response. Some expressed that they "could relate" and appreciated the contradiction that he "hated his father with a passion *and* loved him for no reason." "I liked the way you thanked him for his failures," injected one student, while another underscored the appeal of a piece "written like a conversation." Contributing to the dialectic process, the student-author communicated he would "go home and do some edits tonight." Next the class moved to a discussion of "The Wife of Bath's Prologue" and briefly examined the contradictions of gender illuminated by that text. Interrelating past and present, text and context, student and school community, Randels queried, "Are boys and girls treated differently in this school?" (fieldnotes, 2007)

When I returned later in the year, Salaam and Randels were encouraging students who had written essays on the politics of language to participate in a project being developed jointly with Father Vien The Nguyen, the pastor of Mary Queen of Vietnam Church in New Orleans East. As a result of concerns regarding linguistic and cultural rifts between young and old members of the Vietnamese community, collaboration was under way to translate students' essays from English to Vietnamese and have students share them in a series of radio broadcasts. The teachers further suggested that the translated materials could be used to develop Vietnamese language and history classes at the school. All students, not only Vietnamese students, were invited to participate and graduating seniors in particular were urged to "leave something behind for the school" (fieldnotes, 2008). In these ways, SAC continuously seeks to maintain the bonds of culture, school, and community.

Frederick Douglass High School

Unlike McMain, a school where SAC had only recently initiated its work, Douglass was a place where SAC had roots before Katrina. Yet there, too, a number of substantive post-Katrina changes had occurred, with many of them related to issues that characterized the prestorm context. Consisting of largely working-class African American students, Douglass was one of the lowest ranked public high schools in New Orleans, if not the state. Maria Hernandez, a SAC student whose senior year at the school had just begun when Katrina hit, attests that before the hurricane "the state, using its accountability plan, was trying to shut down Douglass or take it over." Contributing to a much wider national effort focused on educational inequality, Hernandez recollects that she and fellow students at Douglass "were running a campaign called Quality Education as a Civil Right" (SAC, 2007a, p. 17). As a result:

> A lot of people were *finally* looking at our school as more than just a place where criminals are reared, which is the impression you'd get if all you knew were news reports. The media always ran to the school to report a fight, but no one said anything when my classmates placed first in a competition against professional journalists for a series they wrote on public education at the 50th Anniversary of *Brown v. Board of Education*. (p. 18)

Concerning the reign of neoliberal reform, she laments, "We had been fighting to improve from within neighborhood schools that don't have selective admissions. Now, with all schools being charters, no one will have the choice of truly public, neighborhood-based education." What Douglass has become instead is a school operated by the RSD, where only four teachers who taught there before the storm have returned (notably, two are with SAC). The diminishment of pre-storm faculty has been compounded by a corresponding "loss" of students. During the 2007–08 school year, the RSD admitted no new ninth graders to the school, meaning the entire ninth grade cohort consisted of those who had failed the previous year. Pondering the situation in early 2007, before the district's announcement that Douglass might be closed, one teacher with SAC surmised:

> My theory is that they're phasing out Douglass and want to turn it into a charter. They want the building. It's just like my friend says about Nigerian oil—"They want the oil, but they don't want the people." They want the "earl" [the word *oil* repeated with local inflection], but they don't want the people. (interview, 2007)

Another teacher connects this to a much longer struggle around the school: "There was always a segment of this city that would have liked this school to go away—that was going on before the storm" (interview, 2007). Significantly, prior to Katrina the Frederick Douglass Community Coalition, a group consisting of cultural, educational, and political organizations, developed a project to more centrally involve the community in decision making over curriculum and educational policy as well as to make the school available for community meetings (Weaving the Web, 2003). Regrettably, Randels testifies, "There were deeper inroads of parents and students and graduates who were invested in the school and who were here working for it. And so the push back was deeper. That's been stripped away. There's not as much traction here as there was before the hurricane" (interview, 2007). All of this, of course, raises rather serious questions about precisely what "recovery" means for schools in the state-run RSD, especially amid threats to close Douglass—one of the only open access high schools downtown. It certainly calls to mind Freire's (1998) own assessment of neoliberal theory across the globe, which "hides the fact that its ethics are those of the marketplace and not the universal ethics of the human person." He reminds us that "its fundamental ideology seeks to mask that what is really up for discussion is the increasing wealth of the few and the rapid increase of poverty and misery for the vast majority" (p. 114). This unfortunately appears to be the ruling ideology around public schooling in New Orleans.

The question of why such loss and tragedy are unfolding for families as well as schools in New Orleans was taken up during one of SAC's creative writing classes at Douglass. Welling up with emotion, one student read aloud the story of how death has been visited upon her family since Katrina. Her grandfather died on her sibling's birthday, while another close relative had cancer and passed away. Most students closely related to what they called her "tears on paper" and believed that few people outside of the city understood the amount of death that has plagued New Orleans, especially over the last several years. It was far from insignificant, pointed out Randels, that Douglass had 22 security guards, but only two guidance counselors, and he pondered whether or not students might "secure" themselves by getting to class on time and then mobilize for more counselors. As students pondered the idea, Salaam opened up his laptop and proceeded to share two poems he had written, both over a very brief period during which he lost two friends. As I exited the school that day, I commented to Salaam, "This school is like a police state." "No," Salaam mouthed, "it *is* a police state" (fieldnotes, 2007). These exchanges were at the forefront of my thoughts as I drove through the still-devastated neighborhood, where the red lights were not operating more than two years after the storm and houses, schools, and stores struggle to recover, while uptown white elites on high ground have resumed life.

Importantly, Salaam has emphasized with respect to SAC's work, "These are not woe-is-me, feel-sorry-for-us-poor-downtrodden-negroes investigations; rather these are honest explorations of complex situations" (SAC, 2007a, p. 138). This was apparent during a subsequent creative writing class at Douglass, when a student delivered "What I Hope to Do with My Life." Dedicated to a deceased grandparent, the piece detailed her goal of finishing high school—the first in her family to do so—and becoming a preschool teacher. "School's not for me," she candidly wrote, "but I will finish for my family." As the dialogue around kinship proceeded, Salaam added, "I like the way y'all lookin' out for each other. Folks with very little do that. Those with everything are like 'me, me, me.' It's good that's happening [in our community]." Of course, this is not to say that each and every exchange was positively generative or productive in enhancing solidarities. One young man, significantly a ninth grader, was rather resistant. He asked a question to Randels, who, in the spirit of SAC, repeated the pattern. "C'mon man," he uttered with some frustration, "I ask you a question and you ask a question back!" This same student later refused to read his writing aloud (fieldnotes, 2007). Such fits and nonstarters surely reflected the wider context of the school. During my time with SAC, in fact, a day at Douglass was disrupted and then terminated due to an electrical outage in the school. When I queried a security guard about the problem, I was told that the fire chief didn't know what was wrong, but it "could take a week to fix it." Come the next day, the plan was to relocate students to the back part of the building, where power was apparently working. I was told "it shouldn't be a problem" since the school was "smaller" since Katrina (fieldnotes, 2007). Keeping in mind the student's narrative of familial loss, the loss of a school day, and the potential loss of the school itself, the question we need to be asking is: Why? The legacy of racial power and oppression in New Orleans as well as the "freedom dreams" (Kelley, 2002) formed in response provide the grounds for understanding the dominant direction of reform in the city and the contested nature of reconstruction.

FROM THE STUDENT'S HISTORY
TO THE PEOPLE'S HISTORY

A key episode in the history of African American struggle in New Orleans was the central focus of SAC's (1999) first book of student writings, *Resistance*. In 1811, the largest slave revolt in the history of the United States occurred in New Orleans (Thrasher, 1995). In fact, New Orleans was intimately connected to black Jacobinism internationally, as maroon colonies in the swamps beyond the city were responsible for numerous plots and uprisings (see Hall, 1992; James, 1963). One of the leaders of the 1811 Slave Revolt, Charles Deslondes, arrived enslaved in New Orleans in the late 1790s when his master fled the Haitian Revolution. The efforts of

Deslondes and his comrades were commemorated in *Resistance*, which includes the outline of a play that students from SAC ultimately wrote and performed in 2000. In essence, applying dialogical methodology to theater, the play engages all who are present and involves them both in the process of knowledge construction about history and a fuller recognition of present-day solidarities and opportunities for activism.

Envision the following: The play "opens with the plaintive dirge of a funeral procession," while a student-actor announces, "We come to mourn a young man who was my dear and very best friend. . . . His passing should not be without cause. Our job today is to understand that cause. He died because of our complacency" (Walton & Cast, 1999, p. 43). Drawing connections between subaltern experience in the past and the more recent death of "our brothers" in the present, the question is posed: "What happened to the rage of leaders who died before us?" The problem posing persists: "Where are the warriors? Where are the truth tellers? Where are the singers of songs of liberation?" (p. 44). Using the theatrical space to weld reflection and action into wholehearted praxis, the students urge members of the audience:

> If you feel like a revolutionary, stand to your feet, clap your hands to shout and praise our ancestors who carried us through. Shout out not just for Harriett Tubman but for the unrecognized ancestors of the New Orleans area. Some of them stood here in Congo Square to fight for freedom. Shout out for Charles Deslondes (crowd repeats name). . . . (p. 44)

At that point, the wisdom of elders killed in the 1811 Slave Revolt is sought in an effort to better understand more immediate problems. Several revolutionary figures are thus incarnated on stage and offer "historical background as a way to call for present action" (p. 45). Deslondes, for example, proclaims:

> I was aware of the odds against me if I revolted against my oppressors, against the slave masters who enslaved me just as you are enslaved. If you want liberation you must stand firm and show it. Show it by going against the media, which rushes to report fights at your schools but ignores your will to fight intellectually. Which rushes to report when you score a touchdown but is all but invisible when you score high on the ACT. (p. 46)

Of utter import, the historic speeches are punctuated by a "call on members of the audience to testify about oppressions they have endured . . . and ways to overcome them" (p. 45). The play concludes as "poster boards to sign up for community action projects" are circulated throughout the space and a voice rings out: "Ladies and gentlemen of this assembly, if you feel like a revolutionary let's come together . . . by planning solutions to unanswered questions of oppressions within this society" (p. 50). By wedding creative writing, theater, and problem posing, the work of SAC enables the community to consider in quite powerful ways the perennial question "Why?" and to act upon the answers. On a global scale such efforts resonate with the *Theater of the Oppressed* developed by Brazilian activist Augusto Boal (1985), who invented a host of theatrical forms that enable passive *spectators* to become *spect-actors* in a kind of "rehearsal for the revolution" (p. 122; see also Buras & Apple, 2006).

This historical sensibility and its relationship to resistance are reflected in *The Long Ride*, another book produced by SAC (2005). Again revealing the links between SAC and the wider community, students authored this collection of writings for the New Orleans Civil Rights Park—a project initially envisioned by the Crescent City Peace Alliance and destined to take shape at the site of Homer Plessy's arrest on June 7, 1892 (see also Michna, 2009). Plessy was at the center of the historic 1896 Supreme Court case, *Plessy v. Ferguson*, which enshrined the tenet of "separate but equal" and legalized apartheid in the United States. Significantly, he was a resident of New Orleans who had intimate dealings with the Citizens' Committee to Test the Constitutionality of the Separate Car Law, a body consisting of New Orleans' Afro-Creole elite that consciously sought to challenge segregation on railway cars by having Plessy board the white car, declare his status as black, and refuse to move to the soot- and smoke-filled car designated for blacks (Desdunes, 1911/1973; DeVore & Logsdon, 1991; Fireside, 2004). Placing the history of racial oppression and resistance at the forefront, *The Long Ride* includes student and teacher writings that span the colonial history of Africa to *Plessy* to present-day New Orleans.

For instance, writing about the necessity of "recovering the unknown" of Africa, Adrinda Kelly, a student in one of SAC's very first classes, reflects:

> As a young girl, my classmates and I didn't think about Africa often. . . . The truth is there wasn't much a bunch of public school students growing up in one of America's blackest cities . . . could know about a place that we spent so much time trying to disassociate ourselves from. Africa, to us, was Kunta Kinte, slavery, dark skin and big lips. It was the Zulu parade at Mardi Gras with people in black-face handing out coconuts and beads. It was grass skirts and spears, rhythm and jungle. It was a lie, an embellishment, an embarrassment, a fantasy. And we didn't want it. (SAC, 2005, p.8)

For Kelly, overcoming this mis-education became "a kind of birthright" (in SAC, 2005, p. 8). Alternatively, Anastasia McGee attempts to "connect with maroon colonies" by comparing the choices she faced regarding which high school to attend in New Orleans to these rebels' commitment to still-enslaved peoples. She writes:

> The maroons communicated and stayed with the slaves to help free them. . . . It made me think about the decisions I could have made to escape oppression at my current neighborhood school . . . but I resisted some teachers' and students' efforts to try and get me to go to . . . selective admissions high schools. . . . I made the decision to stay at Douglass High School long before I read anything about the maroons and the history, but reading it made me conscious about my decision. . . . Like the maroons I believe in helping other people in my community and not just myself. (SAC, 2005, p. 28)

Historical memory is maintained by SAC through its writings about and for community, and although the opening of the Civil Rights Park has been postponed since the hurricane, Randels nonetheless emphasizes: "In post-Katrina New Orleans, it's interesting to wonder what actions . . . Deslondes, Plessy [and others] would be taking. . . . These are the questions students are beginning to ask" (p. 55).

"NOW WHO'S HOLDING THE GUN?"

While the students with SAC have begun to think through questions surrounding disinvestment and disaster in New Orleans, the United States as a whole has not. Admittedly, there have been attempts to center questions around the meaning of Katrina in U.S. classrooms (e.g., Crocco, 2007), but these are, for the most part, solitary efforts that proceed while an inexcusable silence characterizes mainstream news reporting, accompanied by state neglect. *Katrina and Me*, a collection of student and teacher writings that SAC (2007a) produced, was intended to disrupt these silences by telling the untold stories and ultimately contributed to this book. *Katrina and Me* includes the following words: "Before and After. New Orleans has a new time line. A new zero point." Rightfully eschewing a dehistoricized "post" discourse on New Orleans, a key declaration is made: "To understand post-Katrina, you have to understand pre-Katrina." In contrast to educational policy makers who wish to complete the work of Katrina by destroying the remaining remnants of the old and starting "from scratch," SAC announces: "Students, teachers, and community supporters certainly want much better public education in New Orleans. We just don't believe scorching the earth is the way to do it" (p. 11). Incontestably New Orleans has entered a new era, "but it is not a moment out of time" (p. 12). The past is indispensable if a truly new and more just New Orleans is to be imagined and constructed.

Most important, SAC (2007a) makes clear that the history of New Orleans "is not a story that only those in power will tell" (p. 12). It is crucial that critical race counterstories—the ones experienced and lived by those who called New Orleans home even when they were left to die on its streets—be circulated far and wide. Such counterstories are those told from the margins and in opposition to dominant narratives that ignore or misrepresent the experiences of subaltern groups (Apple & Buras, 2006; Delgado, 2000; Yosso, 2006). I believe they merit not just national but international attention, as readers both within and outside the United States may constitute a kind of tribunal, one that demands accountability from a government that has violated with impunity international treaties on human rights and the United Nations Guiding Principles on Internal Displacement (see US Human Rights Network, 2006, n.d.; Wing, 2006).

Trapped with her family in New Orleans East after the storm, Deborah Carey recollects:

> We listened to the radio about what was going on in the city: nothing, but bad news everywhere. All you could hear was people scrambling for help. National Guards my ass: They didn't even save us.
>
> The so-called criminals of New Orleans saved us, stealing boats, trucks, 18 wheelers, and buses. Society calls these people animals, saying, "They don't deserve to be citizens." . . .
>
> Seeing a big moving truck with at least 30 people in the back, one of the drivers asked us did we need a ride. We didn't even answer. We just hopped on, which reminded me of how slaves were treated: a whole lot of black folks packed up on a wagon escaping from master. . . .
>
> Whatever help we needed the state was supposed to provide. It was like our citizenship went down the stream right along with our houses, all forgotten about by our government. (SAC, 2007a, pp. 29–30)

Conditions are scarcely better now. Even those who have been able to return experience ongoing disarray and difficulty, and discover that the "new" New Orleans is being rebuilt for families who can afford high rent and high ground (Buras, 2005, 2007, 2009a). Another SAC student, Vinnessia Shelbia, elucidates, "Leaving New Orleans was hard, because there's no other place like it. But living in New Orleans post-Katrina is just as bad, because there's nowhere to live" (SAC, 2007a, p. 81). Attempting to stay with relatives, but frustrated due to "12 people living in a one-bedroom, one bath" place, she and her family were forced to move into disparate homeless shelters throughout the city due to escalating rents. These circumstances cause her to articulate sentiments that are sure to resonate with poor youth well beyond the borders of the city:

"It makes me wonder what kind of world we live in when children no older than 14 are experiencing these things" (p. 82). Recalling the violence that typified pre-Katrina New Orleans—violence so often blamed on poor African Americans with white privilege rarely implicated—she poses a penetrating question: "New Orleans really is the murder capital, but now who's holding the gun?" (p. 82). Her words echo those of affordable housing activists, who have protested the planned demolition of thousands of public housing units in New Orleans (Times–Picayune, 2007a, 2007b). In the final analysis, Vinnessia's narrative illuminates the acceleration of state disinvestment in post-Katrina New Orleans and the detrimental effects on low-income communities of color; it also should stimulate questions about the nature of urban "renewal" in other urban contexts (e.g., see Stovall & Smith, 2008).

One veteran public school teacher from Alfred Lawless High School in the Lower 9th Ward, Katrena Jackson-Ndang, laments the school's devastation and states that "for the first time in the school's 42-year history there was no ring ceremony, no prom, no homecoming, no winter formal, no sweetheart ball and no graduation" (SAC, 2007a, p. 70). One year later in July 2006, students and teachers gathered together for a kind of "Lawless Family Reunion"—a composite memorial, prom, graduation, and even retirement party for many "highly qualified educators" who "are not working in the new charter schools and the Recovery School District, because these are using unfair tactics to undermine the professionalism and respect of veteran teachers" (p. 71). Jackson-Ndang adds, "They want to hire inexperienced teachers so they can pay them little or no money and also so they can treat them like sharecroppers or better still like slaves with no rights and no input or say about what happens in the schools." Largely ignored, this teacher cries out:

> The festivities are over for this year, but the questions remain. What's next for Lawless and all the other public schools in the district? Does anybody know? What's next for the highly qualified, unemployed, displaced educators? Does anybody know? Does anybody care? (p. 71)

New Orleans is still unimaginably devastated, with the population cut in half and countless residents unable to return due to strategic disinvestment in public infrastructure during the "rebuilding" process (Buras, 2007; Common Ground, 2006; Greater New Orleans Community Data Center, 2008). Writing poetically, Damien Theodore calls on New Orleans to "wake up." "I finally saw her, and she was asleep," he penned upon returning home two months after Katrina (SAC, 2007a, p. 39–40). He firmly acknowledges:

I got mad when I saw her sleeping,
not worrying about me and my family,
forgetting about her people.
I was mad.
All I could do was hope she was dreaming. . . .

Struck by sudden recognition, Damien continues:

Then I thought about it. She can't do it by herself.
It's gonna take a revolution to wake her up.
If we want her up and alive again, we need to get a move on it.
She will never wake up, if we don't get started now.

What might it mean to reawaken New Orleans, particularly a New Orleans that doesn't forget its people? In terms of education, Maria Hernandez suggests, "If someone asked me about how to rebuild the schools in New Orleans, I'd say set up a school where all the classes have only 15 students and where the 'village' makes the class a family atmosphere" (SAC, 2007a, p. 149). In this way, she proposes that SAC—an actually existing but alternate program within the public system—might cast new light on recovery and reveal that the realization of a more democratic educational system is indeed possible.

Yet clearly most classrooms in post-Katrina New Orleans are worlds away from joining the path charted—not chartered—by SAC. Randels illustrates the promises and challenges that characterized the schools before Katrina and the near overwhelming contests that confront the public schools of New Orleans now. He focuses attention on Z, "a young man who didn't always go to class" before the storm and whose "size and facial expression and body language might seem menacing to someone who sees him around school but doesn't really know him" (SAC, 2007a, p. 189). Z had approached Randels with a request to teach him how to read—a powerful reminder that even before the storm, the conditions that prevailed in the city's public schools were deplorable. One lesson to be learned, Randels points out, is that "young people such as Z are eager to learn, given the right conditions" (p. 190). Tragically, he discloses, "Z won't be with us in the return to New Orleans. Word is he drowned in the storm." Randels' final words, though, push us to find something redemptive amid the destruction that has occurred—in a sense, to unearth what Freire (1970/1993) called "untested feasibility." Recognizing that history is unfinished, I join Randels in issuing his plea: "For the sake of the many young people like Z, I hope policy makers and national experts will listen to the lessons veteran New Orleans educators have learned from Z" (p. 190). That is, youth of color in urban schools want to learn and can, if the physical, economic, cultural, and human infrastructure is there.

I asked the teachers, "How do you conceptualize the role of some of the books and writings the kids are doing as part of the effort to maintain a sense of neighborhood history, community voice, and culture, because so much of this has been disrupted?" Not surprisingly and most appropriately, I was told a story. Drawing implicit connections between global movements against injustice and local efforts in post-Katrina New Orleans, Salaam explained that Jorge Luis Borges, an Argentine writer, "has a story that I think explains" the work of SAC. He began:

> This group of people was beset by invaders and they decided they were going to fight. And they fought and fought, but they couldn't defeat the invaders. And the invaders decided they were going to wipe the people out. And there was a big battle that was coming up and all of the able-bodied young men decided they were going to fight in that battle. The night before the battle, they were preparing to fight and the leader picked one young man and told him, "You have to go away across the mountains." And he says, "I'm here to fight." And the leader says, "No, you have to go away across the mountains." And he says, "What do I have to do?" "You just have to tell our story," the leader explained. "Well, why me? I want to stay here and fight with everybody else." He said, "You're the best story-teller we have. If we lose you, nobody knows our story. So you have to go tell the story." And they had the battle the next day and all of them were killed. And so the way the story ends is "This is my story . . . ." He was the guy who was sent across the mountains and is telling the story.

Salaam immediately concluded: "We have to tell the story. I don't believe we're gonna win this one. I really do not believe we're going to win this one. But I do believe the story is important. We have to tell our story" (interview, 2007).

NEO-GRIOTS WRITING WITH TEXT, SOUND, AND LIGHT

Students at the Center persists under difficult conditions, but remains committed to telling the stories of embattled youth in New Orleans. Part of this effort includes the involvement of students in Neo-Griot Productions, a "New Orleans-based multi-media krewe that produces publications, websites, audio recordings, radio broadcasts, and digital videos." That is to say, SAC builds from the more traditional methods of the griot and incorporates newer digital technologies, especially video, into the narrative process. Thus students are given the chance to "write with text, sound, and light" (e.g., see Neo-Griot Productions & SAC, 2002). At the opening of a class session at Douglass, in fact, a student mentioned *Baby Love*, a video produced by SAC in an effort to dramatize and enliven discussion of some of the issues relevant to teenagers (Neo-Griot Productions & SAC, 2002). One of the teachers retrieved a copy from a nearby cabinet and passed it around so students could view its jacket, which included a brief description of the film, colorful photos, and a list of scenes. *Baby Love* is a feature length film—in this case, Salaam wrote the initial script, while students assumed roles in the film, produced accompanying music, shot the footage, and edited the final copy. Set in New Orleans, *Baby Love* addresses a host of issues that preoccupy teens, from friendship, love, and sexuality to pregnancy, abortion, and HIV, to life aspirations and plans for college. Salaam and Ashley Jones, who played one of the main characters, considered aloud with the class the intricacies of shooting one of the scenes. With curiosities piqued, Salaam queried students, "Would you be interested in making a movie?" A chorus of voices responded "Yes!" Salaam specified that this would require students to first write a script, which led him to query even further: "What do you want to make a movie about?" (fieldnotes, 2007). Not without significance, students were apprised of the fact that a screening of *Baby Love* was planned for students, their families, and community members later in the week. The screening would be followed by an open discussion of the film, highlighting once more the hallmark of SAC's approach: the construction of understanding and knowledge through community participation. In sum, the circulation of *Baby Love* reveals the permeable boundaries between classroom and community and makes visible the processes underlying SAC's ongoing co-productions.

Aside from creating books and films, SAC is involved in the production of *Our Voice* (1999), a "newspaper written by teens for teens about teen issues." Student voices from middle schools and high schools parade across its pages. One is immediately impressed by the range of writings and the community connections that are actively fostered. Take as one example the November issue in 1999. Introducing a student-authored poem delivered at a demonstration for U.S. political prisoner Mumia Abu Jamal, one article begins: "Youth in New Orleans do not just watch the news. They often participate in events in which they air their views" (p. 2). Alongside the poem is a box of announcements for poetry readings and community action meetings. On the very next page, which details upcoming theater events, SAC's play on the 1811 Slave Revolt is listed. One editorial calls for cleaning up a local neighborhood and advocates turning trash-filled lots into basketball courts and gardens. The author makes clear her commitment, writing, "I love the dirty South, and God bestowed it upon me to recognize a mass of riches to be uncovered in the heart of the ghetto" (p. 4). Book reviews and "race news" are likewise a part of *Our Voice*: a review of a book on historic race riots in New Orleans, a photo of students on an archaeological dig in one of the city's oldest black neighborhoods, and a quiz on racism and public education are included (pp. 6-7).

THE FIGHT FOR FREDERICK DOUGLASS HIGH SCHOOL: STUDENTS DON'T KNOW THEIR HISTORY?

The historical consciousness and community activism that are so central to SAC's work make the fight for Frederick Douglass High School, where its own roots run deep, more than a little symbolic. In fact, the story of this struggle resonates with struggles against targeted disinvestment and privatization in many parts of the Global South, whether in Pretoria, South Africa (Ndimande, 2009), Porto Alegre, Brazil (Gandin, 2006), or other urban centers (Davis, 2006). Across these contexts in the "dirty South" oppressed communities navigate and often resist neoliberal policies that promote their cultural and economic dispossession.

Reporting on his return to New Orleans on November 11, 2005, Salaam painfully recounts his response to the destruction before him: "Welcome back, black. Look what they've done to your home." The "they," he clarifies, does not refer to Katrina, but to the politicians, Army Corps of Engineers, policy experts, and urban planners "who did not really give a damn" (SAC, 2007a, p. 43). Regrettably, they still did not two and a half years later, as evidenced by an announcement in early April 2008 that Douglass High School might be closed, with students possibly transferred to trailers at a nearby site, where a Law and Public Safety Academy (that is, a high school focused on military, police, fire, and emergency medical services training) would be opened (fieldnotes, 2008). Fears only deepened when RSD Superintendent Paul Vallas presented a report on the status of elementary and high schools in mid-April—one that failed to even mention Douglass—and "claimed that the community had not cared about Douglass for the last 40 years" (SAC, 2008; see also daLuz, 2008).

In response, teachers, students, members of SAC, Douglass alumnae, community members, and local activists—many affiliated with the Douglass Community Coalition—organized a public meeting with RSD officials to discuss their concerns. During this meeting in early May, district officials emphasized that the School Facilities Master Plan for Orleans Parish, which was under development and due to be released in June, would include "recommendations" regarding which schools would remain open, be renovated, or get closed. One claimed part of the issue was lack of sufficient funds for renovations throughout the RSD (thus the necessity of "consolidating") as well as an estimate provided by a construction company (one responsible for building a substandard police academy in Iraq) that indicated it would require at least $35 million to repair Douglass (fieldnotes, 2008; Myers, 2007). Financial constraints, however, failed to account for why other schools—some in worse condition and some in more affluent areas—were already slated for support or why RSD approval of charter schools had proceeded despite administrative concerns that high school enrollment was "down to 4,000 students" since Katrina. Notably, during the very same meeting, the official also asserted that enrollment was down because "people are looking for alternatives" and stated, without noting the contradiction, that "come June, we're going to have a big enrollment in our high schools." The RSD, the official explained, plans

> to again go out and for all the kids who aren't enrolled and for the kids who were maybe enrolled in schools [read: noncharter schools] and may be interested in reenrolling in other schools [read: charter schools], we're going to in effect . . . have a high school fair . . . and we're going to try to get our enrollment up in our individual [read: charter] schools. (fieldnotes, 2008)

Such contradictions point toward the importance of a question posed by an alumnus and local activist prior to the meeting: "Why would they close the school . . . when there is no other high school in this community and the building itself is a viable building?"

Most significant were comments made by the RSD official regarding the school's history, ones that demonstrated the instrumental role of historical erasure in legitimizing disinvestment and displacement. For instance, one teacher underscored, "This school is probably one of the most historic schools in the city named after one of the most historic black leaders in the USA" (fieldnotes, 2008). An alumnus of the school likewise stressed, "We fought for this school in the '60s, '70s, '80s, and '90s. We have too much history here [to close the school]," referring, in part, to black student protests in the late 1960s to have the school mascot, a Rebel (Confederate solider), changed to the Bobcats (fieldnotes, 2008; interview, 2008). The official responded to such remarks, asserting: "Kids don't know they're going to school at a historical landmark. They just know they're going to a building where the electricity doesn't work, where the technology has been antiquated." Another oft-repeated message of the official, who was consistently distanced from the School Facilities Master Plan, was "I'm not going to get involved in the politics of where schools should go. I'm going to get involved in the politics of what schools should be," as though no relationship existed between the past, the community's sense of place, and the purpose of education. A theater artist, one associated with SAC, assumed the floor and explained:

> Many buildings in this city were destroyed three years ago and this building wasn't, and I think that this is why you're experiencing such a strong resistance about the idea of this building being destroyed or taken away from us. You also have said that buildings aren't really where you are, you are really about academics. I want to share with you that many sacred academic moments have occurred in this building. . . . And one of those things . . . that I can speak formally about is learning about Frederick Douglass, learning about Homer Plessy and the boldness and the work that came from his step so many years ago. And a textbook that has been written about the Civil Rights movement . . . called *The Long Ride* and it was put together by Students at the Center.
>
> I think the biggest strength of the Students at the Center program is that students who are some of the poorest, some of the most oppressed students in our city, have learned how to identify their own oppression. . . . They have learned how to voice that and write about it and teach everyone else about it. . . . If you want to make a difference . . . you will read that book. . . . And you will do everything in your power to save this school and give it back to the hands of the people who built it. (fieldnotes, 2008)

During the meeting, a petition that contested the closing of Douglass and called for a curriculum focused on college preparation, fine arts, and community service—all elements embodied in SAC—circulated. Meanwhile, it was stressed time and again by officials that a "steering committee" had been organized by the principal, and an RSD liaison appointed, to generate a proposal for the school's future, and that "there will be a window of opportunity for the community to provide additional input before the final recommendations are made" in the School Facilities Master Plan (fieldnotes, 2008).

Yet in mid-May, just two weeks after the meeting with RSD officials and *before* the School Facilities Master Plan "recommendations" had been reported formally and the community given the promised window to provide input, Louisiana State Superintendent of Education Paul Pastorek (2008) responded in writing to one of several letters from community activists regarding Douglass's possible closure:

> The Douglass school will be repurposed—reused for another purpose, not demolished. Community involvement will be part of the process of school property disposition. . . . My question to you and your coalition—are you tied to the school building or to creating a world class academic school for the students?

It was stated that a new high school would be built in the 9th Ward, one "focused on civil rights and arts," but details about *when* and precisely *where* the school would be built were not offered, and no recognition was given to the gross contradictions inherent in closing a historic school that took shape during the civil rights era and has housed a program focused on history and communication arts for more than a decade. At a meeting of the Frederick Douglass Community Coalition the very next day, one activist, who was invited to be a member of the "steering committee," expressed concern that the committee itself was "not for input but for rubber stamping" plans that school authorities had made already and reported committee discussion that a "new Douglass" would focus on police, fire, emergency medical services, and the military, despite community opposition. Even more disheartening, she stated that "neither the principal nor consultant [who headed the committee] has any idea of this history of work and have not made efforts to be informed about the strengths of the neighborhood, school, or graduates" (Frederick Douglass Community Coalition, 2008). The struggle continues at the time of this writing, reminding us, in the spirit of Frederick Douglass, Homer Plessy, and Paulo Freire, that we need not accept "a 'well-behaved' present nor a predetermined future."

In truth, neither Randels nor Salaam nor the students are romantic about what will be required to weather this storm. What they do recognize is that they have at their disposal the voices and traditions of ancestors and the bonds of community to sustain and fuel the struggle. One of SAC's (2007b) digital videos entitled *Writing with Light* shows students from Douglass reading essays they penned on the ways that SAC has enriched their lives and communities. One particular image from the video stands out: Salaam is seated on the periphery of the SAC circle, while Gabrielle Turner, a SAC graduate-turned-teacher, assists a current SAC student, who is filming the speech event. Captured here is a visual representation of SAC's genealogy, and the collaborative exchanges that enable students to become teachers and teachers to become students. Standing behind the novice filmmaker, Gabrielle delicately and attentively monitors his use of the camera, sometimes swaying in response to his movements, which are themselves connected to the orators framed by the camera's lens. At the conclusion of this segment, both Randels and Salaam reenter the process and are seen (and heard) offering guidance on film making techniques. All of this powerfully demonstrates what one SAC student has called "initiating and completing the circle of education" (SAC, 2007b). Recognizing the power of critical historical consciousness and counter-storytelling, this chapter has foregrounded the words of SAC students and teachers with the hope that activists who are oceans apart might join and further complete the circle of education by seeing the struggles of pre- and post-Katrina New Orleans through the eyes of the city's youth. They reveal how Freire's pedagogy of the oppressed has taken form in the other South—the one in the belly of the beast and the eye of the storm—and challenge us to consider how solidarities might be built in the fight against the global disaster of neoliberalism (Buras, 2009a; Buras & Motter, 2006; Saltman, 2007b).

CHAPTER 2

Students at the Center: The Word, the River, and Education for Liberation

OPENING REFLECTION

Forming a Mighty River

Kristen L. Buras

CRITICAL RACE legal scholar Charles Lawrence (1995) draws upon the work of Vincent Harding, who wrote a history of black radicalism entitled *There is a River*, and reflects upon what Harding called "the Word." Lawrence elaborates:

> It is a tradition of teaching, preaching, and healing; an interdisciplinary tradition wherein healers are concerned with the soul and preachers with the pedagogy of the oppressed; a tradition that eschews hierarchy in the face of the need for all of us who seek liberation to be both teachers and students. . . . It is a vocation of struggle against dehumanization, a practice of raising questions about reasons for oppression, an inheritance of passion and hope. (p. 336)

From this description, one might presume that Lawrence was pondering the work of Students at the Center (SAC) but of course his work predates SAC. Nevertheless, the vocation of struggle in which SAC is engaged is undeniably a part of the river of black activism that has been raging for centuries. As the words of students and teachers in this chapter demonstrate, the process of education for liberation consists of strenuous work and unsparing critique, yet it is simultaneously informed by an unflagging spirit of hope. Salaam writes honestly about the sense of despair that sometimes takes over and the challenges of "nourishing the dream of teaching youth." Yet he remains steadfast in his commitment: "I do not apologize for my stance: I advocate education for liberation, not education for mainstream socialization." He rightly points out that "some people have developed theories about teaching inner-city youth, and most of those theories are predicated on preparing these youth to participate in the mainstream. Such theories never question the sanity of joining in a system that has oppressed and exploited the very youth we are teaching." Surely the most strident call for the mainstreaming of urban youth of color has been issued by neoconservatives. Their vision of education, however, is far from liberatory (see Buras, 2008). Although framed as inclusive and benevolent, it stands worlds apart from the black activist tradition that Lawrence and Salaam discuss.

A prime example of the neoconservative vision may be found in tracts published by the Thomas B. Fordham Institute under the leadership of Chester Finn. In the "Foreword" to *Sweating the Small Stuff: Inner-City Youth and the New Paternalism*, written by David Whitman (2008) under the auspices of the Fordham Institute, Finn and coauthor Marci Kanstoroom announce that "a healthy, forceful, modern version of paternalism" is what African American and Latino students need. According to them, schools that exhibit such paternalism are "preoccupied with fighting disorder." More to the point, "students are shown exactly how they are expected to behave—how to sit in a chair without slumping, how to track the teacher with their eyes, how to walk silently down the hall. . . . Their behavior is monitored closely at all times" (p. x). This disciplinary ethos "involves much more than telling poor people how to live." It provides them with a "way out of socio-cultural cul-de-sacs" and helps to "change their lifestyles for the better." All of this is allegedly for the greater good, since schools "are supposed to civilize, incentivize and nurture children." Finn and Kanstoroom say we really must appreciate that "schools serving inner-city kids may need to do more of [this] and do it more intensively," that is, placing poor and working-class students of color under "close supervision" and teaching them "how to learn and how to live" (p. vii). This how-to agenda includes a pedagogy that schools students "to embrace middle-class values, to aspire to college, to behave properly, and to reject the culture of the street." At the heart of this project is an invitation to reject the so-called street for Mainstreet, where "a work ethic" and "politeness, neatness, and respect for elders" prevail. But clearly, Finn and Kanstoroom conclude, "poor families cannot pull this off alone." There's good news, though: paternalistic teachers and schools can do this for their "clients" (p. xiii).

Pardon the series of quotes from Finn and Kanstoroom, but I think they expose the deep rift that exists between "liberating" seemingly uncivilized black and Latino youth from their culturally deficient cul-de-sacs (so they can move into a middle-class one on Mainstreet) and engaging in liberatory educational processes alongside students whose voices and cultural knowledge are central to the enrichment of the communities in which they live. In the latter case, politeness does not hold sway over the "impolite" criticism of class and race oppression, while discipline refers not to walking silently, but instead to the rigorous examination of the injustices confronted by students—personally and collectively—under neoliberal policies. This doesn't mean romanticizing the families and communities of students. As Salaam points out in his upcoming account, these aren't "woe-is-me" stories, but rather "honest explorations of complex social situations." But it also doesn't mean "filling up" students with core knowledge, facts, and manners while neglecting to make students think—something Demetria White wisely recognizes in her essay. The silence which is valorized by Finn and his allies represents the same "self-doubt" and "powerlessness" that Ashley Jones sought to overcome through her work with SAC. As she writes in the coming pages, "I entered the program hoping to improve my writing and reclaim my sense of self." In coming to see video production as narrative form, Ashley discovered, "I could make other people look good as well as validate them, just by assisting them in sharing their story. My camera became a mirror through which people could see themselves. . . . My validation came from being able to highlight the beauty and power of others." Echoing the sentiments of Finn, "the larger society told these students they were worthless, having no knowledge or understanding of their own lives. Unfortunately, many of the kids believed it." Gabrielle Turner likewise credits the pedagogy of SAC for instilling a commitment to "passing on the stories" of her family and community and "a passion . . . to capture, preserve, and share this legacy with others." In her exchange with Ashley and Gabrielle regarding "The Power to Tell Our Stories," Adrienne Dixson positions counter-storytelling in the wider tradition of critical race pedagogy and praxis.

This kind of affirmative, historically grounded education for community self-determination sharply contrasts with the standardizing, disciplinary thrust of schooling critiqued by Demetria, who castigates an education that filled her with facts but little knowledge of the "hows" and "whys" behind what is taught. By comparison, the vocation of SAC—its work ethic—is to create spaces where students can speak out and intervene in the struggles of their communities rather than, as Salaam laments, their "being encased in a near zombie-like state of obedience." As Maisha Fisher reveals in her exchange with Salaam over "Education for Liberation Rather Than Exploitation," this is the same vocation that guides the Power Writers, whose work in the Bronx is something she likewise situates in the historic currents of the river mentioned earlier (see also Fisher, 2007b).

Native American activist Winona LaDuke earned a degree in economic development from Harvard University, but never viewed it as a means for escaping indigenous communities. Just the opposite: She has spent much of her life attempting to recover Anishinaabeg land and traditions that were taken by the United States government and logging industry. LaDuke (2002) reminds us:

> Across the continent, on the shores of small tributaries, in the shadows of sacred mountains, on the vast expanse of the prairies, or in the safety of the woods, prayers are being repeated, as they have for thousands of years, and common people with uncommon courage and the whispers of their ancestors in their ears continue their struggles to protect the land and water and trees on which their very existence is based. And like small tributaries joining together to form a mighty river, their force and power grows. This river will not be dammed. (p. 64)

As students, teachers, and critical scholars make clear through their exchanges in this chapter, there are many vital tributaries contributing to liberatory education, and SAC is among them. Together these students share their stories and teach us that they are not "clients" in need of regimentation and marketization: They and their teachers are instead participating in a longer tradition of "soldiering on" despite opposition, as Fisher's insightful history of black literacy organizing and activism attests.

This chapter initiates a fundamental conversation around pedagogy and educational policy, one that sustains the remainder of the book. At the very center of the exchanges are the voices of teachers and students, who are ironically and frequently overlooked as meaningful contributors to the debates and decision making that surround urban education, even though those debates and decisions impinge upon their very lives. Meanwhile, a host of consultants, superintendents, heads of educational management organizations, and think tanks define and weigh in on the issues, only to exacerbate the dispossession that already prevails.

Below Jim Randels recollects what first ignited SAC—at root, a desire to create a community of learners and teachers against a system that seeks to "efficiently" process students en masse, while overworked teachers are scapegoated for their inadequacies under factory-like conditions (the fact that education is made to function like an "industry" or "business" is more than a little significant here). This firsthand account of SAC's beginnings is followed by two sets of exchanges: one focused on "The Power to Tell Our Stories" and another on "Education for Liberation Rather Than Exploitation." Each of these exchanges conveys the meaning of the program through the educational autobiographies of students and teachers, accompanied by the commentaries of critical scholars who emphasize the wider significance of SAC's praxis and its rightful place in an historical continuum of black activism and subaltern resistance.

BEGINNINGS

It's the Working Conditions, Not the Teachers

Jim Randels

"Do you have them?" Portia asked as she darted across the hall, still clutching her graphing calculator.

"I *have* them. The question is have I done anything with them."

"You know what I mean," she sighed, plopping her book bag on her desk.

"Yes. I finished. You can come get your paper and start reading through my comments."

Portia's junior English class was one of my favorites. Although packed with 32 students, well over half of them were eager and serious, itching, like Portia, to have me return their essays so they could begin the next round of revisions. They'd fight over who would read their writings to the class: we only had time for one or two students per day. This limit meant, especially when you add in all the interruptions for testing and assemblies and personal crises and heated discussions about an essay by James Baldwin, a sermon by Jonathan Edwards, or a poem by Ntozake Shange, that each student would be lucky to share her writing with the class once in a month.

As I pulled Portia's paper out of the stack, I could see that the hallways had filled to capacity. The building's a huge factory, packing as many students as possible inside. It's hard not to think of cattle, numbered and tagged, being herded—an impersonal mass. In many ways the best part of teaching are these less packed moments when a student's scheduling allows him to arrive early and grab a minute or two of direct conversation with a teacher or classmate.

Portia glanced at her paper, looked up, and said, "You're much better than any English teacher I've ever had."

Joshua moaned, a sly grin curling the corners of his mouth, "Don't encourage him. I'm rewriting that interview with my mom for the third time."

"They should get rid of the rest of them," chimed in Khaia, the queen of exaggeration. "I'd probably have a full scholarship for college by now, if I'd had you since ninth grade."

I decided I couldn't let this conversation end. My students were beginning to sound like the journalists, insurance salesmen, business people, architects, university administrators, and lawyers who set educational policy for our public schools in New Orleans—schools where few, if any, of them send their children. Occasionally lifting up the individual hero. Usually making simplistic analyses of school failures. Deciding that if two or three "at-risk" neighborhood schools out of 80 or so can raise test scores then all should. Claiming—despite never having taught—that incompetent teachers are the problem.

"What makes you think I'm such a great teacher?"

"Nobody else really thinks about what we write."

"You give us tons of work—and you read it all."

"Other teachers maybe say 'very good' or mark our grammar and spelling mistakes or just give us a grade."

It was clear that my students were products of our broader culture: They went for answers as quick, easy, and unfulfilling as a drive-through. They mimicked what the "experts" said. They took the convenient excuse.

"Y'all have to think about this more carefully. Let's not accept right away that it's just bad teachers or that I'm a great one. What else might explain the differences between teachers?"

We talked about it for the next 15 minutes. In response to their questions, I explained that two years ago I had decided I could not teach well as a full-time teacher. I now taught three instead of six classes a day, 85 rather than 170 students a day. This reduced load allowed me to put in nine rather than 18 hours a day and actually teach my students the way they deserved to be taught—if we were going to stick to the 30 or so students per class that our "efficient," cheap society that devalues education funds.

That conversation led to a fuller discussion of solutions. Out of that class, Students at the Center (SAC) was born. Two of those class members, Kenyatta Johnson and Erica DeCuir, volunteered to work outside of class time to write a funding proposal with me. We decided on a handful of principles:

1. Only the rare mutant superhero teacher would even approach being effective with 180 students a day.
2. Students needed a chance to read and discuss their writings fully, having feedback and full discussion on what they write with peers and teachers.
3. Our city would never fund education the way it needs to be funded and the way national professional organizations recommend: 15:1 student-teacher ratios per class and no more than four classes per day.

4. Students are the most underused resource in any school.
5. Students learn when they teach and when they apply to community improvement and liberation what they learn in the classroom.
6. The best education is a collective and social rather than an individual endeavor.
7. In elective writing classes using a workshop format and with no more than 15 students in a class, students can train to become effective leaders of one-on-one and small-group writing conferences.
8. Writing should take place in all academic disciplines.

That first proposal earned us a $6,000 dollar grant in 1996 to offer two pilot SAC classes at McDonogh 35. Twelve years, 16 books, numerous videos, and over $1.5 million dollars later, SAC is in a handful of schools in New Orleans, featured in national educational conferences, and a model that classrooms in South Carolina, Vermont, California, and Rhode Island are following. And Portia's classmate Erica has since spent two years returning essays and preparing her students to lead workshops in SAC classes at Frederick Douglass High School in New Orleans.

THE POWER TO TELL OUR STORIES

Speaking Out

Randels establishes one basic fact: If the assembly line is constructed instead as a small cooperative, students and teachers can be immensely "productive" in schools and communities. In this first set of exchanges, students share stories in their own words about the history and philosophy of SAC and the educational experiences it has afforded them, particularly in comparison to earlier and more common experiences in school. With her sobering account of classrooms that rarely compel students to question the "whys" behind the memorized facts, Demetria White reminds us of precisely why SAC's pedagogic approach is so transformative (and so desperately needed). In turn, Adrienne Dixson responds by joining students' stories to the tradition of counter-storytelling and critical race pedagogy, arguing that such pedagogy can play a role in disrupting the redemptive images associated with the neoliberal project. That is to say, the power to tell one's own story, to take control of one's own image, is to hold up the "magic mirror" (Hall & Karsten, 2008) that Ashley Jones describes below.

Rain

Ashley Jones

I will never look at rain the same again. Before the storm, rain was something I welcomed with the peaceful calm and quiet giddiness of a child. I would stare at drops, falling from somewhere in heaven, and wonder about what their stories were. I would walk to my car without an umbrella and squeal at the delight of cool splashes of angel tears hitting my face. That was before the storm though. Now, like most New Orleanians who would normally welcome the rain during a second line, a funeral, an outside party, the rain carries a lot of fear and too many memories.

It now reminds me of sleeping in stuffy hotels and wakening to my mother's call to see my city submerged under water. As long as I live, I will never stop seeing people on rooftops, or wading through sludge with their babies and bags of the few things they could salvage from a full lifetime of relics, keepsakes, souvenirs. The images of people, and places I had driven or walked past all my life, startled me. I'm sure that for some, those images showed the human suffering and pain that lingered in the air those horrific days after the water rose. But what frightened me was that for those of us who had gone through the experience, those images represented powerlessness where it could have showed strength.

I have battled with self-doubt and powerlessness ever since the fifth grade, when in front of all of my peers one little boy howled, "Hey Ashley, you have a Beavis and Butthead nose." He destroyed me that day, by comparing me to an image he saw on television. When my eighth-grade teacher told me about Students at the Center (SAC), I entered the program hoping to improve my writing and reclaim my sense of self. My teacher was able to see my worth.

I was a reclusive 15-year-old when I entered SAC. SAC's philosophy is that students are the most valuable resource for their own learning. The program validates young people's experiences and encourages them to analyze history, literatures, and current world events. By sharing writings and ideas about educational reform with the larger community, students also become leaders and agents for social and educational change. Suffering from the "ugly duckling" syndrome, I barely muttered a word in the class, even though I was quickly identified as one of its most talented writers.

Eventually, writing became the weapon I used to slay my feelings of self-consciousness and doubt. I quickly became a resource to my peers. Implementing one of SAC's ideas of quality education, I began peer teaching, critiquing writings, and mentoring my peers, from freshmen to seniors.

By my senior year, SAC had already become a model program for what education could mean to a city grappling with social and educational inequality. After having distributed countless student-written chapbooks and produced radio spots in conjunction with WWOZ, a jazz and heritage radio station vital to New Orleans' musical legacy, SAC started making movies.

With two other students I formed Newbian Productions, an all-female crew and the first media production group in our high school's history. I was the first to try my hand at cinematography.

The moment I slid behind the camera, I became in control of whoever was caught between the light and my lens.

The camera, which first appealed to me because it provided a hiding place, became a way that I could express. It was empowering knowing that I could make other people look good as well as validate them, just by assisting them in sharing their story. My camera became a mirror through which people could see themselves. In turn, people would become mirrors for whoever would sit and watch.

It was also transformative for me. My validation came from being able to highlight the beauty and the power of others. A large part of SAC's philosophy, which has now become a part of mine, is that we can all learn from each other's experiences. And I was learning, with every shoot, how to look at myself and mirror the "me" I was hiding inside.

I would continue to build my self-confidence through SAC even while in college. I dedicated every summer of my college career to teaching young people and veteran educators about the power of video production.

Part of my duty as a SAC graduate is to also teach to those coming after me the craft that has played a major role in my own social life.

I began to work closely with Frederick Douglass High School, one of the lowest performing schools in the state of Louisiana. Most of these kids suffered from unbelievable trauma. A number of them had parents who were either behind bars, drug-addicted, or dead. Most experienced violence and murder on a daily basis.

The larger society told these students they were worthless, having no knowledge or understanding of their own lives. Unfortunately, many of the kids believed it. It was clear in the way they second-guessed themselves and downplayed the wittiness and insight that comes from learning by experience. I saw myself in them a lot.

The students had stories but believed they were not valuable. So they lived like their lives were just as worthless. They felt invisible, as I do sometimes. They were a group not in control of their own images. Television, the school system, the larger society were telling them who they were.

Teaching them how to take their own experiences and express them through images forced them to analyze their lives. Every image says something distinctive, so one has to be conscious of the message an image can transmit. In thinking critically about how to shoot a fight with a family member, a hard decision made, these young people begin to think critically about who they are and what they can become.

Becoming a mentor to these young people and being that person they can talk to has only sharpened my own dreams of who I could be and where I hoped to end up in life. Giving them the tools to use their voice helps me find my own.

Because of my close work with these kids, my dream was to create media initiatives across the world that would give people around the world an opportunity to share their stories, becoming other peoples' reflections.

At 22, I graduated from college and like most young people I was ready to spin the world on its head with my talents. I had just started my job at SAC. I was going to devote a whole year to working with Douglass students as a co-teacher. Then, of course, Hurricane Katrina happened.

I stared at the images of people who represented me and felt absolutely weak. For months I couldn't stand the nationwide news broadcast. I was feeling the same fatigue as everyone else from my city, but the fatigue didn't come from sheer boredom of the same old story. It was out of a community's need to move past the waters and rebuild its spirit in a world that only cared about demolished homes.

I've always believed that images were powerful enough to shape the consciousness of whole societies. The community did not have the power to tell its own stories. The government and media broadcast images did not reflect who we really are.

I had a college degree and dreams about running media organizations all across the world. But in the wake of the storm, I lost confidence. I began to wonder, as many people did, in the hours, days, weeks, and months after Hurricane Katrina, if I could be whole and feel like the world had a place for me. Mentors pushed me to apply for graduate school, and although I tried, I couldn't find the strength to move on from this thing that sought to deform my spirit. I was that ugly duckling again.

It would be students from Douglass and a new school, Eleanor McMain, who would remind me that I had a purpose still. Just like the rains had taken me back to feelings of inadequacy, the storm also reopened wounds for many of our students. The pain of a brother's death, a parent's incarceration, the ghost of a suicide resurfaced. While most teachers were trying to instruct kids as if the disaster never happened, SAC encouraged them to use their experiences to advocate for better schools and communities in post-Katrina New Orleans.

Helping them process their feelings and getting them to the point where they can create a video piece with the understanding that their stories can help others has been my saving grace.

Because of them, I am more confident that I can move past the old hurts that losing New Orleans has caused, because the students remind me of the things we can always reclaim, like dreams and goals.

It is my belief that we all carry stories inside that are just as valuable to someone else as they are for us. When we allow ourselves to be that mirror others can look into to figure out their own lives, then we allow those wounds to begin the process of healing.

There are people all over this world feeling powerless, but that's just because I haven't found them yet. My goal is to start an international film organization for the disenfranchised and the unheard, because everyone should have the power to tell their own stories.

My real power is in being able to give others the strength to control their own lives, and knowing that helping others find their voice does not diminish my own.

Rain will always evoke memories of the storm for me; the important thing is that I welcome the rain as something that can cleanse me instead of drowning me.

"Just Fill Me Up"

Demetria White

Throughout my entire schooling career, I was always a student at the top of my class: placed in the gifted program in the first grade, valedictorian in sixth grade, and number one on the principal's list in 11th grade. Oh, wait, I forgot to mention my first-place victories in the schoolwide science fair in third, fourth, and sixth grade, and my district fair invites in ninth grade for physical science and 10th grade for geometry. Boy, wasn't I smart! Something like a modern-day genius, I would say. Anything my teacher told me, I could repeat it in a matter of seconds. So, if my second-grade teacher "accidentally" told her entire class that New York was located in New Jersey, then New York was located in New Jersey. Who cared about the logic? We didn't know to think about what the statement said, or even meant. We were only second graders memorizing what we needed to know for that particular test. Guess what? When that question appeared on the test, New York was definitely located in New Jersey. It was even approved with a little red check. When I learned, better yet, memorized how to add, subtract, and multiply integers, I simply recorded the process and repeated it when necessary. Still to this day, as a high school senior, I don't know why a negative multiplied by a positive produces a negative. So, is it really my fault?

Is it my fault I didn't take the initiative to learn what I needed to know and not act as my teachers' receptacle, letting them fill me with facts and not knowledge? I say the teacher is to blame. Anything that happened in grammar school is the teacher's responsibility. He should take charge and explain to the student the whys and the hows behind everything he teaches. So, if he says, "Iron rusts when placed in water," he should follow with "because oxygen molecules bond with the iron molecules causing a chemical change that alters iron's chemical formula." Explaining the logic at an early age results in a student inquiring about the logic later on.

In the society we live in everyone just wants the answers. It's okay to want to know just the answers; however, at some point it is essential to know the whys behind the answer. If the majority of society continues to demand a specific answer, educators who want our learning to mean more than just a test score, like Paulo Freire, will never be heard.

I am a victim of teachers' neglect to make students think. For the past 13 years, I haven't thought about anything I was taught. I just repeated what the teacher wanted to hear. I was fooled into thinking I was smart. To tell you the truth, I have no knowledge at all. All the awards and honors I received truly belong to my teachers. Everything they said, I recorded, memorized, and repeated in order to get the grade. Now that I am a high school senior, school is a total burden. It's extremely hard because I feel that I don't know anything. I am being asked to think about calculus. Who would have thought a math test question would be, "Justify why Y=3." For so long, I've been given the answer, but now I have to find a process, and I just don't know how.

The Stories in Me

Gabrielle Turner

Rushing up the stairs to the third floor, I thought, "I would hate to be late for the first day of class." Hurrying through the crowd of students standing in the hallway as if they had no place to go, the bell sounded, "Ding, Ding, Ding." I whispered to myself, "Room 304, 305, these classrooms are always confusing. There it is, 306."

I walked in the class and a couple of people were sitting having conversations. Catching my breath, I quietly took my seat. "I hurried to class and the teacher ain't even here yet," I whispered under my breath. I looked around to see if there was anyone I knew. No one looked familiar, so I buried my head into my folded arms and rested for a moment.

"Good morning."

My head popped up to see a white man walking hurriedly into the room. He combed through his long brown hair with his fingers and said, "I'm Mr. Randels."

He looked as if he rushed to get to class just as I had.

"OK, let's push these desks a bit closer together into a circle, and we'll introduce ourselves."

Everyone stated their names, classifications, and something they were interested in. This was new to me, because I had never been in a class where we introduced ourselves. Instead, the teacher would pass out forms and call roll. I preferred his method, because by the end of the class I didn't know everyone's life stories, but I knew something about them. From that moment I knew this would not be the average class, and it wasn't. It was challenging, but I liked this challenge. We were encouraged to think critically and apply everything we read or discussed to our lives. We shared our readings and writings with one another. This also was different. I was not used to sharing my thoughts, feelings, and opinions with other students. During these 50-minute classes, I learned to listen and understand the other 15 students in my class. Of course, we did not always agree. We had heated discussions, which at times escalated into debates. These were healthy quarrels. They helped us to appreciate and respect one another.

Not only did we read our personal pieces, but we also read other student writings, writings of well-known authors, and some unfamiliar authors. We read quite a bit. I was not familiar with a lot of the authors we studied, such as Alice Walker. I hadn't read in a while.

When I was a little girl, my mom would assign my sister and me books to read and papers to write. My favorite book was *Why the Sun and the Moon Live in the Sky*. As I got older the assignments stopped. So my interest in reading and writing dwindled. I was hoping that this class would reignite the fire I once had for these useful tools.

One of the first assignments was to read *In Search of our Mothers' Gardens* by Alice Walker (2003). I had to read it four times by myself and once with my mother to really get an understanding of the reading. It dealt with how our ancestors, mainly our mothers and grandmothers, had passed on but they didn't die alone: Their stories and talents were buried with them.

This reading exercise led me to do some digging of my own. I can hear my dad's voice right now: "Girl, you walk on your tiptoes just like Mae Lee" or "You remind me of Heck."

Mary Lee was my grandmother and Heck, which was her nickname, was my great-grandmother. I never got to meet either. I have a crisp and clear memory of my maternal grandmother. The only thing that tied me to my paternal grandmother was a dress. I still have the dress. I want people to understand what that dress means to me. I want people to feel what I feel when I see that brown and white cowhide dress. So, I did the one thing that I knew: I wrote. I wrote a piece about the dress and how it helped me gain personal, in-depth, heartfelt memories. I interviewed family members and friends to learn more about the woman who contributed to my big round eyes and the gap between my two front teeth. My grandmother was an amazing woman. She gave birth to 14 children, five of whom died sometime after birth. My father was the first surviving child. She raised these children with a fourth- or fifth-grade education. She kept a clean house. She believed in cleanliness. I believe I have acquired that from her. I do not think her spick-and-span habits came from her simply enjoying not seeing a speck of dirt. Cleaning houses was not a hobby for her. It was a task. She was a housekeeper-sharecropper. She was my grandmother, a woman I hardly knew anything about until I understood the importance of passing on stories and that little weird dress.

I believe that passing on stories is one of my life goals, whether the stories are movies, radio commentaries, or journal entries that my daughter will one day read. My mom said her legacy to her children was reading and writing and passing on the stories. That legacy awakened a passion in me to capture, preserve, and share this legacy with others.

A door of opportunity opened for me when I was introduced to Students at the Center (SAC). This organization allowed me to be "Gabe" in an environment that preferred everyone to be like everyone else. Because of the skills I've attained by being in SAC, I know that my stories, gifts, and talents will always live on and will not be buried with me. SAC is still helping me. I am still sitting in circles learning, discovering, and digging up stories.

Commentary

Making Sense of Race Through Counter–Storytelling as Pedagogy

Adrienne D. Dixson

New Orleans had always been a mythical place for many of my family members and me. Although we lived in Los Angeles, we grew up on a steady diet of red beans and rice on Mondays, boudoin sausage, etouffee, gumbo, and jambalaya on any of the other days of the week. Linguistically, my grandparents' household was also very rich. They spoke in a southern Louisiana patois that to a child, sounded like they were singing rather than talking. As a result of this cultural blending, my own speech is a blend of a southern Louisiana "lilt" with a Watts "edge." Words like *gris-gris, beaucoup, cher, ma–ma,* and *pa–pa* and phrases like *comme ci, comme ça* became a natural part of my lexicon. From my grandparents and other relatives who also migrated to Los Angeles in the 1940s, I heard stories about a time when people were baptized in the blue waters of the Mississippi River. My first actual visit to the area was as a college freshman at Southern University and A&M College in Baton Rouge, the largest of the Historically Black Colleges and Universities in the nation. My decision to attend Southern University was a sort of homecoming for many in my extended Los Angeles family and those who remained in New Orleans.

As a jazz studies and flute performance major, Southern's proximity to New Orleans, an hour's drive by car, enabled me to take in the Big Easy nearly every weekend. At the age of 17 years old, I had fallen in love with New Orleans and reclaimed it as my home. Upon completion of my degree, and convinced that I could hold down a "day job" and also be a jazz musician, I returned to New Orleans as a Teach For America Corps member to become a public school teacher.

It is against this backdrop that my interest in urban education and the pedagogical practices of African American teachers grew. I left teaching (initially temporarily) for graduate school hoping I would gain skills that would help me understand the challenges of public education, especially public education in New Orleans. While I have not yet found the answers I had hoped for, I found a theoretical lens to help me make better sense of what I experienced and witnessed both as a teacher in New Orleans and as an African American mother with sons who attended public schools. Critical race theory (CRT) has been an informative theoretical framework that I believe helps document the history of racialized educational inequality and uncover the insidiousness of race in the United States (Dixson & Rousseau, 2006; Ladson-Billings & Tate, 1995; Tate, 1997). One important tenet used by CRT scholars is counter-storytelling. CRT legal scholar James O. Calmore (1995) suggests that it is important for people of color to tell our stories, or to "give voice" to our experiences as racialized people, because these stories perform a very important knowledge production purpose and because our stories are

> a very personal expression that allows our experiences and lessons, learned as people of color, to convey the knowledge we possess in a way that is empowering to us, and, it is hoped, ultimately empowering to those on whose behalf we act. (p. 321)

In the spirit of CRT, I will tell my own story about public education in New Orleans, connect this story to the stories of Ashley, Demetria, and Gabrielle (Gabe), and explain how counter-storytelling can be a powerful pedagogical tool for examining racialized educational inequity—one that Students at the Center (SAC) has used in truly compelling ways.

I gained valuable experience as a sixth-grade teacher at Charles E. Gayarre Elementary School (later renamed Oretha Castle Haley) in New Orleans in the early 1990s. Gayarre was located on the corner of N. Robertson and Franklin Avenue, "just before you cross over the bridge to the 9th Ward" as we commonly described its location to native New Orleanians. I taught in a public school that, like others in the district, was plagued with chronic absenteeism and persistent low achievement, although the school was more successful than others in overcoming these issues. Most of our students qualified for free or reduced-price lunch and had been retained at least once during their elementary schooling, quite often as a result of not passing the Louisiana Educational Assessment Program (LEAP). In spite of what seemed to be typical but formidable challenges of urban school districts, I was fortunate to have been hired in a school with a strong principal and a dedicated group of veteran teachers. My senior colleagues also demonstrated an interest in helping novice teachers develop their teaching skills. In many ways, I view my experiences at Gayarre as being an apprenticeship into the teaching profession. One profound lesson I learned from teaching at Gayarre was the intricate connection between pedagogy and a teacher's understanding of student and local culture, or what Ladson-Billings (2009) describes as "culturally relevant pedagogy."

Desperate to find a way to address the myriad issues that seem to engender students' apparent disengagement with school, the district decided to investigate a new curriculum: Molefi Asante's Afrocentric Curriculum. Although other racial groups were represented in the district, African Americans comprised nearly 95% of the student population. In my third year I was elected to be the Upper Division Chairperson for my school and charged with the responsibility of conducting professional development workshops for new district initiatives. I attended a number of districtwide workshops on infusing more culturally relevant materials into the social studies and language arts curriculum. I became increasingly more aware of the contradiction between curriculum initiatives that seem to "trickle down" from the district and teachers' implementation of initiatives into their everyday classroom practice (Apple, 2004). Although I believed the tensions related to the chasm between district policies and teacher practice had an impact on student achievement, I became increasingly more aware of how the sociopolitical context of New Orleans also contributed to the disparities.

The glaring disparities between the wealthy and working classes seemed to contribute to the educational inequities in the district. The racial demographics of the schools belied the property ownership that provided the majority of the fiscal support for New Orleans Public Schools. In particular, while African Americans were and still are 65 percent of the city's population, African American children were and are 95 percent of the student population in the city's public schools (Cowen Institute, 2008). Nearly all of the students who attended Gayarre lived in rental property owned by absent white landlords who neglected their properties. These same property owners repeatedly voted against raising the millage rate and property taxes that many knew were needed to repair and update antiquated school buildings that lacked central air conditioning; yet, they sent their children to one of the many private or parochial schools in the city. Although my school was equipped with central air and heat, we only had one overhead projector in a school that serviced nearly 800 students and approximately 25 teachers. My classes routinely had more students than I had desks or textbooks, and if not for the fact that I rarely had 100% attendance, I would not have had room for all of my students on any given day.

The actions, or inaction of property owners coupled with the city's weak economic infrastructure, seemed to negatively impact New Orleans Public Schools in a number of ways. My gross annual salary, while above the poverty line for Louisiana, was only $20,000 my first year of teaching. After five years of teaching during which I received a raise each year, I left the classroom and New Orleans with a gross annual salary of $22,000. At the time, Orleans Parish was the highest paying district in southern Louisiana. In addition, the maximum reimbursement to teachers for purchasing instructional materials out of their personal funds was $30 per year. Moreover, although the district offered to pay up to $600 per course for its employees who wanted to pursue additional degrees or training, generally, the allotment in the budget was not enough to accommodate all of the district's employees. The financial constraints undoubtedly impacted the district's ability to retain teachers.

While I was concerned about curricular changes that could aid in addressing the achievement disparities, I also became aware of, on a smaller scale, how a teacher's political action can make a positive impact on students' engagement with school. In my teaching I drew upon the funding disparities, the drug epidemic, and the rising homicide rate, among other issues that touched my students' lives. These experiences, coupled with my interest in pedagogy and curriculum, profoundly shape my understanding of the challenges of urban public education, especially as it impacts communities of color not only in New Orleans but also across the United States.

My counterstory helps to speak back to the dominant narratives told by both neoconservatives and neoliberals about communities of color, ones that cast them as dysfunctional and deviant and in need of "saving" and/or surveillance and control. Legal scholar Charles Lawrence (1995) asserts that "we must learn to trust our own senses, feelings, and experiences, to give them authority, even (or especially) in the face of dominant accounts of social reality that claim universality" (p. 338). The stories presented here—my story, Ashley's, Demetria's, and Gabrielle's—are rarely told. While not the simplistic, "teacher as hero" stories with the happy endings that Hollywood loves to tell about "troubled" urban schools, these stories illustrate the complexities and nuances of urban educational contexts. Remembrances of a New Orleans Public School District that was both beloved and despised is the complicated truth of trying to make a way out of a nearly impossible situation. That teachers like Jim Randels and my former colleagues taught along with other teachers who merely had their students regurgitate information is not dissimilar to what happens in other schools throughout the United States—urban, suburban, rural, and private. That these pedagogies are assumed to be the *only* ones in urban schools is the dominant narrative that we attempt to disrupt. Through Ashley's and Gabe's stories we learn that African American youth do care about and value education. Ashley's own struggles with self-esteem, a familiar theme in the coming-of-age narratives of young women, did not deter her from challenging herself educationally and pursuing her goals. More important, Ashley's story shows us the dedication that African American youth have to the notion of racial uplift and the compassion they demonstrate in light of a horrific tragedy like Hurricane Katrina. Gabe's story illustrates the way that writing our own story helps us find out who we are and how we are connected to something much larger than ourselves. If we only listened to and believed the mainstream media's portrayals of African American youth, Ashley and Gabe would be anomalies. Yet their descriptions of SAC and its commitment to intergenerational work with other youth show us that the descriptions of African American youth as prone to violence and resistant to education are the exceptions and not the rule.

Demetria's experience is an unfortunate by-product of being educated in an urban district placed under the panoptic watch of state administrators who hold them accountable to testing machines designed only to measure what students do not know, not what they do know. Yet, her story of teachers who did not challenge her is far too common for students of color in urban school districts (Lipman, 1998). Her story illustrates the complexity of urban education—the challenges that Demetria will face in a society obsessed with "measuring" knowledge and conferring opportunities based on the inherently racist notion of merit. How can we expect Demetria to compete on a playing field that is inherently unfair? As resources and access to higher education become more and more restricted and embattled, students like Demetria, who have had far too many experiences with poor teaching, will be blamed for not working hard enough. Their parents will be blamed for not caring; and their communities will be blamed for not being supportive. Counter–storytelling can and does expose the racist practices that attempt to justify marginalizing students of color. Yet, these stories cannot be told in isolation. Demetria's story, while illustrative of the neglect students of color experience in urban schools, must be told alongside Ashley's, and Jim's, and mine.

That only one skewed picture of public education in New Orleans has been the most dominant story told to date is not surprising. The presumption of black inferiority is what gives such stories currency. The stories we tell about our city and our schools are often missing and suppressed, yet they provide an important counternarrative. It is also important, as these stories demonstrate, that teachers provide and claim a space for students to tell their stories. It is equally important that we analyze these stories for what they tell us about race and inequity. How do students understand what is happening to them? What are the implications of particular practices and policies that appear to be "normal"? How can we create opportunities for them and ourselves to resist and disrupt racism? This work is crucial to reclaiming the educational landscape that was nearly washed away when the levees were compromised on August 29, 2005.

EDUCATION FOR LIBERATION RATHER THAN EXPLOITATION

Speaking Out

In this second exchange, Kalamu ya Salaam echoes Dixson's concerns regarding educational inequity. He lays out a damning critique of the school-to-low-wage-labor pipeline and prison-industrial complex on which neoliberalism depends, alongside a strikingly honest assessment of the challenges and irrefutable stakes involved in building democratic educational spaces. His testimony serves as a crucial reminder: It is imperative to foreground the voices of revolutionary educators who speak with the passion and commitment that generally characterizes those zealously advocating free market reforms. Importantly, Maisha Fisher responds to Salaam and contextualizes the efforts of SAC teachers and students within a history of black activism rooted in the "Word," taking us from New Orleans to New York City and Atlanta. In this way, the pedagogy of the oppressed represented by SAC is better understood as part of a mighty and enduring river of resistance.

We Stand by Our Students

Kalamu ya Salaam

Our Students at the Center (SAC) class stood around in small clumps outside the school building. With the temperature an uncomfortable lower-50s and an annoying light rain falling, the weather was not welcoming. Tiesha stood unsmiling under a blue umbrella. I told her to hold that pose with her face booted-up and scurried over to my black leather briefcase to get the digital camera. I wanted to take her picture. "You really going to take my picture?"

After taking four or five shots, I moved under the sparse cover of a tree, but it offered scant protection. The rain still fell on us. Tiesha smiled as she inspected the small screen on the back of SAC's digital camera.

Jim pulled out the heavy African American literature book from his backpack and proceeded to continue the last discussion we had before the fire alarm went off. What did Alice Walker mean about fruit awakening taste buds in the poem about her sister Molly?

Greta, the coordinator of the Smaller Learning Communities educational program, called on my cell and wanted to know where we were. Shortly she joined us and jokingly admired Jim's tenacity as chilly raindrops wet the book's pages. "Y'all really going to try and hold class amidst all this?"

"Yeah, why not?" Jim casually replied, pushing back his long, dark hair that helps earn him the semisarcastic nickname of "Jesus." Three out of the eight or so students in class that day gamely struggled to answer the questions.

We were outside because someone had set fire to the second-floor bathroom. And eventually we were all called into the gym and dismissed for the day. This was the new principal's second day in charge; a not-unusual, even if atypical, day at Frederick Douglass High School.

Every day working in the public school system I battle the demons of despair; most times I eat that bear, but sometimes brother bear takes a deep bite out of my rear, and on such days, nursing my wounds, I retreat home to repair, often in the process questioning myself: why in the hell do I return to this day after day?

I love the youth, especially the students at Douglass and I know that I as an older black male make a major difference, especially as I do not represent authority types, but rather, in many, many ways, am but an older version of them, or at least a version of who they can become once they achieve critical self-consciousness and commit themselves to lifelong learning.

Any of us who work in a major American metro-area, inner-city public school intimately knows Mr./Ms. Despair Bear, knows the challenge of maintaining in the face of a system whose normal state is either chaos unreigned or else the even more sinister, terrifying silence of lockdown. But here is where we go every day, somehow nourishing the dream of teaching youth.

Some people have developed theories about teaching inner-city youth, and most of those theories are predicated on preparing these youth to participate in the mainstream. Such theories never question the sanity of joining in a system that has systematically oppressed and exploited the very youth we are teaching. If preparing them to simply be "productive citizens" of the status quo is the bottom line of what we do, then we might as well be teaching courses in suicide.

I do not apologize for my stance: I advocate education for liberation, not education for mainstream socialization.

I am interested in coaching youth to engage reality in two ways: (1) Know themselves and (2) decide for themselves what they wish to become. Those two simple objectives are the foundation for my praxis—the pedagogical theories I develop/adopt/adapt, and the day-to-day practice I use to engage the reality of public education.

Education is ground zero in the systemic exploitation of black people in New Orleans—ground zero because public schools are the direct feeder for the necessary, albeit unskilled, labor needed for the tourist-oriented economy. For those not fortunate enough to work in a hotel, the public schools prepare them for the penitentiary. I will not recite the alarming statistics; it is enough to note that in New Orleans they are building more hotels every day—where will the bellhops and maids come from? If you are reading this, I assume you are already aware of the statistical fact that more young black males are in prison than college.

Teachers who would educate black youth but either shy away from making or else are incapable of making a political-economic critique of the school system, such teachers are themselves impediments, if not downright opponents of education for liberation. If we are not prepared to at least intellectually confront the implicit racism of using test scores to fail students whom school systems have systematically mis-educated, if we are unwilling to recognize the utter underpreparedness of system administrators and the lameness of their solutions, if we are afraid to address the difficulties of middle-aged whites trying to educate black working-class youth, in other words, if we are unwilling to face what is really happening in public education, all of our "innovative" programs will fail because they are not addressing the real problems.

We are at war for the future of our students. In New Orleans, tourism is the number one (two and three) industry. Our schools are the way they are because the economy continues to need drawers of water and hewers of wood, continues to require a labor force to clean, cook, and serve. And though they cannot articulate it in political language, our students know. The ones at the selective admissions schools, encased in a near zombie-like state of obedience, work to escape the neoslavery of tourism via college and a "good job" somewhere else in America. Those at the open access schools rebel or else go through the day in an alienated state of nonengagement with the curricula, which they generally (and too often not incorrectly) perceive as a waste of time. This is the context within which SAC works as a creative writing elective.

Everyone who visits our classes, or looks at *Our Voice* (a student-run newspaper we publish), or reads the chapbooks and poetry collections we publish, or views one of our numerous videos, everyone marvels at the work and wants to know how we do it. I smile. Although we employ specific techniques, there is no secret ingredient. It's the fruit of protracted struggle, the fruit of the hard work of encouraging the students to take their lives and their futures seriously.

Three of our basic principles: (1) No class larger than 15 students. (2) Sit in a circle. (3) Require each student to participate in discussions. We also encourage students to engage in peer teaching with their fellow students who are not in a SAC class or with middle or elementary school students, including those in after-school programs. We strongly urge students to get involved with social change organizations and agencies, a number of which are active partners with SAC.

In addition to reading our work aloud and taking turns reading a wide variety of materials, we teach active listening skills by talking about how to ask questions and by our example of asking questions. Silence is death; no student is allowed to not participate. While we do not accept rote responses, at the same time we do not reject any honest response as "wrong" or "inappropriate." We are not working on what Paulo Freire calls the "banking" concept wherein we as teachers have fed our students the right answer and are prodding them to give us back that specific "right" answer. Instead the SAC methodology is to begin at the beginning.

We begin with the experiences and real thoughts and reactions of our students. We begin by affirming the importance of their existence, their personalities, howsoever and whatsoever they may be.

One particular tool in this affirmation process is the *story circle*, a technique developed by John O'Neal and others in the Free Southern Theater. We sit in a circle and take turns telling a story about a selected topic.

To be successful, we must actively listen to our students. This process is one of building community. It is not reductively a one-way process of simplistically asking our students to spill their guts to us while we silently sit in judgment. Indeed, in SAC we all participate as equals; we teachers tell our stories when our turn comes. We all tell stories and we all listen to each other.

Whether a person intends to or not, if they honestly participate, they end up doing two things. One, we all learn more about each other, and we thereby become closer to each other. Two, we learn to articulate ideas and emotions that previously had never been publicly expressed. For many students, this is their first experience in an educational setting of being embraced for who they actually are rather than for how close they are able to come to some external standard that is set before them as a kind of educational Holy Grail.

We then encourage our students to write. Again, we do not require any one-to-one write-the-story-you-told process. Rather we ask them to write about a variety of topics, and even encourage them to write on a topic of their own choosing if it is a topic they strongly want to express. When we combine the story circle technique with the prompts and inspiration that come from the reading assignments, invariably students produce a richer body of literature than if they were simply asked to respond to abstract writing assignments. Here is an example from Maria Hernandez, a sophomore at Frederick Douglass who presents a brilliant social critique of the effects of violence that is also an unsparing and startling self-critique:

"Just Like Him"

They say when you're around someone for a long time, you start looking and acting like that person. The problem is that I didn't want to be like him in any way, but what can I say? I have his eyes, his hair, and recently I've acquired his personality. Lately I go crazy and snap. I bitch slap my little brother and on more than one occasion I've drawn blood from my little sister's lips. I didn't want to be like him, but I did it anyway. And something inside me is telling me that I let him win.

When you review student writing at this level, the work forces you to confront yourself. You cannot stand before this student and just go through a rote exercise. What do you do?

We publish the work and encourage her to do more. Just as our students learn from us, we as teachers learn from our students. The experience of liberatory education is necessarily a reciprocal relationship. We learn to know our students as fellow human beings with whom we share our lives and experiences, rather than solely seeing students as blank slates upon whom we teachers are trying to inscribe particular lessons.

When we say start with where we are at, we are saying a mouth full. Our students have many, many problems. An upcoming publication is called *Men We Love, Men We Hate*. Recently during a discussion of an excerpt on black manhood from bell hooks' new book, a quick, informal poll demonstrated that only one person of the 12 or so students lived in a two-parent family with a male as the head of the family. We were discussing patriarchy, which is a bit tricky when there are no patriarchs present in their day-to-day lives—and that was at the school whose reputation is petite-bourgeois, many of them are literally the children of first-generation professionals and lower level managers.

Although functional enough to do their class work and to pass standardized tests, even these students, the so-called best and brightest, suffer social stress and trauma at sometimes unimaginable levels. Sexual molestation, dysfunctional families, suicide, drug (especially alcohol and tobacco) abuse, sexually-transmitted diseases, and warped senses of self-esteem are endemic, indeed near pandemic, across economic strata. Without falling into the trap of either pitying or being repulsed by their problems, our task is to encourage the students to articulate the realities of their day-to-day existence. Unless and until they can honestly recognize and confront their own realities, they will never be able to truly transform themselves and their communities.

These are not woe-is-me, feel-sorry-for-us-poor-downtrodden-negroes investigations; rather these are honest explorations of complex social situations. For students, these investigations are a brave and ultimately inspirational example of self-transformation through confronting social issues at the personal level. Neither Jim nor I try to weigh these projects with overt political views. Our tack is to ask questions. We encourage them to dig deep within themselves and be as truthful as possible.

Because we are not a core curriculum class and because we are a "creative writing" class, we have more latitude with lesson planning than do most of the regular classes. Although one might suppose this means that we are less rigorous in an academic sense, all of the students will tell you that, except for a handful of their other teachers, our SAC class requires them to work much harder than do their regular classes.

Even though they have to read more, write more, think more, they come back, some students taking our class two or three times during their high school matriculation. Last semester at Douglass we encountered the phenomenon of male students cutting their assigned classes to sit in on our writing class. One of them eventually persuaded his counselor to switch his class, while another student, Bruce, got a note from his mother saying that it was okay to skip one class so he could be part of our SAC class.

Later in the semester when Bruce was selected as one of two students to represent Douglass at a statewide conference on "agenda for children" where our SAC duo recited poetry, one of the counselors wanted to know how in the world could that happen since Bruce was failing every other class. Bruce has severe problems with text. His spelling is on an elementary level and his grammar is almost nonexistent, but he has a sharp mind and easily grasps concepts such as metaphorical consistency, which he calls "m-c." When it is time to publish Bruce's work, we patiently sit with him and correct each misspelled word. We question him about grammar. We do what editors have traditionally done for many highly rated writers whose manuscripts would be unpublishable without significant editorial help. One of my favorite images of Bruce is his head buried deep in a dictionary trying to find out the correct spelling of a word he wants to use. His academic shortcomings notwithstanding, Bruce has the fire and determination to improve himself, and his family supports SAC partially because they know the value of our work—one of Bruce's older cousins had previously been an editor of *Our Voice* newspaper.

There is a misconception that undereducated students are not ready to grasp philosophy, political economy, subtleties of high art, and so forth. However, just because the school system has failed to educate them, that does not mean that our students are stupid and/or uneducable. That they score poorly does not mean they cannot think and do not have analytical skills. Indeed, their environment forces them to develop very sharp discrimination skills.

They are able to easily spot insincerity and incompetence. They know with the accuracy of a finely tuned Geiger counter that teachers are simply collecting a paycheck or impersonally teaching from a textbook without being concerned about the student as a human being. Students learn early how to dodge the bullies and con artists who daily confront and try to hustle them both in and outside the classroom. They develop all sorts of evasive techniques to avoid physical harm and/or incarceration by police, guards, and other authority figures whose sole responsibility is to maintain law and order, a law and order that demands mindless obedience and compliance with arbitrary rules and regulations. In many, many ways our students are far more realistic about their educational situation than are we who would teach them but who do not take the time to understand them or their world except as either an abstraction or with a pejorative view of their environment.

A sure sign that many of us do not understand our students is our refusal to understand that even if students can't spell, they can reason, even if students can't pronounce multisyllabic words, they can express themselves. How well a person does on a standardized test is no indication of that person's character or desire to learn.

Thus we read and discuss Plato's "Allegory of the Cave" or excerpts from Paulo Freire's *Pedagogy of the Oppressed* alongside of Toni Morrison and excerpts from the writing of Frederick Douglass; we read Sandra Cisneros and Birago Diop as well as Alice Walker and Langston Hughes. We not only read these authors, we discuss the relationship of the text to their lives and follow up with assignments that, for example, ask students to write about their own "cave" experiences.

I want to make sure no one romanticizes SAC and the struggle we wage. Students deserve far more than we are able to give them, even though we, they, and their families recognize that SAC has given them far more than they would have normally received in their matriculation through the jungles of public education.

We realize that not every class can operate the way SAC does; however, we are certain that public education can be significantly improved by specifically focusing on the needs of the students, which, for us, means including the views of students. We believe another world is possible. We believe students are a resource and not just an object of education. We encourage the students to become agents of their own education, and we struggle with other teachers and administrators to make these changes. Unavoidably, this is sometimes a contentious and even bitter struggle. There are teachers and administrators who actively fight against what we are doing.

Some people say SAC is successful because we work with only a handful of students, and SAC is elitist because we pick only the best students. In the second semester of the 2003–04 school year an antagonistic counselor assigned us two special education students, plus one student who was a serious discipline problem, plus three students who needed upper level English to graduate and who also had to pass the LEAP (Louisiana Educational Assessment Program) test but had failed the English portions previously, all of this in addition to those who were assigned to us "just because," even though we are supposed to be an elective course and even though the counselor did not include some students who requested our class. Meanwhile, we have a handful of students who want to learn how to write, two of whom are intent on becoming writers.

So we circle the chairs and soldier on. And though we have our problems, despite stumbles and setbacks, despite backbiting and resentments (the inevitable result of struggles to create change), despite having to deal with a wide range of student attitudes and capabilities, despite all of that, our students produce and their work is both our defense and our offense. Their work is the answer to the question of can public education be improved. We proudly stand by the work that our students do.

Commentary

Soldiering On: Black Literate Lives Past and Present

Maisha T. Fisher

In a 1979 essay entitled "Notes from a Banana Republic," Kalamu ya Salaam reminds the *Black Books Bulletin* readership, "for poor working class Black people New Orleans is the anti-thesis of [the] Big Easy" (p. 15). Salaam, like many black poets and writers who emerged during the Black Arts Movement, cultivated the important traditions of "agitating, educating, and organizing" (Fisher, 2009) by not only naming social and economic injustices in America's cities but actively engaging in struggle against these injustices. Salaam's essay begins with a story of him driving a Sudanese ambassador to the Paris UNESCO office through New Orleans' Lower 9th Ward where Salaam was raised. The ambassador compared what he was seeing in the Lower 9th Ward to African townships and declared it "looked like the Third World." This comparison was no surprise to Salaam who responded, "This *is* the Third World." Salaam's love for New Orleans is evident in his work then and now as an educator, institution builder, and griot. However, Salaam critiqued the structural inequities that forced New Orleans natives, mostly black, to work for little while tourists dropped in to enjoy a masquerade without any comprehension or care for how difficult New Orleans residents' lives really were. "Living below sea level," wrote Salaam, "New Orleans is a lot like scuba diving, periodically and without fail, you've got to come up for air, or else you will drown" (p. 17). Then and now, Salaam has worked tirelessly to create opportunities for the young people of New Orleans to "come up for air" using the medium of poetry, performance, and most recently the combination of text, sound, and light through digital media. There could not be a more urgent moment for Salaam, his coteacher Jim Randels, and the passionate young people in Students at the Center (SAC) to do this work. This work is especially important as young people continue to grapple with how to reinvent themselves and their communities in a post-Katrina New Orleans. As the Recovery School District (RSD) seeks to reestablish schools in New Orleans, scholarship has duly noted the "lack of basic human and tangible resources essential for success in any educational environment let alone one formed after the worst natural disaster in American history" (Tuzzolo & Hewitt, 2007, p. 60). In fact, New Orleans and consequently its schools are not only in the same condition Salaam and his guest described in the 1970s but much worse. In a study examining the prevalence of the school-to-prison pipeline in pre- and post-Katrina New Orleans, Tuzzolo and Hewitt found that an increase of zero-tolerance policies in New Orleans elementary and secondary schools, coupled with security guards and police officers outnumbering teachers as well as high suspension rates for "petty infractions," has contributed to efforts to manage, control, and push out the small number of students who have returned to the city. However, students need more resources to facilitate healing and learning rather than more security, which often exacerbates circumstances: That is, "New Orleans schools should focus on enhancing educational opportunities and addressing the lingering and unaddressed trauma and grief that many students continue to face over a year after the hurricanes ravaged the city" (p. 67).

The "liberatory pedagogy" (see Chapter 1) of SAC is one space where youth have an opportunity to address the "lingering and unaddressed trauma" of being uprooted from their homes and left to put all the pieces together on their own. Ashley Jones, a New Orleanian and SAC student once looked to the rain as something she welcomed yet now faces it with "a lot of fear and too many memories." As Ashley, along with her peers, grapple with the experiences of powerlessness felt during and after Hurricane Katrina, she turns to SAC and the opportunity to write and "reclaim [her] sense of self." While the idea of writing as an act of reclamation may not be new, it is an act that has become increasingly more critical to urban youth throughout the United States. Literacy research has begun to examine how teachers create opportunities for youth to use writing to confront issues like gentrification and racism in their New York City neighborhoods (Kinloch, 2007b; Fisher, 2005, 2007b), use playwriting and performance as a way to examine issues in the juvenile (in)justice system (Fisher, 2008; Fisher, Purcell & May, 2009), examine and thus celebrate the linguistic practices of their families and communities (Alim, 2006), and build on themes found in hip-hop music to improve their critical reading, writing, and thinking skills (Hill, 2009). In this book youth use their writing to speak out and speak back to the "benign neglect" the city of New Orleans is facing (Buras, 2007). Demetria White solemnly reminds us that this "benign neglect" is the culmination of years of mis-education in New Orleans public schools. Demetria recounts her experiences with a banking-model education; she got through junior high by memorizing and regurgitating facts only to learn that this was not enough for high school and beyond. Through her work with SAC she has been able to name and critique her mis-education, writing, "If the majority of society continues to demand a specific answer, educators who want our learning to mean more than just a test score, like Paulo Freire, will never be heard." As Demetria painstakingly shares her testimony of being tricked into thinking she was learning, Gabrielle Turner's story demonstrates the important shift students in SAC made from mis-education to reeducation. Gabrielle conveys a sense of surprise when she got to class late along with a white man, Jim Randels, who as it turned out was her teacher. Randels asked students to arrange their desks in a circle; not only did he change the space physically but he also changed it psychologically. Turner and her classmates learned about each other for the first time in their high school careers. Like teacher Joe Ubiles and his Power Writers—a collective of student poets in the Bronx who wrote about their lived experiences and exchanged writing with their peers—Randels refused to colonize students; rather he encouraged and exalted their voices (Fisher, 2005, 2007b; Fisher & Ubiles, 2009).

Gabrielle's depiction of meeting Randels mirrors my experience meeting Salaam. Prior to meeting Salaam in person I met him through the poetry and songs of a young poet, Gabrilla Ballard, in Northern California during my study of participatory literacy communities, or PLCs, including spoken word poetry open mic events (Fisher, 2003, 2004, 2006). Ballard was a singer, songwriter, and talented musician who credited her family and mentors in New Orleans for cultivating her talent. Ballard had attended Ahidiana, a black community school co-founded by Salaam. When I interviewed Gabrilla about her writing and participation in PLCs, she made it clear that Salaam and Ahidiana had greatly impacted her life:

> [Ahiadiana] was a school that was based in African, African American culture. It [was] an independent school and the curriculum was structured by the teachers but it was very holistic. It was hands on; it taught us to have love, respect and just honor for who we are as Africans-Diasporic Africans. You know that's important because many of [the teachers] had Pan-Africanist views; we didn't feel separate from the continent, you know what I mean? And some people argue that the school prepared us for a world that doesn't exist. I don't agree with that. I feel that the school created—prepared us to create—the

world that we wanted to exist because what other reason are we teaching anyway? (quoted in Fisher, 2004)

Ballard later joined Salaam's NOMMO Literary Society which was a forum for poets and writers to exchange their writing using a workshop format, read a wealth of materials, and listen to music. I e-mailed Salaam prior to a trip I planned to New Orleans in 2002. When I informed Salaam about my interview with Ballard he invited me to visit NOMMO. With all the kindness and grace imaginable, Salaam picked me up at my hotel and drove me through Treme, a historic black neighborhood where NOMMO was housed. Our interview took place among the endless shelves of books and bottomless drawers of CDs—most of which were lost during Hurricane Katrina—that were available to NOMMO members. Salaam's stories and kindness transported me to cities throughout the United States in which poets and writers worked hard to build and maintain independent educational institutions, establish arts programs, and preserve spoken and written words. However, what was even more impressive was his continued commitment to cultivating young people, also known as neo-griots, who tell their stories using modern video technology. I consider Salaam to be a soldier—his commitment to the children of New Orleans is unwavering. Elsewhere, I discuss the soldiering of black poets and writers committed to cultivating a new literary generation. These soldiers do their work beyond traditional classroom walls—often in coffee houses, black bookstores, and cultural arts centers. Poet and author Michael Datcher perceptively notes:

> Every city I've been to, there is this kind of black person who is conscious or who is like a real soldier. And it seems to me every city has soldiers. Our challenge is getting those soldiers together. And we have no collective plan, no army and no national agenda. But we have so many soldiers, so many charismatic people with integrity. (quoted in Fisher, 2007a, p. 140)

This definition of a *soldier* shared by Datcher emerged from a renaissance of organizing literacy communities in urban epicenters that mirrored the work of Salaam and others during the 1960s and 1970s. What has changed since I interviewed Datcher is that many of these "soldiers" do have a collective plan and agenda to do whatever is necessary to educate youth in school settings and in out-of-school settings. SAC is part of the growing movement to ensure urban youth have "power not programs" (Brown, 2008). Randels and Salaam are not merely transferring power, they provide a forum for the youth whose voices rise from these pages to teach us—if only we will listen.

CLOSING REFLECTION

Toward a Critical Reading of the Privatized City

Kristen L. Buras

If we listen keenly, there's something pivotal to be learned here. Ashley is clear—crystal clear—that representation matters. Her camera became the means for producing images of fellow students, ones that mirrored and validated their experiences rather than depicting them through the more common lens of fear and depravity. "They were a group not in control of their own images," she writes, continuing, "Television, the school system, the larger society were telling them who they were." The wounds inflicted by dominant imagery only deepened after Katrina, as she and many others were perpetually assaulted by portraits *about* but not *by* them. The persistent problem, which ultimately fueled Ashley's work with grassroots media, was the fact that the community lacked adequate means to craft and disseminate its own story.

This suggests a more fundamental question, of course. *Whose* images prevail of youth of color, their schools, and their neighborhoods? Ashley's camera, Gabrielle's commitment to "digging up stories," and the overall commitment of Randels, Salaam, and Students at the Center to "the Word" and pedagogies of voice, cast light where shadows usually masquerade as reality. As Leonardo and Hunter (2009) suggest, images of the urban—or what they call the "urban imagination"—assume various forms, some of which are raced, classed, and gendered in exceptionally problematic ways. All of this matters because *what* precisely is imaged or imagined has pedagogic and policy implications which follow. One prevalent image is that of the "urban jungle," a place where civility is far less common than deviance, pathology, and violence. Yet not all city dwellers are prone to such tendencies, rather working classes and communities of color allegedly are. This is why, as Salaam, Dixson, and Fisher point out, we are told that youth of color need to be managed and controlled, and, if all else fails, pushed out, removed, or incarcerated.

The other image, perhaps equally as prevalent, is the "sophisticated urban space." In this image, "the future meets the city" as cosmopolitan and often white middle-class consumers vibe in a culturally, racially, and linguistically diverse playground where they can partake in cultural difference without bearing the burden (Leonardo & Hunter, 2009). More pointedly, they can eat "ethnic" foods and don "urban" fashions, and all the while never be subjected to what neoconservatives have advocated as the new paternalism (Whitman, 2008). They are not mired in a culture of permissiveness and poverty that requires educational discipline. Neither does their presence indicate the need for urban renewal. To the contrary, the sophisticated urban space is dependent on their presence and the deeper they dig in their high heels, the higher the rents they pay to live in places of "controlled difference" (Leonardo & Hunter, 2009), the more civilized the jungle presumably becomes. This is the neoliberal image of the renewed and largely privatized urban landscape, where disorder has been contained and boundaries are never breached.

Yet the counterstories in this chapter and the next one present a third image, one grounded in the realities experienced by economically and racially oppressed communities. Here students and teachers are not simply authors of images and stories, but *authorities*. That is to say, they speak with knowledge and conviction about the countless ways that they, their families, schools, homes, and communities have suffered as a result of the images and policies advanced by neoliberal reformers. These are stories of defiance in the face of abandonment and dispossession, and through candid detail and unsparing critique, they firmly represent what Fisher calls "writing as an act of reclamation." In this respect, students' stories are very much like tributaries to a mighty river of resistance. In the shadow of ancestors and elders, they stand on the bank of the Mississippi and provide a critical reading of the privatized city—one from which they refuse to be removed.

CHAPTER 3

Race and Reform
in the Privatized City

OPENING REFLECTION

Capitalist Dreams

Kristen L. Buras

IN THE 1940s, Langston Hughes penned the poem, "Still Here":

I've been scarred and battered.
My hopes the wind done scattered.
Snow has friz me, sun has baked me.
  Looks like between 'em
  They done tried to make me
Stop laughin', stop lovin', stop livin'—
  But I don't care!
  I'm still here! (Hughes, 1994, p. 295)

It is truly difficult to imagine words more apt for describing what many working-class youth of color in New Orleans and elsewhere are enduring under neoliberal insurgency: an undisguised attempt at dispossession and removal. This is the "capitalist dream" that Harvey (2006) alludes to when discussing the enforcement of what one U.S.-appointed member of the Coalition Provisional Authority in Iraq called "free market fundamentalism." In this instance, the U.S. government sought to "work with appointed representatives who would be as pliant as possible in locking down these free market reforms before direct democracy (which would almost certainly reject them) took over" (p. 10). Standing amid the winds of free market fundamentalism—not those of Hurricane Katrina alone—the young neo-griots of Students at the Center defiantly assert, "I'm still

78

here!" To be sure, the scarring and battering caused by neoliberal and neoconservative policy makers has been painful—a reality put in relief by the testimonies in this chapter.

The winds are strong and they carry with them the remnants of a racial past, which then become part of the foundation for current reforms. In the tradition of the eugenics movement of the early twentieth century (Gould, 1996) and *The Bell Curve* more recently (Hernstein & Murray, 1996; for a critique, see Kincheloe, Steinberg, & Gresson, 1997), Louisiana state legislator John LaBruzzo, who is white and represents a suburb of New Orleans, has considered proposing legislation that would support paying poor women $1,000 dollars to have their Fallopian tubes tied (and poor men to have vasectomies). LaBruzzo "worries that people receiving government aid such as food stamps and publicly subsidized housing are reproducing at a faster rate than more affluent, better-educated people who presumably pay more tax revenue to the government," and that such patterns will lead to economic collapse (Waller, 2008, para. 3). But his proposal wouldn't stop there. He has also pondered "tax incentives for college-educated, higher-income people to have more children" (para. 6). LaBruzzo claims his proposal is not racist because there are more whites than blacks on welfare. Yet people of color are disproportionately represented among the poor even if the absolute number of poor whites is greater, which means his plan disproportionately targets low-income African Americans. Significantly, the number of low-income welfare recipients as a whole has declined due to exactly this kind of racialized attack on the social democratic state. With the inauguration of Workfare (or "welfare to work" legislation) in the mid-1990s and a five-year lifetime cap on benefits—it is worth noting that Workfare is the prototype for the paternalism that Chester Finn advocates (see Chapter 2)—many were pushed into poorly paid work while social supports vanished. In Louisiana, for instance, the monthly average for the Family Independence Temporary Assistance Program (FITAP) was 280,177 recipients during 1990–91; in 2006–07, the average was 13,504 (Moller, 2008). Whatever the case, LaBruzzo contends that "education reforms" have done little to help the children of the poor out of "generational welfare," leaving two alternatives: sterilization or the future collapse of the economy. The fact that the federal government intervened in the market with a subsidy of billions for predatory lenders in the banking industry is apparently overlooked (while the monthly grant for a qualifying mother with two children under FITAP is a meager $240). The underlying premise of such a proposal is to gut and cut those things perceived to be drags on the functioning of the free market. That is, state administration and funding of public welfare is to be eliminated and those "dependent" on so-called handouts are to be eliminated—selectively, of course, since forms of state intervention for the wealthy are not viewed as welfare at all.

Offered in this chapter are the counterstories of students who reveal the racial dimensions and profound costs of living in *Neoliberal* Orleans, where capitalist dreams take form as the state is selectively and strategically gutted and public infrastructure in poor and working-class communities of color is abolished. There's a stunning coalescence between Langston Hughes's words and the experiences of Vinnessia Shelbia and her family, literally scattered throughout the city of New Orleans in various homeless shelters. Because "the prices for rent are outstanding and standing out," her hopes for her mother finding an affordable place to live have been daunted. In the same moment, her anger and indignation about the circumstances she confronts, and her willingness to speak out, serve as a startling critique of the so-called ethics of neoliberalism, which racialize and privatize the right to home. She raises a fundamental question about state culpability when she asks "who's holding the gun?" Here it is essential to think back to Robin D. G. Kelley's (1993) notion of *infrapolitics*, or the hidden forms of resistance in which racially oppressed communities engage. The stories told in the coming pages do indeed represent voices from below, voices with deep roots in New Orleans, voices that rise to the surface in protest even when, as Deborah Carey puts it in reflecting on abandonment after Katrina, "our citizenship went down the stream right along with our houses, all forgotten about by our government."

These processes of systemic uprooting are occurring as workfare, gentrification, and educational choice prove to be the ultimate "invisible hand" or "force of nature." Uprooting has occurred in the arena of public health care (Charity Hospital has never reopened) and in public housing (many housing projects have been demolished or are slated for demolition). In contrast to Finn's (Finn & Kanstoroom, 2008) presumption that the communities from which African American and Latino students emanate should be abandoned for the middle-class milieu that he and LaBruzzo valorize (the former being a cultural eugenicist of sorts and the latter a biological one), Tyeasha Green discusses the profound loss she feels as a result of one such "missing project." "My old neighborhood taught me so much," Tyeasha writes, emphasizing that "the government should be building up not tearing down." Yet in city after city, including Chicago, as Pauline Lipman shows, the impetus has been to tear down and to rebuild for middle-class families deemed worthy of convenient and habitable housing in the inner city. And many ask: Why not? Plans for newly constructed mixed-income housing assert that the "values" lauded by neoconservatives will rub off on the poor who supposedly will live side by side with those already imbibed in a culture of politeness, discipline, and work. Alas, poor black folk will now be in a position to make better "choices."

Yet as Kirsten Theodore illustrates, the "choices" on offer are not always better. Theodore makes readers aware that long before Katrina, she attended a school of choice that attempted to strip her of the desire to become a teacher of students like herself—youth whom some of her teachers deemed worthless. Veteran teacher Katrena Jackson-Ndang expresses similar concerns about post-Katrina "pushing" of charter schools by the government at the same time that the Orleans Parish School Board was urged by the state to fire nearly all of the teachers in the city. These teachers, Jim Randels reminds us in his essay, constituted a substantial portion of the black, college-educated middle class in New Orleans. Jackson-Ndang argues that the charters only "want to hire inexperienced teachers so that they can pay them little or no money and also so they can treat them . . . like slaves, with no rights and no input or say about what happens in the schools." That is to say, choice has become a way to destroy open access neighborhood schools, as Maria Hernandez reluctantly points out in the pages ahead, and to discontinue collective bargaining agreements and weaken the union in which so many veteran teachers were invested. This is the same union that neoliberals say obstructs innovation and free market reforms. Unfortunately these attacks pay little heed to the historic racial struggles fought by the teachers union in Jim Crow New Orleans—a history that Randels shares in recollecting a visit with two early black teacher unionists, and which Vanessa Siddle Walker connects to other earlier struggles for African American education.

In light of racially inspired expulsions from schools, homes, and communities, Damien Theodore worries that he may "never get the chance to teach in the neighborhood" where he grew up. His worries are well-founded, unfortunately. The School Facilities Master Plan mentioned in Chapter 1 has slated more than 60 schools for indefinite closure under the somewhat vague notion of "landbanking" (Kilbert & Vallas, 2008), thereby creating an opening for the commodification and privatization of public property and the conversion of the commons into the exclusive possession of the few. This is all part of the "experiment" that Whitman (2008) and other conservative reformers are so grateful Katrina enabled (for a critique, see Saltman, 2007b). In fact, Whitman considers it promising as well as lamentable that New Orleans is "perhaps the only big city in the nation without a viable teacher union" (p. 291). New Orleans, he tells us, is also a space into which "many of the nation's best known charter school and education reform groups rushed," including the Knowledge Is Power Program (KIPP), Edison Schools (privately managed, for-profit ventures), and Teach for America. He praises the fact that Paul Vallas, Superintendent of the Recovery School District, stepped into the re-mix, pledging that this would "be the greatest opportunity for educational entrepreneurs, charter schools, competition, and parental choice in America" (quoted in Whitman, p. 291). Yet the writings of students reveal that in their neighborhoods, the "choices" seem few and far between while the agenda of racialized dispossession advances. Will historic schools be renovated and sold to middle-class whites and blacks as condominiums just blocks from the riverfront? Whiteness, property, and accumulation do indeed seem to be part of a "master plan." Who will have the right to claim, use, and enjoy the assets of the city, and who will be excluded? Concerns over precisely who has the right to choose or decide are taken up quite seriously by Michael Apple in his response, which aligns the marketization of education in New Orleans with disinvestment and privatization globally.

The capitalist dream, it turns out, is a nightmare for all but the wealthy elites who plunder the urban landscape and appropriate historic schools and neighborhoods for themselves. Maria Hernandez speaks out: "I've lost my home, my friends, and my school. . . . But the worst part of it all is that the public officials—both elected and hired—who are supposed to be looking out for my education have failed me even worse than the ones who abandoned me in the Superdome." In the pages ahead, students' counterstories capture the destructive confluence of schooling and housing policies under neoliberalism and the struggle to maintain an infrastructure of culturally knowledgeable veteran teachers—ones capable of inspiring youth to become educators and contributors to an ongoing battle over community welfare. Participating in exchanges with students focused on various aspects of the neoliberal agenda, including "State Abandonment and the Privatization of Education," "Forceful Expulsion and the Exclusive Right to Home," and "Suppression of Veteran Teachers' Labor," Michael Apple, Pauline Lipman, and Vanessa Siddle Walker respond to the issues raised by students and teachers and consider the repercussions of current reforms. They also unmask what is at stake if we don't wake up, providing an invitation to reflect on the poetic declaration of Damien Theodore, who concludes this chapter by echoing Hughes's courageous defiance with a call to action and an assertion of subaltern rights to the city.

STATE ABANDONMENT AND THE PRIVATIZATION OF EDUCATION

Speaking Out

As I have argued elsewhere (Buras, 2007), state neglect and disinvestment constitute a racialized strategy of genocidal proportions: Sometimes the effects are immediate and at other times gradual, but the effects are real and not infrequently calculated by conservative policy advocates. Below we are reminded of both the violence of immediate physical abandonment of communities of color as well as the implications of the slow but equally destructive replacement of open access, neighborhood-based public schools with selective admissions charter schools and school choice. Even more concerning, these stories raise the issue of what it means when displacement, deregulation, and privatization of education combine as a tripartite policy regime—a regime with global dimensions, but one about which too few seem to care.

Forgotten by Our Government

Deborah Carey

It was August 28th of 2005. You know when you are alone in the house you hear extra noises as if it could be a ghost in there? Well, that's what it was like. I heard someone fooling with the door. But it was dad, mom, and my sister coming into the house from the garage. I went into the garage, and I saw a whole lot of wood from Home Depot. My daddy usually boards up the windows when a storm is coming. But I also saw some sandbags, which gave me an idea that the storm would be coming for sure.

We left my house on a Sunday. I remember the day because we didn't go to church. This surprised me because daddy made sure we never missed a Sunday. We left to go by my sister's house. She lived on the third floor in a one-bedroom apartment in East New Orleans. Nine people were in the apartment just waiting and watching the storm through the window of my sister's balcony. Nobody knew what would happen next. A couple of days passed. We listened to the radio about what was going on in the city: nothing but bad news everywhere. All you could hear was people screaming for help. National Guards my ass: They didn't even save us.

The so-called criminals of New Orleans saved us, stealing boats, trucks, 18 wheelers, and buses. Society calls these people animals, saying, "They don't deserve to be citizens." You ask me, we should be afraid of what they call National Guards, certified to BYHO ("Blow Yo' Head Off!"). If you ask me, the people known as criminals should have been the city leaders.

Finally we were rescued from my sister's apartment by a boat full of strangers. Not knowing who they were, it didn't even matter. They dropped us off on Chef Mentur Highway, one of the driest places in eastern New Orleans at the time. We met up with some of my little niece's family. They let us spend the night on the floor of their one-bedroom apartment. By then there were 19 people packed in an even smaller apartment, some of us sleeping in hallways.

Staying there for only one night on a wet, stinky, crowded floor made me sick. I remember how we had to shit in a bag on the toilet. When it got full, it would stink up the whole house, because the water had stopped working in the building. When we were told that we had to evacuate, I nearly messed up my legs. I had to help get bags and bags full of clothes and blankets through the water. I was trying my best not to let them get wet. Once again we did not know the next stop on our little journey. But I figured since we made it this far why just be afraid and give up now.

Hitchhiking was our next source, because we know ain't no way in hell we could have made it to the interstate. Besides just a bunch of old people were with me. I had to be the youngest besides my two little nieces and my nephew. Seeing a big moving truck with at least 30 people in the back, one of the drivers asked us did we need a ride. We didn't even answer. We just hopped on, which reminded me of how slaves were treated: a whole lot of black folk packed up on a wagon escaping from master.

While driving we saw hundreds of stragglers covering the streets. They were chasing after the truck like starving wolves running after pieces of meat. Seeing that made me realize we were luckier than some others. It was like leaving the weak behind and picking which ones would stay alive longer. Finally my family and I made it to the Convention Center. While driving there, we heard many voices, such as: "Say, lil daddy, let my mamma on." Or a weak voice that dragged, saying, "I've been walking for two days now. Please stop." Hearing that made me cry as my grandmamma would say, "Girl you droppin' watermelon tears." I swear it was watermelons rolling down my face. When we got to the Convention Center, I thought it was the promised land. I thought the people who were supposed to rescue us would bring us to the land of milk and honey. Instead it was nothing, but "Chaos!" with a capital C.

People screamed for help and passed out, stinky and dirty. There were looters and snipers with AK-47s around babies no older than 3. Old people, young people, sick people, and, last but not least, survivors. Day after day passed. We sat waiting impatiently for the National whatevers to come and rescue us.

Whatever help we needed the state was supposed to provide. It was like our citizenship went down the stream right along with our houses, all forgotten about by our government. We're used to hearing about how unjust the city of New Orleans is on a daily basis. But actually encountering it took me by surprise. Question: Where were the city's so-called leaders for that week, for those days, for those nights, and for those moments?

I'm not sure what day it was, but I remember waking up and feeling like I was in a nightmare rather than having one. The people were screaming for help, passed out, stinky and dirty, sick, old, young, and even the looters—all demanding Help! Something that the Black American should've been doing way before this time, demanding "Help!"

Worse Than Those Six Days

Maria Hernandez

When Katrina hit New Orleans, I was two weeks into my senior year at Frederick Douglass High School. My friends and I were frantically trying to keep our school from closing. Douglass was one of the lowest ranking schools in the district, so the state, using its accountability plan, was trying to shut it down or take it over. We were running a campaign called Quality Education as a Civil Right, doing our part in this one-year-old national campaign by continuing the work we had been doing at Douglass: involving more parents and students and community members in working together to improve the school and to demand all the resources we needed to do that.

A lot of people were *finally* looking at our school as more than just a place where criminals are reared, which is the impression you'd get if all you knew were news reports. The media always ran to the school to report a fight, but no one said anything when my classmates placed first in a competition against professional journalists for a series they wrote on public education for the 50th anniversary of *Brown v. Board of Education.* But for folks who knew what we were doing and spent time with us, you could see them actually smiling when Douglass was mentioned.

In the midst of all this, I was extremely bummed out. I was bored of walking the same old halls and knowing everybody who walked by. I was ready for a change. I got more than I bargained for when Katrina hit.

Looking back on the last few days of August 2005, I still can't believe we spent six days in the Superdome, the stadium that housed thousands of hurricane victims, without knowing if my dad was dead or alive. We had to sneak out of the Superdome and swim past corpses and bayou animals to find him. I sliced my leg in the process of avoiding a dead woman floating.

We found my dad, and my uncle, who was with him in the old neighborhood. They had survived by swimming from roof to roof. It was a relief to find all of them okay, but there's nothing worse than walking into your 'hood and not recognizing it: water waist deep, the stores all looted, or in the process of being looted. I couldn't help but let tears fall.

As they say, home is where the heart is. So I guess my heart is 20,000 leagues under the sea. That would be a good explanation for the emptiness that comes through my chest and expands to my body and words. It's hard to keep going and pushing when you don't even know if what you're looking for is still there.

This uncertainty that's strangling me is also undermining Douglass, the school my friends were fighting to make better. When we gathered for a weekend reunion on October 8–9, 2005, we learned that all the New Orleans Public Schools would become charter schools this year. We had been fighting to improve from within neighborhood schools that don't have selective admissions. Now, with all schools being charters, no one will have the choice of truly public, neighborhood-based education.

And worse than that, the only public high schools open on the East Bank of the city, where the hurricane hit the hardest and where probably over 80% of the population, including my family and all of my friends, live, have selective admissions criteria. How can these decision makers open two high schools on the East Bank, but none for common folk like me, who either can't get into or don't want to get into selective admissions high schools?

I've lost my home, my friends, and my school. I'm always on the verge of tears. But the worst part of it all is that the public officials—both elected and hired—who are supposed to be looking out for my education have failed me even worse than the ones who abandoned me in the Superdome. My family and friends have food and water and the kindness of strangers. But we still don't have control of our lives, and we're still being abandoned by local, state, and federal officials.

I'm in the same situation I was before Katrina: but now I'm fighting to reopen Douglass and other neighborhood high schools in New Orleans and to provide quality education for people like me.

Does Anybody Know?

Katrena Jackson-Ndang

On July 15, 2006, dark clouds gathered and lightning and thunderbolts filled the New Orleans sky. But neither dark clouds, thunderbolts, nor rain could keep eager students, faculty, staff, and parents from gathering at Southern Oaks Plantation to celebrate the end of the school year for Lawless High School.

Alfred Lawless High School, the only public high school in the Lower 9th Ward, was devastated by Hurricane Katrina. For the first time in the school's 42-year history there was no ring ceremony, no prom, no homecoming, no winter formal, no sweetheart ball, and no graduation. So the July 15th celebration represented many different milestones. For some people this was a Lawless family reunion. It was a graduation for the class of 2006. For the class of 2007, this was a junior prom. The classes of 1986 and 1996 took this as their class reunion, and for 20 of the 68 faculty and staff members, this was a retirement party. For those going back to distant places like California, New York, New Jersey, Florida, Georgia, Tennessee, and Texas, it was a bon voyage party. But sadly, for many others gathered there, it was a memorial for the four Lawless loved ones who died during the storm.

This celebration was for the Lawless family, but the sentiments of the whole city were felt in that room. For you see, there are so many parallels between what happened in the city in general and what happened to Lawless and New Orleans Public Schools in particular. Lawless lost four family members due to the storm, while the city lost more than 1,500 family members. The school district, which had more than 100 schools before the storm, lost all but 4 of its schools as a result of a state takeover of public schools in Orleans Parish. Charter schools became the buzzword for what was needed to reform the school system in New Orleans. Even schools that were already exemplary became charter schools.

Pushed by the state, the school district terminated more than 4,000 educators. Twenty Lawless faculty and staff members were among the 2,000 educators forced to retire. I am among the 20 retirees from Lawless, and I can say, like many others, I was not ready to retire, but was forced to in order to maintain some semblance of benefits and peace of mind. I am highly qualified according to the No Child Left Behind Act, because I continually upgraded myself in my content area. In fact, I was lead teacher on a U.S. Department of Education grant to the New Orleans Public Schools to improve the teaching of American history. This massive termination of educators caused the current shortage of qualified teachers. Furthermore, New Orleans lost at least 8,000 people who were part of its middle-class tax base. In other words, at least 4,000 highly qualified educators will educate children in other states and districts because they have been denied jobs in the new charter schools and the state-run Recovery School District.

Many highly qualified educators are not working in the new charter schools and the Recovery School District because these are using unfair tactics to undermine the professionalism and the respect of veteran teachers. The test that they administer is an insult to the profession of teaching. Orleans Parish is the only district in which such tests take place. In any other school district, the state deems its certification system, which includes the national Praxis exam, a good measure for hiring teachers. I worry that these new schools only want to hire teachers who have never taught before. They want to hire inexperienced teachers so that they can pay them little or no money and also so that they can treat them like sharecroppers, or better still like slaves, with no rights and no input or say about what happens in the schools.

For three hours on July 15th the Alfred Lawless High School family forgot about the troubles of hurricane-ravaged New Orleans and concentrated on the school's happier days and memories. In fact, someone had a flashback and began to shout the Pythian (the school mascot) victory yell: "L- A- W- L- E- S- S, Buck 'em up, Buck 'em up, Pythians, Buck 'em up!" The festivities are over for this year, but the questions remain. What's next for Lawless and all the other public schools in the district? Does anybody know? What's next for the highly qualified, unemployed, displaced educators? Does anybody know? Does anybody care?

Commentary

Making Schools "Right" Again:
Whose Choice Is the Education Market?

Michael W. Apple

During the war in the former Yugoslavia, I spent time in refugee camps in what is now Slovenia. Thousands upon thousands of people fled over the mountains to escape the murderous and merciless shelling of Sarajevo. When the people crossed the border into Slovenia and reached the refugee camps—really just decaying army barracks that were the only home they would know for months—they immediately organized two things:

food distribution and schools. Both were seen as absolutely essential for them and for their children.

I use the word *refugee* with great hesitancy, for words like *refugee* can do damage to reality and to one's humanity. These were *people* who were forced out by state-sanctioned murder, by official policy. They were people who cannot be adequately described by that one word—*refugee*. These were teachers, builders, nurses, shop owners, store clerks, farmers, children, fathers, mothers. The concept of "refugee" is too anonymous and can act as part of a larger process of dehumanization. And there is more linguistic politics at work here. The conflict that led to the murders and the fleeing—the "ethnic cleansing"—is itself cleansed and made more acceptable by describing it by that incredible oxymoron "civil war."

What happened—and continues to happen—in New Orleans is also cleansed. The word *refugee* was applied to state-abandoned residents of New Orleans who were fleeing for their lives (mostly, and not incidentally, people of color), and the murderous circumstances that ensued were described as a "natural disaster." Terms such as *natural disaster* are ways in which dominant groups dismiss their own culpability in the creation of situations such as these (Apple, 2000). It is all too painfully obvious that there was very little about what happened that was natural, as Deborah Carey and Maria Hernandez testify in their stories about the very real nightmare they endured as the so-called National Guard disregarded their lives. This was the result of decades of neglect, economic attacks, racializing policies, and a regime at all levels that saw in this socially created disaster an opportunity to transform New Orleans through the application of the religion of the market.

I say "religion" here, because *neoliberalism*—a vision that sees every sector of society as subject to the logics of commodification, marketization, competition, and cost-benefit analysis—seems to be immune to empirical arguments, especially, but not only, in education. As I demonstrate in *Educating the "Right" Way* (Apple, 2006), in very few nations of the world has setting the market loose on schools and other social institutions led to greater equality. Indeed, it has often led to the reproduction of existing hierarchies and the creation of new inequalities.

The religious status of neoliberalism assumes particular things. Choice, competition, markets—all of these supposedly will lead us to the promised land of efficient and effective schools. The key word here is "supposedly." This is a crucial caveat, since we know that school choice policies, especially those involving marketization and privatization, often involve schools choosing students and parents as much as parents choosing schools (Apple, 2006). In New Orleans, it is obvious that it also involves destroying existing schools and shedding the teachers who worked in them. The dismissal of unionized veteran educators, such as Katrena Jackson-Ndang, and closure of Lawless High School are hailed as signs of progress. Anything that existed before is "bad," everything that replaces it is "good." It is not to romanticize the realities of schools as they were before Katrina and its aftermath, to recognize the fact that these schools and these teachers had long histories, with many victories associated with them. These schools and these students and teachers carried with them the collective memories of struggles. They provided a living, breathing history of oppressed peoples' never-ending collective attempts to create and defend institutions that speak to their and their children's realities, histories, cultures, and dreams. In contexts such as this, "choice" functions as the partial destruction of collective memory.

But this institutional destruction and the shedding of teachers so that everyone is more efficient and effective is not all. We also know that such policies on the ground do not work as smoothly as market proponents assume in their utopian dreams about efficiencies and accountability. Indeed, it has become clear both nationally and internationally that markets can indeed not only reproduce existing inequalities but that they can create even more inequalities than existed previously. When they are combined with an increased emphasis on national and state testing—which usually accompanies such proposals in a considerable number of nations—the results from this combination of neoliberal market initiatives and neoconservative pressure to standardize and impose a supposedly common culture and also to mandate reductive accountability measures can be truly damaging to the most oppressed people (see Apple, 2006; Buras, 2008).

The class and race specificities of these tendencies are increasingly visible. There is an emerging body of international research that documents how middle-class parents are able to use choice plans for their own advantage (Ball, 2003; Lauder & Hughes, 1999; Power, Edwards, Whitty, & Wigfall, 2003). This should not surprise us. As Bourdieu (1984) has elegantly demonstrated, middle-class and more affluent actors have a "natural" habitus that makes them considerably more able to employ strategies that enable them to play the market game. Their store of cultural, economic, and social capital privileges them in the complicated conversion strategies surrounding choice. Similar racializing effects are all too visible as well, as choice programs foster a set of strategies in which dominant groups are able to protect their children and themselves from the body and culture of the "polluting Other" (Apple, 2006; Gillborn, 2008; Lauder & Hughes, 1999).

But of course this is the point, isn't it? Making New Orleans a nice "safe" city for the middle class and "whitening" it so that the city becomes even more of a theme park for tourists with money, becomes one more instance in a long history of the relationship between markets and their vision of rational individual choice and race (Mills, 1997). In saying this, I want to be careful, however. The language of the free market and choice is partly counterhegemonic. In a time when the common stereotypes that circulate so widely in the media and in white common sense picture African Americans as dangerous and irrational, the vision of the rational individual consumer embodied in the ideology of the market offers a different identity to oppressed people than the pathological ones seemingly so easily accepted among those in society who view themselves as the norm, as the "human ordinary" (Apple & Pedroni, 2005; Pedroni, 2007). However, in the long run, as has happened to people of color in other countries, the gains associated with this partly counterhegemonic identity can be easily washed away and may be more than a little temporary (Lauder & Hughes, 1999).

Behind my arguments in this reflection on the articulate voices of the students and teachers included in this exceptional book are a number of points. But one of them stands out for me. Language makes a difference. How someone or some situation is described, especially by powerful forces who wish to remain in power, is crucial. The language employed carries with it a whole raft of assumptions of course; but it also creates boundaries for what is seen as legitimate action and what is seen as not useful, not efficient, not workable, and quite often too radical. Neoliberalism is no different. It opens a space for certain identities and closes down others. It gives people *one* option of who they are: They are *consumers*. They are to be motivated by one thing: individual gain based on one's choice of "products." Collective responsibility and an immediate concern for social justice—these things will take care of themselves. This is a desocializing sensibility. Do not think of oneself as a member of a group of oppressed people who have a long history of struggling for social justice. Think of oneself instead wholly as a "chooser" of goods and services. Consumer choice will ultimately provide for all—even if you and your community have little say in what these choices are or actively refuse to include the institutions that have had partial victories associated with them. The message is "Trust us." "We" are the reformers; we will give you what you don't yet know you want. We will transform schools so that (for now, selective) children will get schooling that will be better.

Of course, the "we" here are the powerful, the true believers, and at times simply the profiteers (see Burch, 2008). The "non-we" are those who are told to trust the market and the choices it makes available. And the students and teachers in Students at the Center (SAC) in New Orleans are definitely part of the non-we. This entire situation reeks of something that has a long history. It is one more instance of dominant groups speaking the language of transformation at the same time as power shifts even more radically into their hands. Let us be honest. This is simply political authority masquerading as the margins.

But while criticism of these policies is absolutely essential, it is not enough. The defense of powerful alternatives that have been built, such as SAC, and the continued day-to-day battles to create and defend other practical examples of an education that is worthy of its name—this is clearly just as important. There *are* critically democratic alternatives to the "reforms" that are being imposed in New Orleans. Critical educators, community activists, students, and others know that such programs exist because they live in them every day. These alternatives embody many of the principles that are so visible in SAC. They offer ways of organizing curricula and teaching in powerful and personal ways, ways that call forth the voices of students and teachers as co-responsible subjects. Indeed, as the voices of the teachers and students demonstrate in the grassroots book that James Beane and I put together, *Democratic Schools* (Apple & Beane, 2007), these alternatives work in real situations where the forces of the powerful in this society have decided that marginalized people only deserve certain choices, choices that seem more and more to look like marginalized (or no) schooling for marginalized people.

Yet, as the real people who came over the mountains from Sarajevo documented, people will build schools for their children. Community members, activists, teachers, students, and many more will mobilize, will collectively sacrifice to create educational institutions, even under the destructive and disastrous conditions created by the storm of neoliberal policies. And, once again, there's a key word here—"collectively." Neoliberalism's attack on collective identities, and on educational experiences that are rooted in re-creating such identities, can be resisted. The voices of students and teachers of such programs as SAC document why this is so important.

FORCEFUL EXPULSION AND THE EXCLUSIVE RIGHT TO HOME

Speaking Out

As Apple reveals above, educational choice functions as a cover for a host of maneuvers and policies by the classed and raced state not simply in New Orleans, but under conditions of uneven neoliberal globalization affecting countrysides and cities worldwide. The students who speak out in this exchange push the bounds of the conversation beyond schools by relaying the experiences they've had on the home front—that is to say, what they have confronted amidst the loss of housing, neighborhood, and community. Their stories compel us to examine how educational policies and markets have correlates in the domain of housing, an arena where the state has been equally culpable in pursuing an agenda of displacement, disinvestment, and privatization. Long before Katrina, as one example, thousands of families were expelled from the St. Thomas Housing Development in New Orleans when federal funding was granted through the HOPE VI program to build mixed-income housing in place of the long-neglected housing project (see Buras, 2005). Pauline Lipman considers students' stories in relation to similar patterns around housing in Chicago and the ways these have been wedded to disinvestment in the public schools and broader plans for community reconstruction.

Missing Project

Tyeasha Green

When I'm down or confused, I find myself driving back to Mazant Street and looking at the blank windows of my old apartment building.

I miss walking outside, always seeing somebody I know. It was like a family that you were born with. Because no matter whom you fussed with, fought with, liked or didn't like, or anything like that, it didn't matter. When you were hurt or someone was messing with you outside the neighborhood, the other Florida Project residents always had your back.

Yes, there were killings over the most stupid things like a dice game, a dogfight, or the most stupid of them all, "he said, she said" mess. But still the project was a place where people lived, learned how to bond, and understood what a community should be like. We learned how we should stick together as a black family and how we should respect other blacks as people not like dogs or someone you walk over and don't care about. We learned not to mistreat other people just because we could.

My old neighborhood taught me so much. I would really hate to see it go. That's why I hope that officials from New Orleans, the state, or the federal government do not tear down my old home. The project is a place where people can go and learn so many new things about the people who live there.

The government officials should be building up not tearing down. Most of the teachers at my school are not even living in their old homes. A lot of them are staying on university campuses or with friends. Restaurants and other businesses are looking for workers, but most low–income workers don't have an affordable place to live.

It's been over 18 months since Hurricane Katrina, but it feels like years. Now, people like me who love our old homes in the Florida and other projects are living in new neighborhoods. We have to deal with new schools and lots of loss—of people, not just property. So we're depressed, confused, and lost. And in the middle of those struggling feelings, we don't have the old neighborhood and family support, which is really the main thing poor people like us have to keep us sane.

Who's Holding the Gun?

Vinnessia Shelbia

Leaving New Orleans was hard, because there's no other place like it. But living in New Orleans post-Katrina is just as bad, because there's nowhere to live. There are places to sleep, but nowhere to live.

When I came back to New Orleans after living in Georgia for one year, leaving my immediate family behind, I went to stay with my relatives living closest to New Orleans. That was my father's mother whom I had never lived with any of my life. Staying there didn't last long, but what could I expect: 12 people living in a one-bedroom, one-bath don't add up.

So I turned to my last resort: a homeless shelter. None of my relatives lived in the city. I had only one close friend from middle to high school. I couldn't stay at her house. It was overcrowded with her family members. If you would have asked me where I saw myself in the future, I wouldn't have said a shelter.

Around this time in their lives, other teenagers are happy and planning their senior year, but not me. I was worried about will I get raped by one of these homeless men who are sleeping right on the other side of the room. And because these worries are keeping me up, will I be rested enough for school tomorrow. And while I was thinking about school, I'd also worry how will I get there, since there are no more bus tickets that permit me to ride the bus for free. The yellow school buses come when they want, for whatever reason that is. So many school days go unattended, and my teachers ask why . . . and where's your mother?

Well, my mother has finally pawned everything that she can to feed my brothers. And she has filled out so many applications. But for what? The people who take her applications have no direct contact, since she can't afford to keep a phone on. I can remember times when I was in New Orleans and I would have to call my brother's friend and hope that he was at my mother's house so I could talk to her. My burned-out mother did the only thing she knew: Sell everything in the house to get tickets back to New Orleans.

Writing this makes me angry. It makes me wonder what kind of world do we live in when children no older than 14 are experiencing these things.

Even though my mother came back recently, we remain homeless because the prices for rent are outstanding and standing out. So now my whole family is homeless: mother and sister at a woman's shelter and a week later my sister Angela gets put out because she can't find a job and that's one of their requirements. So luckily Angela found a shelter that was not overcrowded and was taking women without children.

My youngest brother Savion was living in Boy's Town. Maybe once out of every three weeks I would talk to him, and he would ask me the same thing: "When mama gon' get a house?" I would tell him what she would tell me, "Hopefully soon." I didn't know, and she didn't know either. Those conversations were like a reality smack, waking me up to see that we were just hoping and wouldn't be getting a house anytime soon.

New Orleans really is the murder capital, but now who's holding the gun?

Commentary

Racial Reform on Chicago's Home Front

Pauline Lipman

It is a warm July evening but the auditorium at the Center for Inner City Studies, an African-centered educational institution in Chicago's historic Bronzeville area, is still packed. Parents, teachers, principals, and community members have been lining up to speak for over three hours. The official sent by Chicago Public Schools to appease concerns about the plan to close 20 of the Midsouth area's 22 schools is sweating and visibly frustrated. Ms. B (a parent and Local School Council chair) takes the mic: "We want to know what you're going to do with our children. You tore the houses down [public housing projects], children moving from place to place. Somebody's looking out for someone else!" (fieldnotes, 2004)

This scene has repeated in African American and Latino communities across Chicago since 2004 when Chicago's Mayor Daley announced Renaissance

2010, a plan to close "failing" or "underenrolled" schools and turn them over to charter school operators or make them into selective enrollment schools. The goal is to close 60–70 public schools and open 100 new schools, two thirds as charter or contract schools (similar to charters). Community resistance by an alliance of parents, teachers, unions, school reform groups, and African American community organizations forced Chicago Public Schools (CPS) to drop the Midsouth closings, and there have been more victories since, but as of 2009, the plan overall is running ahead of schedule. CPS leaders, the mayor, and their partner in this project, the Commercial Club of Chicago, boast they are creating "a new market in public education." (The Commercial Club is an organization of the city's most powerful corporate and financial leaders.) New Orleans and Chicago have been ground zero for market-based education "reforms" which are going national with Arne Duncan, former CEO of Chicago schools, heading up the U.S. Department of Education. Education markets are a core of the Obama administration's education agenda. Tyeasha Green and Vinnessia Shelbia's powerful testimonies and Ms. B's charge speak back to a national, even global, agenda to remake the city for capital accumulation, racial exclusion, and "conquest" by the upper middle class (Smith, 2002).

In Chicago, as in New Orleans and other cities, housing and school policies are intertwined in neighborhood destabilization, gentrification, and displacement of communities of color. Closing schools that are anchors in their communities makes a community less liveable and creates additional pressures for displacement. The loss of neighborhood schools and uncertainties of a shifting market of unproven charter schools and selective schools with complex admission policies and limited enrollments can be the tipping point pushing families out of neighborhoods. At the July 2004 hearing in Chicago, community members insisted that Renaissance 2010 was designed to further their community's gentrification. Their claim was grounded in the fact that the area was experiencing some of the most intense gentrification in the city (Lipman & Haines, 2007). For example, Michaels Development Company (whose projects are partially financed with public HOPE VI money in cities across the United States) has a $600 million investment in Legends South, a new complex of over 2,300 houses and apartments on a two-mile stretch of land where the Robert Taylor Homes public housing complex stood. Michaels is just one of the investors in the area.

The groundwork for HOPE VI was laid by a nexus of real estate and banking practices, housing policies, and corporate decisions going back to the post–World War II period and extending through the 1980s. The logics of capital and race combined to promote white flight and to disinvest in, deindustrialize, and racially segregate central city areas with large African American and, in some cases, Latino populations. In New Orleans the hurricane provided a massive new investment opportunity for developers and banks. But long before the storm hit, there was a prolonged scourge of public neglect and private disinvestment that plagued low-income working-class communities of color across the United States. In many cities, public housing was allowed to deteriorate until it was uninhabitable, justifying demolition, while neighborhoods were stripped of businesses, grocery stores, public amenities, and jobs. This was the precondition for public housing demolition and "revitalization" as mixed-income developments.

The conditions that justify closing schools in low-income African American communities are also products of a nexus of investment decisions and public policies. Despite real gains of the civil rights and black liberation movements, decades of racial segregation, insufficient resources, inequitable funding, neglect, and mis-education set up schools for failure under high stakes accountability policies (Lipman & Haines, 2007). Underenrollment, another justification for closing neighborhood schools, is also rooted in policies that push out working-class families (e.g., gentrification and loss of affordable housing). Our mapping of school closings onto patterns of racial segregation and gentrification in Chicago reveals the connections between disinvestment and reinvestment in housing and schools and the displacement and exclusion of low-income people of color (Greenlee, Hudspeth, Lipman, Smith, & Smith, 2008; Lipman & Haines, 2007). It mirrors the connection between the failure to reopen public schools in New Orleans' black communities, policies that prevented Vinnessia's and other families from returning to and rebuilding their houses, and the investment opportunities opened up by the new housing and education markets.

This dynamic is located in what geographer David Harvey (2001) calls the "spatial fix": "Capitalism perpetually strives, therefore, to create a social and physical landscape in its own image and requisite to its own needs at a particular point in time, only just as certainly to undermine, disrupt and even destroy that landscape at a later point in time" (p. 333). The urban built environment is "junked, abandoned, destroyed and selectively reconstructed" (Weber, 2002, pp. 520–521) through downtown development and strategic reinvestment in previously devalued areas. The territorial organization of capital—the location of production facilities, the built environment of cities, housing, schools, and places of consumption—is destroyed and rebuilt elsewhere in order to establish a "new locational grid" for capital accumulation (Brenner & Theodore, 2002, p. 355). New Orleans makes clear how deeply racialized this process is in the

United States. Disinvestment, neglect of physical infrastructure and the built environment, coupled with racial segregation, prepare the ground for a new round of profitable reinvestment that excludes working-class people, particularly low-income people of color.

The $5 billion HOPE VI federal housing policy to dismantle public housing, disperse residents, and replace it with mixed-income developments to which only a percentage of former tenants are relocated is a major tool in this process. Under Chicago's version of HOPE VI, the Plan for Transformation, demolition of over 19,000 units of public housing is nearly complete with the tenants dispersed to the private housing market in the city and impoverished ring suburbs or out of the Chicago area altogether. The land where public housing stood is now an enormously valuable commodity. Mega complexes of housing, recreation, and upscale retail, all largely out of reach of public housing tenants, rise up in their place. Meanwhile, displacement of thousands of families, mostly African American, has torn apart the social fabric of communities and bred homelessness and instability. To use Tyeasha's words, "depressed, confused, and lost" links families from New Orleans to Chicago.

Before communities can be gentrified, they have to be devalued, prepared for redevelopment, and reimagined as places of value. To do so, it is necessary to construct a reality of "easily discardable people and social life" (Wilson, Wouters, & Grammenos, 2004, p. 1181). Race is at the center of this process. The historical web of economic structures and public policies that enforced racial segregation and disinvestment in communities of color were undergirded ideologically by racially coded discourses of social pathology and danger associated with the "inner city" (Wilson, 2007). This is the discourse underpinning the rationale to dismantle public housing: Concentrations of poor people breed social pathologies that produce poverty. This logic is relentlessly reinvigorated by corporate media and public officials who invoke metaphors of pathology and violence to describe public housing and low-income African Americans in particular. In Chicago the destruction of thousands of family units of public housing in the Robert Taylor Homes complex on the city's South Side was applauded as a solution for a "gang-infested" area that needed to be "cleaned out" and "revitalized" (e.g., Grossman & Leroux, 2006). The state institutionalizes this discourse by labeling areas "blighted" as a precondition for seizing them under eminent domain and assisting private real estate redevelopment and gentrification (Weber, 2002). "Blight" is racially loaded. For example, buildings on the African American South Side of Chicago were more frequently categorized by the city as substandard even though they were not as old as those in other parts of the city (p. 526). Representations of black urban space as pathological are knitted to the supposedly regenerative and disciplining effects of the market. In the neoliberal context, "public" and "private" have become racialized metaphors—private equated with "good" and "white" and public with "bad" and "black" (Haymes, 1995, p. 20).

The logics of capital and race converge to project black communities as simply sites of capital accumulation rather than political and cultural contexts invested with socially produced meanings. This negates the history of black urban spaces as central to a culture and politics of resistance (Haymes, 1995, p. 10) and African American schools as centers of community (Walker, 1996). Struggling working-class communities of color may be pathologized by the media and social policy discourses, but as Haymes argues, they have far more complex meanings for those who live there as spaces of collective identity, material survival, and community. Tyeasha makes this point vividly: "But still the project was a place where people lived, learned how to bond, and understood what a community should be like." Her voice echoes in the lament of a Chicago teacher at a school that received many displaced children: "I think the greatest impact is that there's no longer this sense of community atmosphere." Closing down neighborhood schools and housing breaks a web of human connections in which the social and cultural practices of daily life are rooted, race and class identities are formed, and community is constituted. Mindy Fullilove (2005) describes the trauma of displacement due to urban renewal as "root shock," or the "the traumatic stress of the loss of [one's] lifeworld" (p. 20).

Vinnessia asks, "Who's holding the gun?" Neoliberal policy makers who have produced the greatest concentration of wealth in the fewest hands in human history have reshaped cities globally. The urban landscape is marked by contrasting zones of wealth and poverty, centrality and exclusion, that are economic, cultural, social, political, and spatial—and, in the United States at least, racialized through and through. Urban policy is dominated by efforts to attract capital and prevent capital flight, to compete for investment and tourism, to create large-scale development projects such as waterfronts and tourist attractions. City governments subsidize capital to relocate and invest in the city, privatize public services and infrastructure (e.g., schools and housing), and redirect resources and create policy to support real estate development (Hackworth, 2007). Facilitated and funded by city government, gentrification is a pivotal sector in neoliberal urban economies and a central factor in the production of spatial inequality, displacement, homelessness, and racial containment. Good government means supporting, working with, and acting like corporations while bypassing democratic participation in favor of public-private partnerships and corporate bodies that make fundamental decisions about schools, housing, and community development with no public accountability. The Bring New Orleans Back Commission and Chicago's Renaissance 2010, which is co-lead by CPS and the Renaissance Schools Fund, an offshoot of the Commercial Club, exemplify neoliberal governance.

HOPE VI, Renaissance 2010, and the forced relocation of New Orleanians to make way for development expose the racialized social engineering inherent in neoliberal urbanism. People are objects to be manipulated according to a plan devised elsewhere. As Tyeasha states, "The government officials should be building up not tearing down." Genuine "choice" should also mean enhancing "the right to stay put" (Imbroscio 2008, p. 120) through the development of quality affordable housing and schools in one's community. The struggle for "the right to stay put" is part of a larger democratic struggle over not only access to housing, jobs, and schools but also the right to cultural and political space, the right to decide what the city will become.

SUPPRESSION OF VETERAN TEACHERS' LABOR

Speaking Out

When schools and homes are lost to neoliberal initiatives, so are people and communities, as Tyeasha makes very clear. In this final exchange, teachers and students explore what it means to "lose" a specific part of the community—black veteran educators—as a result of forceful expulsion combined with weakly regulated charters and racially inspired union busting; the latter is surely the hallmark of neoliberalism, which promises to liberate schools from the unnecessary restraints imposed by labor and state bureaucracy. Rather problematically, the rhetoric about "uncaring" teachers and the need for improvement through free market innovation hides a deeper reality: Many of New Orleans veteran teachers have fought since the era of Jim Crow for the right to vote, equal pay, and the improvement of the public schools. Rather than constituting the "problem," as neoliberal reformers would have us think, these teachers have worked under the most challenging of conditions, and have used their knowledge of community to challenge unjust conditions in the process. To threaten that legacy by recruiting itinerant laborers (e.g., transient, uncertified teachers through Teach for America) is gravely concerning. Vanessa Siddle Walker documents what stands to be lost by providing historical perspective on the cultural assets of black teachers in the Jim

Crow South, a history that makes all the more understandable why students themselves energetically assert their desire and their right to follow in these teachers' footsteps.

Passing on a Torch

Jim Randels

I keep thinking about Ed and Leatrice Roberts. Kalamu, Ashley, Maria, and I spent a couple of Saturdays at their home this summer. Maria, a rising senior at Frederick Douglass High School, sat between the two white-haired elders with dancing eyes and mischievous grins. They were on the couch, beneath the photograph of Dillard University's College of Education Class of 1948. Maria's head was bent over her notebook, except when she threw it back, braids and beads and all, laughing with Ed and Leatrice about crazy Ed dragging Leatrice on dates to union meetings or voter registration drives. Or when she looked straight at Leatrice, accepting and appreciating her elder's stern, gentle question about how the boys were treating her.

The Roberts' house is gone now, like the other homes in Pontchartrain Park, completely flooded out by the breaches in the London Avenue Canal. And the story of their neighborhood hasn't really been told in the national media. It's easy to see the poverty and racism and downright evil unearthed by Katrina. What we don't see is that the largest group of black, college-educated homeowners in New Orleans was teachers. What happens to this group when public schools are shut down?

I doubt that Ed and Leatrice carried out the old diplomas from the first graduating class of McDonogh 35 High School, of which Mrs. Reed, Leatrice's mother, was a member. I expect all the photographs and memorabilia from Amozion Baptist Church, the Lower 9th Ward church down the street from my fiancé's house and where her family and Leatrice's family have been members since the Reconstruction era, are gone now. Leatrice was head of the history committee and had enlisted the digital media crew of Students at the Center to help with the 135th anniversary celebration in October. And Dr. Keith Ferdinand's drawings, the ones he did as a kid in the late 1950s, are probably gone. Most of them were lost in 1965, when Hurricane Betsy flooded the Ferdinand home in the Lower 9th Ward. Ed and Leatrice, dry back in 1965 in their new Pontchartrain Park home, had some of the few surviving youth drawings of their godson—a cardiologist known for his community-based health advocacy in New Orleans.

But if I know Ed and Leatrice, their hearts are especially heavy about the threats to American Federation of Teachers (AFT) Local 527 that the post-Katrina state of public education in New Orleans have laid bare.

I remember Maria putting down her pen and smiling with pride and mischievous conspiracy when Ed talked about how his elementary school classroom became an adult literacy center. Ed and his union colleagues knew that developing literacy for their students needed to include parents. But they also knew that in the Jim Crow South, the education had to be political too. Parents needed to register to vote, and the classrooms were important spaces for developing democracy.

Maria practically cheered when Leatrice explained that she started teaching in 1949, the year that black teachers finally won equal pay. Maria had just finished a new writing on Veronica Hill, one of the teachers who helped launch the first white-collar union in the South, AFT Local 527. This black union had as one of its main goals to pursue the struggle for equal pay for teachers in the Jim Crow South.

And Maria had been angry when she read the headlines in the local newspaper that the school district was considering dropping its contribution share (employees also contribute from their salaries) to the Health and Welfare Fund. The Roberts and their fellow teachers had fought for this union and district partnership—not just for the dental and vision benefits but for the professional development provided by the teacher center. This center (now the Center for Professional Growth and Development) has been the most stable avenue for improving teaching practices and sharing resources that black or white teachers in New Orleans have had for the last 30 or 40 years.

Maria concludes her essay on Leatrice, entitled "Sharing a Life, Passing a Torch," with these paragraphs:

> "Just because you retire doesn't mean you stop being an activist."
> That's the reason she founded the retiree chapter. Ms. Leatrice and Mr. Edward struggled their whole lives to get teachers the benefits they deserved through the Health and Welfare Fund. They succeeded, but now everything they worked for is on the brink of getting destroyed as the school system considers cutting the Health and Welfare Fund to balance its budget.
>
> "I've done all I can, but before I'm gone I want someone to pass the torch to," Ms. Leatrice said.
>
> That's why I went to see her. I wanted to let her know that we students appreciate her and that there are a few of us who would gladly receive the torch and run with it.

I am proud of Maria's resolve and know that her words aren't hollow. She's already planning to move back to New Orleans in January, to carry the torch the Roberts have passed. She understands that this may mean getting a GED, since schools that honor the democratic institutions that Ed and Leatrice and other black teachers fought to establish will probably not be open. And I will be proud to be there with Maria and her classmates, working as hard as ever to give them the best education possible and one that preserves what storms and post-Katrina opportunists cannot wash away.

I Don't Want To Go To That School

Kirsten Theodore

"Why can't I go to Douglass, Auntie Nise?"

"Because it's not the school for you."

"What do you mean, not the school for me?"

"Look, I'm not about to explain myself to you. You're just not going."

"Damien and Shannon went. And Damien's already finished two years of college successfully. Why can't I go?"

"They didn't have options, and you have two, so I'm choosing one for you."

"So what. What's the difference between Douglass and Signature? Can you answer that?"

"Signature is better."

"How do you know? There's no proof. Douglass has had ups and downs and you judge it, but you don't know anything about that experimental school that's been open less than a year, and you're ready to send me there."

"Yep."

I was in eighth grade when we had that conversation, and I still remember it like it happened this morning. To people like my aunt, who had never been there and just looked at the test scores, Douglass didn't have much to offer. But I wanted to go there for several reasons: (1) My cousin and sister went there and always came home excited about their writing class or the journalism club or the choir; (2) Douglass was only a hop, skip, and a jump away from my house; and most of all, (3) I had spent most of my afternoons in an after-school program called Urban Heart that was set up and run by the community, teachers, and high school students like my cousin.

Urban Heart is also where I discovered that I wanted to be a teacher at Douglass. I wanted so much to be a part of the Douglass family, but it was ripped away from me when I was sucked into Signature High.

At this "choice" school my dream to be a teacher slowly faded, because the majority of my teachers told me I was crazy for settling for something so low and I shouldn't want to help students who give up on themselves and would end up selling dope. I kept wondering how my auntie could think Signature was better than Douglass when all Signature did was put down people like me.

When we returned to New Orleans in October 2006, a couple of months into my 11th grade year, one of the only open schools with space for students was Frederick Douglass. So now it was my auntie who didn't have a choice. My whole world lit up when I found out that I'd be going to Douglass.

Like most things in New Orleans, however, Douglass had changed after the storm. Now the state, which had never before run a school, much less a school system, had taken over Douglass. Only five teachers who had taught at Douglass before Katrina were left. About half of the teachers were uncertified and teaching for the first time. And there were security guards everywhere. In fact, at the beginning of the school year there were more security guards than there were certified teachers.

Despite all the ways that the state takeover has made Douglass worse than when I dreamed of going there, I'm actually happy to get out my bed every morning to learn from the half of my teachers who are certified. These veterans of neighborhood public schools in New Orleans are always there to help me where I lack. If it wasn't for Ms. Adams, I would not know that Huey P. Long and Claiborne were governors, not just roads. Ms. Haines taught me not only what a parenthetical citation is but how to blend many sources and stories together into a unified essay. And Mr. Randels, the same writing teacher with Students at the Center (SAC) who taught my cousin Damien six years ago, has trained me to go to the elementary school across the street, the one where Urban Heart used to be, and lead writing workshops for seventh and eighth graders with my fellow SAC members.

Best of all, being at my neighborhood school has me back on track with a vision and purpose for my education. Once again I want to become a teacher, and I'm really glad to be in a school that supports me in this vision rather than looking down on me for it.

Commentary

African American Teachers in the Old South and the New

Vanessa Siddle Walker

Could Maria Hernandez and Kirsten Theodore be magically transported to the annual convention of the Louisiana Colored Teachers Association (LCTA) in Shreveport in November 1937, they would recognize with even greater clarity the rich legacy to which they are heirs. At that meeting of black educators, the former president of the National Association of Teachers of Colored Schools (NATCS), Mary McLeod Bethune, assumed the platform to deliver one of the keynote addresses for convention attendees, a group representing approximately half the black teaching staff in Louisiana (Middleton, 1984; Perry, 1975). Could Maria and Kirsten have been part of the audience, they would have heard Bethune's indignant expression of dismay at the horrific differences in expenditures in the education of black and white children. Bethune cited data documenting the details of her claim that black children received only about one eighth the funding spent on the average American child, then used the statistics to challenge a system that provided fewer resources while expecting similar outcomes from black children. "Booker T. Washington once said," Bethune observed, "that it's too great a compliment to the Negro's intelligence to suppose he [or she] can learn eight times as easily as his [or her] white neighbor" (Middleton, 1984, p. 63).

Imaginarily settled in the midst of attendees, Maria and Kirsten would no doubt recognize the tragic parallel between Bethune's assessment of state officials who were implicated in the educational inequality in 1937 and the state-hosted inequalities existing in their own day. Could they have seen the report that the State Department would issue a few years hence documenting the extent of the problems the LCTA confronted in its desire to elevate the educational status of black children, they would likely have been even more struck by the parallels. Among the challenges were "securing more teachers, better teachers, and better salaries; providing improved educational facilities accessible to all the children; establishing a full school session; adapting the educational program to community needs" (Middleton, 1984, p. 75). One can only imagine the shake of young heads as they listened. The actors and times might have changed but this new generation of student activists would immediately recognize the ways in which some challenges remained the same.

Of course, less obvious to Maria and Kirsten would be the political and professional activities LCTA had used for decades to redress the inequities in black education. Maria and Kirsten could not easily observe from the convention session the ways in which executive officers of LCTA at the 1937 meeting were not merely listening to Bethune's critique of the limited opportunities for black children but were simultaneously challenging the structures that made such inequalities possible. Following a tradition of blacks seeking equality of schooling opportunity that dated from Reconstruction (Baker, 1996), LCTA formed in 1901 specifically because "black parents and educators clearly recognized the serious problems the state educators were ignoring" and decided to initiate change (Middleton,

1984, p. 54). Modeling black teacher associations in other states at its onset, LCTA intended to provide the organizational structure for black educators to "deal intelligently with the various problems that were stifling the educational productivity of black educators and students in Louisiana" (p. 54). In the years leading up to the 1937 convention, and until its subsequent demise in 1977, the LCTA (renamed the Louisiana Education Association in 1947) would be "linked inseparably with the growth and progress of education in the state," including launching attacks on racial inequalities, salary equalization, desegregation, voter registration, curricular differentiation, and teacher-pupil welfare (p. 11).

To the larger public, many of the advocacy activities of LCTA were concealed. Yet, the activity of LCTA is evident in the stories Maria and Kirsten know and admire. McDonogh 35 High School and Dillard College (first known as Straight University) are institutions and activities interconnected with the life of LCTA. The Center for Professional Growth and Development likely has its conceptual genesis in the professional development of teachers that was part of LCTA's ongoing professional development. The voter registration and other advocacy activity of Leatrice and Ed mirror earlier LCTA activities. Even names such as the Civic Improvement League typically camouflage advocacy led by black educators (see Walker, 2009a, 2009b). Maria and Kirsten would not know these historic roots and the ways they connect to the stories and people they do know. As captured in a 1983 interview, "the full record of [LCTA's] involvement in public education is so substantial" that the "full story" has not been told (Middleton, 1984, p. 121).

Importantly, the tradition of concealed black teacher advocacy evident in Louisiana is not unique to this state. As I argue elsewhere (Walker, 2005, 2009a,), black educators in the South were in the forefront of efforts to achieve equality in schooling. Through their organizational structures, black educators were overtly political, demanding that the promises of democracy be applied to black children. They consistently fought against inequality in school bus transportation, school facilities, textbooks, school terms, and other areas in which black children were receiving less than their share of funding and resources from state agencies. In some settings, black educators also advocated for housing and election of specific public officials (Walker, in preparation).

This multitude of advocacy across time and geographic region provides a strong historical context to support Maria and Kirsten's desires in the present. Maria's ambition, for example, to pick up "the torch" of Ed and Leatrice embraces an aspiration that has deep roots. However, unlike the beginning point she imagines, her predecessors' work did not originate in the late1940s nor is it confined to the legacy of the two deserving educators she knows. Rather, Maria's torch will be lit from the embers of a more longstanding legacy that includes the struggle of multiple forgotten black educators. In the New Orleans in which she lives, as Buras has argued convincingly in the introduction to this book, neoliberal policies trump equality and justice for children. In fact, the state-created inequalities in personnel, resources, school terms, and access in the current era are new iterations of similar concerns during the segregation era. Clearly, the need for new torchbearers to address old struggles is dire.

Just as Maria wishes to engage the legacy of black educational advocacy, Kirsten's desire to become a teacher is similarly rooted in this history. In addition to serving as advocates for black schools, the tradition of black educators is also one where attention was focused directly on the importance of educating black children well. Despite poorer facilities and resources and the well-documented neglect of school boards, black educators repeatedly, in myriad settings, structured schools to encourage the success of black children (see Walker, 2000, 2001; Walker & Tompkins, 2004). Through interpersonal and institutional caring, strong parental involvement, professional degrees and support, well-connected school principals, and strong professional networks, black educators muffled the larger societal claims about the inability of black children and generated in the students a belief that they could excel. In Louisiana and across the South, the school climates they populated reflect consistency in beliefs about children and in implementation practices. Because the black educators were themselves products of black communities holding similar values to those communities whence their children came, they believed in the potential of the children and many committed themselves to creating opportunities for children who looked like them and collectively had the same success potential they had. "We know, don't we?" Mordecai Johnson postulated when encouraging black leaders throughout the South to return to their communities and seed change. "We must be the agents of what we know" (Walker, 2009b, p. 99).

Like Maria whose focus is advocacy, Kirsten also has a dream that builds on the twin legacy of teacher inspiration that characterized the endeavors of black educators. Kirsten values the legacy of Frederick Douglass High School, where her sister and cousin could be motivated by teachers in a writing class, journalism club, or choir. Extracurricular activities like these were the hallmark of institutional caring in segregated black schools. They highlighted student talent and encouraged leadership as the school collectively used varied forums to communicate to black students the extent to which their potential mattered to the larger black community. In her attachment to Douglass is the lingering manifestation of a long tradition of black educators.

Moreover, Kirsten recounts a contemporary portrait of Douglass where her teachers, the "veterans of neighborhood public schools in New Orleans are always there to help me where I lack." In fact, she credits these educators with getting her "back on track with a vision and purpose for my education." In this description, Kirsten also evokes the images of black educators of the past. Often described as being "hard" on students, black teachers traditionally encouraged and supported black students in individual settings *to* excel but never relinquished their demanding high expectations that students *would* excel. Kirsten's excursion across the street to teach seventh- and eighth-grade students, facilitated by her teachers at Douglass, melds seamlessly into this tradition of black education.

Sadly, Kirsten's experiences at Signature High School also foreshadow the reality of a New Orleans that will relegate the precious resource of its own children to schooling structures where children may not be fully appreciated for the cultural traditions they bring (United Teachers of New Orleans et al., 2007a). Left with Signature's imprint, Kirsten might never have been able to embrace the heritage of black teaching that is rightfully hers. In the multitude of schools with inexperienced teachers, incomplete school terms, and stifled access to public schools, one wonders how many other students like Kirsten are being educated to abandon the communities from which they come, rather than being encouraged to reclaim a heritage.

To be sure, those educators of the past would applaud loudly Maria and Kirsten's desires today with the same enthusiasm they received Bethune's talk. The issues have an eerily familiar ring; the urgency is as great. However, even as they embrace a history, Maria and Kirsten must recognize that the history provides no easy road map. Among the difficulties LCTA confronted were leadership disagreement and fractures in vision that helped germinate AFT Local 527 as LCTA embraced organizational affiliation with the National Education Association (see Middleton, 1984; Walker, in press). Yet the hint of the footprint left by previous generations of black activists should inspire confidence. Maria and Kirsten are beginning journeys on a well-trod road. May they fare well.

POETIC DECLARATION OF RIGHTS TO THE CITY

In one way or another, the preceding accounts address the means by which familial and communal assets in working-class African American neighborhoods are converted into exclusive rights exercised along class- and race-based lines. Along with students and teachers, Vanessa Siddle Walker charts the legacy of struggle to build and maintain educational spaces guided by an ethic of collective rather than private welfare. In the process, she demonstrates that the weakening of cultural bonds and community ties through racialized policies of dispossession is immensely concerning. Poet Damien Theodore recognizes this when he declares, "It kills me to think that I might never get a chance to teach in the neighborhood I grew up in," and concludes, "THAT IS MY RIGHT!" His recollection of cherished cultural practices and their potential demise as a result of neglect and disinvestment—or what he refers to as a city "forgetting about her people"—serves as damning testimony against the neoliberal project. In the same moment, his declaration of rights to the city and his commitment to fight the dismissal at the heart of this project provide the ideal segue to the next chapter, where students and teachers elaborate on the freedom dreams that they believe should guide pedagogy and policy in New Orleans—and perhaps Chicago, Harlem, Washington, DC, and other centers of racial and economic redevelopment.

Wake Up

Damien Theodore

After two months I finally saw her, and she was asleep.
Lifeless, lethargic, and asleep.
Not a worry in the world and asleep.

I got mad when I saw her sleeping,
not worrying about me and my family,
forgetting about her people.
I was mad.
All I could do was hope she was dreaming.
Dreaming about the days of second lines and jazz funerals.

The days of seafood gumbo, jambalaya, and boiled crawfish.

I know she dreamt of her schools and police department.
They needed improvement, but I know she would wake up
just to play with them again.

She had to long for the hot summer days, with kids eating snowballs
and dropping cool juice on her skin.
She had to miss that.

She had to miss the violence and drugs.

She could do without it, but that's what made her, her
and she needed that.

She had to miss the people living in Treme and in the 9th Ward.
They loved her as much as she loved them,
and they were loyal to her.

She couldn't enjoy all of these things, because she was asleep.
It pissed me off that she just lay there, letting people from all over
the world walk all over her: Rearranging her image.
How could she just let them do that?

But just when I thought I had too much,
she turned over and whispered in my ear,
"I can't wake up by myself. I need your help."

Then I thought about it. She can't do it by herself.
It's gonna take a revolution to wake her up.
If we want her up and alive again, we need to get a move on it.
She will never wake up, if we don't get started now.

I miss her too much to let her stay asleep.
The thought of not going to another parade kills me.
It kills me to think that I might never get a chance
to teach in the neighborhood I grew up in.
THAT IS MY RIGHT!
To never eat another hot sausage po–boy is unbearable.
I love the stuff that was naturally New Orleans.

I NEED HER AWAKE NOW!!!!!

Then I decided to leave her again,
and as I left I realized that I must and I will wake New Orleans up.
It may take me the rest of my life to wake New Orleans up,
but she will be alive and well before I die.

She will second line again, she will bunny hop again,
she will be New Orleans again.

WAKE UP NEW ORLEANS, WAKE UP!

CLOSING REFLECTION

"I've Been Scarred and Battered":
Warnings from Harlem, Washington, DC, and Beyond

Kristen L. Buras

Damien's poem describes a city in need of radical redemption, but not the kind provided by elite programs of urban "renewal" and free market fundamentalism, both of which heavily rely on a scorched earth policy and the vicious dialectic of dispossession and accumulation. Instead, he vividly portrays a New Orleans that requires the restoration of valued and long-standing cultural traditions rather than allowing itself to be trampled upon. By contrast, under the neoliberal regime, as Apple points out, the old is "bad" and the new, especially those things offered for private appropriation and (re)consumption, is "good." Only several years after the initiation of aggressive, marketized educational experimentation in New Orleans, one mainstream news report—a story surely not of the community's making—proclaims that there's finally a sense of promise in the city. This is due to Paul Vallas, head of the Recovery School District, who "hired a small army of young, motivated teachers from across the country through the organization Teach for America—some of whom replaced veteran teachers who were considered underperforming" (Callebs, 2009). Such a move, however, runs roughshod over the rich legacy of black educational activism that Walker documents, the same legacy that's inspired Maria and Kirsten as student activists and to which Jackson–Ndang is herself a contributor. But that's the way of the world under neoliberalism, where race is wedded to political-economic interventions and urban development schemes premised on whiteness as a form of property. We are asked to participate in a narrative that requires the following: *Forget* the fact that black veteran educators and the communities they represent fought for educational equity, invested faith in black children despite an inequitable balance of economic resources, struggled for voting rights, equal pay, professional development, access to housing, and "all of those human rights, liberties, powers, and immunities that are important for human well-being" (Harris, 1995, p. 279). This is a new day, a new New Orleans, and "we" should be thankful for its promise—never mind if the government is effacing your history, closing your school, and tearing down your neighborhood under the banner of regeneration.

Of course there's an unmistakable problem with this account of educational reform and urban development. It fails to raise an integral question: Who has a right to the city of New Orleans? This question is relevant to many other cities as well. In Chicago, Lipman shows, low-income communities of color exercise neither a right to neighborhood public schools nor a right to public and affordable housing (see also Lipman, 2008). The same goes for black veteran teachers in the city, who filed a lawsuit against the Chicago Board of Education for dismissing them by the thousands in lieu of "a much younger, much whiter, and much less experienced corps of instructors," one that will supposedly help to "turn around" failing urban schools (Dixon, 2009, p. 2). What's more, as in New Orleans, the "wholesale replacement [of neighborhood public schools] with charter and other special schools has destabilized vast residential areas of the city and greatly contributed to gentrification" (p. 4). It's no coincidence that Paul Vallas, Arne Duncan, and a host of conservative foundations, such as Gates, Bradley, and Walton, had a hand there too.

Writing during the Harlem Renaissance in the 1930s, Langston Hughes' poetry captured the historic give-and-take between racially oppressed communities and more powerful groups. In the present era of neoliberal insurgency, the "scarring" and "battering" to which he refers assume dimension on quickly gentrifying streets. In her ethnographic work with black youth in Harlem, Kinloch (2007b) reports an exchange between Kavon and Quentin:

> *Kavon:* Right across the street from my projects are condos
> with balconies. . . . They believe that what's going on in our
> community is like a second renaissance . . . another Harlem
> Renaissance.
> *Quentin:* . . . . Don't get me wrong, there's a lot of newness in Harlem,
> some for the good, some for the bad, some I just don't understand
> yet. But how can the new replace the old: condos versus projects,
> whites versus blacks, balconies versus fire escapes, silence versus
> community gatherings, not knowing neighbors versus having
> people's backs. And this is a renaissance? (p. 43)

According to Quentin, this is less a renaissance than a "white-ification of the hood." This process of gentrification is advanced through the racist invocation of Harlem as a "jungle" that's "dirty, dangerous, lots of crime, criminals, poor blacks on welfare, people not caring about where they live, schools on lockdown" (in Kinloch, 2007a, p. 64). In juxtaposition, Quentin, much like Damien in New Orleans, declares that Harlem has stories that haven't been adequately told and "shouldn't be forgotten"

(p. 63). He firmly asserts, "This is my home. . . . I got a right to this place, and my right runs deeper than theirs" (p. 65). Kinloch urges that such counternarratives be put front and center in the contest over urban space (see also Maurrasse, 2006). It's hard to imagine that Maria, Tyeasha, and Vinnessia would disagree. In fact, Kavon and Quentin's disbelief about the dramatic changes occurring on their block is reminiscent of Maria's neighborhood after Katrina. "There's nothing worse," she writes, "than walking into your 'hood and not recognizing it."

The same may be said of many other cities across the United States, including the nation's very own capital. In Washington, DC, neoliberal experimentation in schooling, housing, and health care has promoted widespread dispossession. Open access, neighborhood public schools were replaced by selective admissions, corporatized charter schools and vouchers. Public sector employees, including teachers, were attacked as the New Teacher Project, also operating in New Orleans, advanced rhetoric about ineffective teachers and the problem of unions. Public and affordable housing was replaced by private upscale developments paid for with public monies. The public hospital was closed as well. As in New Orleans, Chicago, and New York City, "this approach to economic development has displaced entire communities through outright demolition of affordable housing and, more insidiously, through the closure and repurposing of neighborhood public schools" (El-Amine & Glazer, p. 55). In a turn of events that is strikingly close to an effort in New Orleans aimed at "reinventing" the riverfront—a public-private venture that I'll discuss in the next chapter—DC has sought to redevelop its waterfront through an initiative that includes an $800 million, publicly financed baseball stadium (p. 55). El-Amine and Glazer rightly compare such privatization to global structural adjustment programs implemented by the World Bank. This is an issue I will take up in the concluding chapter, where I discuss the relationship of reform in New Orleans to policies in the Global South more generally.

For now, it's essential to remember, as Apple urges us to do, that the utopian dreams of capital are not the only ones in play, even if the field of power is grossly uneven. He is perfectly correct that while criticism of these privatizing tendencies is essential, so is "the defense of powerful alternatives that have been built." In this regard, we next move to consider the freedom dreams and concrete educational interventions that have been developed by Students at the Center and other movements for urban educational justice.

CHAPTER 4

Putting *All* Students at the Center: Charting an Agenda for Urban Educational Transformation

OPENING REFLECTION

From Capitalist Dreams to Freedom Dreams

Kristen L. Buras

IN LEARNING ABOUT the work of black teacher unionists Ed and Leatrice Roberts and their historic contributions to educational struggles in New Orleans, Maria Hernandez assured them: "There are a few of us who would gladly receive the torch and run with it" (see "Passing on a Torch" in Chapter 3). This is precisely what students do in the current chapter—they assume the torch carried by elders who spent their lives fighting for equitable schools and present a vision for the future of public education in New Orleans (one that is relevant to democratizing education in cities across the nation). Clearly, however, the freedom dreams that they articulate are strikingly different from the capitalist dreams that elites are working to materialize. While many have hailed deregulation, school choice, and privatization as the penultimate solution for struggling schools and communities (Hill, 2002; Ravitch & Viteritti, 1997, Whitman, 2008), the students here reveal that such reform instituted to scale raises rather serious concerns. Moreover, they complicate dominant notions surrounding what schools should teach and the purposes they should serve.

In "A Talk to Teachers" (written in the early 1960s), James Baldwin (1970) declared:

> We are living through a very dangerous time. . . . We are in a revolutionary situation, no matter how unpopular that word has become in this country. The society in which we live is desperately menaced. . . . So any citizen of this country who figures himself responsible—and particularly those of you who deal with the minds and hearts of young people—must be prepared to "go for broke." (p. 82)

As he goes on to forcefully argue, the dangers of the period were not wholly new. Rather African Americans pledging allegiance to a nation promising "liberty and justice for all" have been perpetually subjected through the schools to the notion that "he has never contributed anything to civilization—that his past is nothing more than a record of humiliations gladly endured" (p. 83). In short, the root of the threat was not the revolutionary Negro (although clearly his aspirations threatened whites, who were hell bent on retaining racial power), but the historic hegemony of whiteness itself.

Along these lines, Bruce Coleman—a present-day Baldwin—provides his own talk to teachers and policy makers, explaining: "Something was always missing from my education. . . . I mean we didn't have a conscious mind or awareness of our history or for that matter that it even existed." Bruce condemns the "lack of education that draws from what is already inside of us" and issues a call for curriculum that links learning to critical cultural and historical consciousness. Erica DeCuir echoes and elaborates upon Bruce's philosophy of knowledge, sharing her own family's story as evidence of the "muted existence" of black folk that so often results from class and racial oppression. In contrast, she recollects the way in which Students at the Center (SAC) centered her own and other students' voices as they questioned why they had never "taken a stand":

> Why didn't we confront security men in department stores when they followed us around? Why didn't we react when there were injustices facing us? There was ample talk of fear and acceptance. There was talk of hopelessness. Students began to passionately recall situations where they could have done something, should have said something, but didn't. The cycle of black pain, black fear, and black hopelessness came full circle. . . . I realized that my parents' silence was much bigger than them. It was a pattern of deferred dreams and dead uncertainties.

The counterstories of Bruce and Erica thus contain within them a curricular vision, one that positions the voices, cultures, and histories of traditionally oppressed groups at the very core of schooling. Post-Katrina New Orleans, Ashely Jones urges, has "the opportunity to learn from the SAC community." I think that goes for urban schools elsewhere, too.

It wouldn't hurt to remember the words of Carter G. Woodson, as Bruce does. Woodson (1933/2000) warned that "to handicap a student by teaching him that his black face is a curse and that his struggle to change his condition is hopeless is the worst sort of lynching. . . . It kills his aspirations" (p. 3). SAC has ignited and bolstered the dreams of youth in New Orleans, who are prepared to wrangle over the norms and forms that public education will take up. As racial and economic conditions only worsen with rising energy costs, declining wages, home foreclosures, school closures, and the like, the situation may indeed be revolutionary. But the revolution is neither fought solely from below nor is its root cause to be found there. The "powers that be" are advancing on the home front, and they too have revolutionary plans and aspirations. For instance, the School Facilities Master Plan for Orleans Parish, which was officially released in late August 2008 for a 30-day period of public comment, provides a rather disturbing "blueprint" for the twenty-first century. Here it is essential to mention the conception of schools at the heart of the plan. Much as RSD officials repeatedly framed their comments during the May 2008 meeting with community members at Frederick Douglass High School around the potential fate of the building (see Chapter 1), the master plan adopts a highly technical discourse as well. We are informed that "the master plan describes the maintenance and development of an infrastructure and physical plants that will support the needs of educational delivery" (Kilbert & Vallas, 2008, p. 13). The report, in fact, is not about school communities at all but about "inputs," "outputs," the need for "avoiding redundancy," "deferred maintenance," "Facility Condition Index (FCI)," "population trends," and "recovery profiles," the last of which is extremely concerning since one of the "selection parameters" for determining which schools will remain open is enrollment projections, which do not account for the way in which class, race, and state policy have enabled and disabled the return of specific neighborhoods (or the fact that it's even harder to return when there's no school nearby). As one longtime neighborhood resident and musician makes clear, "What it has gotten to is the fact that if we close down all of the high schools and you know your children have nowhere to go to school, then you'll leave. They've tried everything that they can to get people out" (interview, 2008), and I'd add, to keep them from even returning. This is the underbelly of the neoliberal city.

In sharp contrast, the students in this chapter recognize that the issue is not *buildings* but *communities.* Reflecting on her concerns over selective admissions schools, Ashley stresses:

> If we are serious about creating a better New Orleans and we understand that a better school system is an important factor in that, then we know what we have to do. There is only one way to eliminate low–performing schools for good: Get rid of those schools that separate and destroy the potential of community.

Chris Burton puts it another way when he critically reflects on his own experiences as a gifted African American student in the city's public schools and expresses concern that he "cheated," meaning he had "received aid and attention that should have been directed also at the children more in need of it." He warns that only "when every last student is taken care of and able to get the attention reserved for the few" will New Orleans schools improve. Indeed, Chris says he returned to New Orleans because he believes "charter schools . . . will widen the education gap more than [particular selective admissions schools] were doing before the storm." This privatization of student interests and educational institutions is something that Bruce calls the "new segregation" based not simply on race, but also "academic ability, economic class, and parental involvement." Such concerns are warranted. While isolated charter schools have created a space for sometimes progressive educational experiments, there is also a good deal of evidence that on the whole they exacerbate educational inequities and fracture school communities (Dingerson, Miner, Peterson, & Walters, 2008; Scott, 2005; Wells, 2002). This certainly seems to be the case in New Orleans, which has a density of charter schools unsurpassed by any other city in the country. As mentioned in Chapter 1, the majority of these schools either have formal or informal selective admissions policies.

All of this has led the Frederick Douglass Community Coalition, with which SAC is very closely affiliated, to develop an alternative plan for educational reform in New Orleans. The coalition is committed to providing resources and support to "schools that have no selective admissions requirements, honor the collective bargaining agreement of AFT Local 527, and are part of a public school system that plans and fights for equitable and high-quality education for all students" (SAC, 2007a, p. 194). They also provide some dynamic suggestions for and examples of wedding schools to communities through interdisciplinary curricula, such as SAC's involvement in New Orleans Civil Rights Park (see Chapter 1) and the Creole Cottage Program in which students learn math and other subjects while working to build homes in the city. Importantly, they recommend that the school be made the center of the community, a place where a variety of grassroots organizations can congregate and where democratic participation in policy making can occur (see SAC, 2007a).

These freedom dreams will not be realized easily. The School Facilities Master Plan (Kilbert & Vallas, 2008) recommends that Frederick Douglass High School be "landbanked." This means the school will be closed, with it and other landbanked "sites" either "retained" or "redeveloped for other community purposes," or "converted to housing, offices, or other public or private uses" (p. 58). All future high schools will have citywide enrollment, which the plan conceives as part of an approach called "total community" education. More to the point, there will be no neighborhood high schools and, rather crucially, "the actual attendance policies will be established by school governing bodies" (p. 9). Each high school will be themed as well, with one focused on science, another on medicine, another on military discipline, and so on. It's not terribly difficult to read between the lines: some of the schools will be free to enforce selective admissions policies, while the "unfit" will likely be sent off to the open access military academy.

This makes the educational vision of Students at the Center and the Frederick Douglass Community Coalition all the more pressing. The students and community activists who "speak out" in this chapter are a part of the historic river of black resistance about which Charles Lawrence (1995) wrote. Before considering their words, however, I should mention that there's another river—the one that gave the Crescent City its name. That river, the Mississippi River, is one that certain city leaders and private power brokers in New Orleans plan to develop. While Douglass is landbanked, the bank of the Mississippi River (to be precise, some six miles of riverfront) is to be developed as part of a $294 million public-private venture to "Reinvent the Crescent" funded partly through a $30 million Disaster Community Development Block Grant (see Reinventing the Crescent, 2008b). Part of this development is to occur just blocks from where Douglass High School currently sits. It appears the "building" might be a really nice place for a new community, one consisting of what is called the professional *creative class*. Investment on the riverfront between 2008–2016 is meant to "encourage an augmented housing stock," "revitalize existing neighborhoods for renovation and redevelopment," "promote a more active tourist industry," "attract new residents" (Nagin, Fielkow, & Cummings, 2008, p. 14) and capture "new industry and entrepreneurial capitol" (Reinventing the Crescent, 2008a). Clearly, there's an affinity between the school district's master plan and urban developers' efforts to invent the neoliberal city. Right after the storm, in fact, there were rumors that Douglass "was going to be turned into a condominium" (interview with neighborhood resident-musician, 2008), a fact that heightens the seriousness of the struggle and the salience of the agenda charted in the counterstories and commentaries that follow.

CHALLENGING THE SUPPRESSION OF IDENTITY AND KNOWLEDGE

Speaking Out

Neoconservative reformers, such as E. D. Hirsch (1987, 1996), have asserted the need to restore cultural stability and curricular coherence, which allegedly have been threatened by "divisive forms" of multiculturalism and the kind of progressive education represented by Students at the Center. What is needed instead, according the Hirsch, is *core knowledge*—a tightly controlled curricular framework that includes the "facts" that all students need to know to be culturally literate and upwardly mobile. Over the past two decades, this educational vision has guided the nationwide core knowledge movement including hundreds of schools teaching the knowledge that Hirsch claims is common and shared. To nurture wider investment in core knowledge, the curriculum has even come to include portions that reflect the history of traditionally marginalized groups (see Buras, 2008). Yet none of this even remotely comes close to the curricular vision articulated by students here. They recognize what Hirsch and so many advocates of core knowledge fail to acknowledge: The curriculum in schools is not neutral, common, or shared. It is a selective tradition in which only the most watered-down traces of subaltern history are included, if at all. Rather than either accepting the total absence of black history or cooperating with a distilled and piecemeal version that can only be described as *rightist multiculturalism* (Buras, 2008), students join Joyce King in challenging the suppression of black voices and experiences. These testimonies reframe the debate over what exactly should constitute the core of what students learn.

No Black History in School

Bruce Coleman

Through my childhood, something was always missing from my education, my development. When I would sit in class, my fifth-grade teacher would talk about Christopher Columbus discovering America. She never told us about the native people or about black people coming here first.

Instead of seeing Malcolm X or pictures from the Black Power movement, teachers would decorate the classroom with the Easter Bunny and Santa Claus. We were brainwashed through school. When I say brainwashed, I mean we didn't have a conscious mind or awareness of our history or for that matter that it even existed.

The term *education* is derived from the Latin word *educere,* which means "to bring out." "The process of education is therefore the process of bringing out knowledge which is already inside of you," said Anthony T. Browder (1989). From my earlier experience, many classrooms cause our minds to atrophy from lack of African-centered education, from lack of education that draws from what is already inside us.

Eight years later I see the same effects of this type of education in my high school. Today I look at why my school is in such bad condition. I look at the students who come to class to go to sleep and those students who come every couple of days to class.

I feel like it is in such bad shape because students are not motivated to want an education. Maybe many teachers themselves suffered from a lack of black education when they were coming up. Carter G. Woodson (1933/2000) seemed to believe this even way back in 1933 when he published *The Mis-Education of the Negro.* Students need more Malcolm X, David Walker, and Ida B. Wells and less Easter Bunnies and Santa Claus.

Elementary and junior high just were not challenging enough. Is it more than being challenging? Is it just as much connecting learning to life and history? Or maybe it's the way school is set up—class size and school size contribute to schooling not working. Also contributing to the poor quality of education is the new segregation. Private and magnet schools as well as college and work programs for high school students too frequently pull leader students away from neighborhood schools. Our schools suffer from an imbalance, a new segregation not just by race but also by academic ability, economic class, and parental involvement.

In Mwalimu J. Shujaa's *Too Much Schooling, Too Little Education* (1994), the contributors tackle many of these issues. They describe one of the strengths of preintegration schools as being the neighborhood setting, where parents, teachers, and students all interacted outside of school. We have lost that as well as having too little black history in school.

These gaps in education contribute to some of the bad things we see in school. Instead of being in class, some students are cutting class. Some students prefer finding a job to getting in the books. They weren't taught properly when their seed was growing. Now it is hard to fertilize them with knowledge.

This problem hit home to me earlier this year. My teacher asked us if we knew of Ida B. Wells when we were beginning to study journalism.

All the students said no. Ida B. Wells researched lynching and wrote the book *The Red Record* (Wells-Barnett, 1895/2009). She was instrumental in forming the National Association for the Advancement of Colored People (NAACP) and developed an activist spirit when she confronted racism, especially the lynching of her friend, Thomas Moss. Moss had opened a grocery store in Memphis. The white man who owned a nearby store began losing business to Moss and his partners. These three black men turned up lynched. It broke my heart and made me angry when I heard this story—not just for Thomas Moss, but for my classmates and me, who after 11 and 12 years of schooling did not know this history.

I went through elementary school acting up in the class, not really interested in what teachers were teaching. Maybe if I knew what our people did to get us a better education, I would have taken it differently.

Maybe if I knew about Fredrick Douglass, I would have educated myself, especially if I wasn't getting it all in school. A white woman first educated Frederick Douglass. When her husband came and saw this, he said, "You can't teach them [slaves] how to read. If they learn to read they will want power and will learn how to get it." When Douglass learned this, he went on to educate himself by stealing books from the slave owner and tricking the owners' sons into teaching him a little.

Today we don't have to steal books. We have the freedom to read them. Before we can read these books we have to have someone to let us know they exist. Someone had to inspire Frederick Douglass to want to read even with all odds against him. So often we are stuck with teachers and school curriculums that don't give us our full history.

Once I took this Students at the Center writing class taught by Mr. Jim Randels. His class opened the world of black history up to me. I learned about the black holocaust. I learned about Egypt as an African origin and the real beginning of African American history. Black poets such as Langston Hughes, Gil Scott Heron, Nikki Giovanni, Etheridge Knight, and Kysha Brown started speaking to me as we studied them in class. I learned about revolutionary leaders such as Malcolm X, the Last Poets, and the Black Panthers. Mr. Randels is the teacher I never had in elementary school. He is not the only one like this in the schools. For instance, my classmate Glenda Baker describes all the black history she learned from Mr. Blunt at Drew Elementary School. But teachers like this are too few and far between. Or they are too overburdened with large classes, pressures for testing, and students who face difficult home environments to teach as well as they can.

All this study of history and writing got me involved in a poetry contest in which I won $500 for first place and a trip to New York. Through Mr.

Randels's guidance, a classmate and I became leaders of a writing workshop in New Orleans where we would help teens on parole write essays. Eventually we published a book of teen writing based on the workshop. The book is called *Writing Not Drowning* (SAC, 2001). I was so involved, I didn't have time to get in trouble; I was more focused on learning my missed history.

Before I knew about my identity through black history, I was like a body without any blood in it. When I started reading, my blood came back—I became alive.

After I began seeking knowledge, I reflected on my elementary times. Back then, they gave me crayons and paste and smiley faces, but I did not get any black history. Is this why students when they reach high school don't want to sit down and write a page or two about life? It is hard to grow a seed if it's not planted in its own garden.

Breaking Free of Our Muted Existence

Erica DeCuir

It took me a long time to overcome the "speech impairment" inherited from my parents. In elementary school I would listen silently to cruel jokes and constant teasing about my hair, shoes, eyes, nose, and mouth. My mother would tell me to just ignore them, sit with other quiet students or alone if possible. When I was ten years old a cashier in the local grocery store accused me of stealing gum. There were other students in the store stealing candy and because I was wearing the same uniform and walked in with them, I was a likely accomplice too. My father told me to forget about it, to never go back there again. I grew up watching my parents do this in all aspects of their lives: Avoid the bill collectors, ignore the unruly neighbor, be patient with the family members who take advantage of you. My parents had succumbed to a common trait of tired black folk in the Deep South: don't question authority, be honest and hardworking, and focus on the struggle for survival.

I've never witnessed my father speak up for himself. He would either leisurely suggest another way of working out the solution or gravely plead for leniency. As a result we always received the bad part of a deal: the car payments with outrageous interest rates, the overtime worked but paid at regular wage, the contractors who spent months completing house renovations. When not talking about bills, or car repairs, or maintenance to the home, he fell silent.

Contrary to my father, my mother spoke all the time. She talked about friends, family, births, and deaths. She talked about her job and asked about our day at school. She talked about Halloween parties and what to cook for dinner. She talked about everything except her thoughts, her dreams, her wishes, her interests. She skirted around problems with happy faces and trips to the ice cream parlor. When my sisters and I got into a fight with other girls in our neighborhood in the Lower 9th Ward, she took us out for dinner and told us to forget about it. My mother believed that anything could be cured by looking away from it.

My parents had five girls. We have all inherited speechlessness from our parents in some way or another. I struggled with my family's muted existence until high school. Actually, I began breaking away in junior high when I entered a new school determined to be popular. I "played dumb," got involved in makeup and jewelry, and became one of the disruptive kids who lagged behind in the back of the class. Well, I wasn't one of them. I was their groupie. I would sit in the back and laugh at their jokes, occasionally chiming in with my own put-down of the unlucky target of the day. My determination to be cool and popular played a big part in gaining my voice, though in a negative way. I began to roll my eyes and talk back to teachers. My mother, increasingly alarmed, forced me to apply to the competitive academic high school, McDonogh 35, at the end of my eighth-grade year. I went to the entrance exam, tried to fail it on purpose, and wound up getting a place in the new freshmen class of 1994.

In high school my new environment pushed me to focus on academics. The school has been a hub of the black intelligentsia within New Orleans for many decades. It prided itself on excellence in academia, a Blue Ribbon school, and boasted more black college graduates than any other in our community. Because of the extreme dedication to academics, popularity came from your rank in the class.

I began to write in high school. I had always written things down; it was my secret voice in the silence of my home. When I was in elementary school I would write my responses to all of the kids who teased me. I would write my hopes and dreams, silly things in a diary about famous rap singers, and my frustrations. But in high school I began to actually *write*. I learned how to construct meaning from texts. I learned how to recognize and convey analytical thought by weaving together multiple texts. I learned how to question the writing of my peers and provide constructive criticism. I learned how to value my voice.

In my English honors class we read Toni Morrison's *Beloved* (1988). I was 16 years old. Through the complexities of hegemony and repression under the slave regime, the decision of Sethe in killing her children became powerfully clear—and understandable. In Sethe, and with later comparison of Celia the Slave, Harriet Jacobs, and Sojourner Truth, I saw the extreme lengths these women made to secure their voice. It was so valuable to them. Some made profound statements with their actions, like Celia and Sethe, and others strongly protested orally and in writing, like Harriet Jacobs and Sojourner Truth. They fought so hard for the ability to shape their own lives, to determine their own fates, and to achieve this under the somber realities of their lives. It was amazing.

My teacher, Jim Randels, told us to write not only in the traditional discourse, but by providing our own experience as an analytical tool for literary interpretation. We sat in a "story circle" and first gave stories about our lives and commented on the decisions these women made. I remember feeling very small and self-conscious—I had never taken a stand in my life. I wasn't taught to do that. I was taught to accept, to adapt, and to deal with whatever life gave me. When I told Mr. Randels that I didn't have anything to contribute, he told me to talk about just that. Talk about why you have never taken a stand in your life. Then write about it. Many of the other students talked about defending someone against a bully, or giving help to someone in a situation, but none of us had really taken a stand on something in our lives.

Our conversation then took another turn: Why didn't we? Why didn't we call the police and report domestic abuse when we heard shouting from our neighbor's home? Why didn't we confront security men in department stores when they followed us around? Why didn't we react when there were injustices facing us? There was ample talk of fear and acceptance. There was talk of hopelessness. Students began to passionately recall situations where they could have done something, should have said something, but didn't. The cycle of black pain, black fear, and black hopelessness came full circle. We analyzed historical factors of repression and hate, we examined color consciousness and notions of inferiority, we acknowledged the role of survival and the determination to maintain some kind of peace. I realized that my parents' silence was much bigger than them. It was a pattern of deferred dreams and dead uncertainties. It was a cycle of promise and disappointment, a sequence of ideal hope and unfortunate realities. Under the burden of it all my father fell silent. The weight pushed my mother to place all hope in her children and give up on herself.

When I began to write, I became intrigued with the role of history in shaping our current lives. I saw myself in subject matter and began writing from deep inside myself. I compared myself to the "crazed" women described by Jean Toomer and Alice Walker in her *In Search of Our Mothers' Gardens* (2003). And, like Pecola (Morrison, 1993), I shared my own secret childhood fantasy of blue eyes (mine were green). Inspired by journalist Ida B. Wells, my classmate Adrinda Kelly wrote her own tribute to Wells and lynched black men, showing how our use of literary devices grew stronger as our connection to legendary black women deepened. Our classroom became a haven for free thought and comparative analysis to all things: text, self, world. Higher levels of thinking developed. Intricate writing styles formed. Diverse opinions were valued. Teacher became co-learner. Students became co-teachers. A radical concept soon emerged: Students at the Center (SAC)—a pedagogical strategy that combines reciprocal teaching, cooperative learning, and critical thinking based upon a firm belief in the value of students' voices. We took part in shaping curriculum and saw firm connections to our daily lives. Our papers were goal oriented and purposed to include reflection and comparative analysis.

Particular to the teaching of history, this last factor was key. If history remains alone, static, and removed from contemporary society and reality in students' lives, it is nothing. It remains a dusty manuscript on an old bookshelf. No one learns from it. Its mistakes are repeated. Its lessons go unheeded. If my historical study did not question my willingness (or unwillingness) to take a stand in my life, I never would have valued my voice. I never would have analyzed the phenomenal black women who faced insurmountable tasks to determine their own destinies. And I definitely could not have made sense of my parents, my community, my life.

An environment that welcomed diverse opinions and personal reactions to text and curriculum also taught me the value of other voices in the classroom. Their stories supported (or contradicted) my own, and we balanced each others' perspective. Alice Walker and Harriet Jacobs were only the beginning. Eventually Plato's *Republic* sparked heated conversations on the role of government. And later, Chaucer's *Canterbury Tales* led to a debate on the essence of women in "The Wife of Bath's Tale." We soon moved fluidly through course content—sometimes meeting the state standards, sometimes not—and covered everything "from Plato to Tupac." Writing styles improved as we interwove multiple texts and differing perspectives.

Six years out of high school I reflect on my learning style a lot. Now completing my master's degree in social studies education at Teachers College, Columbia University, I frequently observe high school classrooms and advise teachers on new studies and methods in the teaching of history. I am always wary of quiet classrooms where students sit listening with hawk eyes. Are they learning? Or are they mentally checking off their "to do" lists? When I introduce SAC methods, the class wakes up. I see in them the same engagement, excitement, and passionate writing that I have witnessed in my own students as a history teacher at Frederick Douglass High School. I try to create for them an environment that supports students' voices, produces role models and experiences relating to their cultural identities, and interprets present situations by analyzing history.

With my family, I break their silence with a very soft, whispering hum—the type of humming that occurs when pop songs are played over and over on the radio until eventually you yourself begin to sing the tune. Sometimes it's Zora Neale Hurston's *Their Eyes Were Watching God* (1937/2006), given to my mother on her birthday. Or weekly phone calls to my dad to talk about sports, my nephew's little league baseball game, or the fillings I received at the dentist's. My sisters and I build on our relationship by reading together, arguing together. To get them going I bought each of us a copy of Toni Morrison's *The Bluest Eye* (1993), a novel that I chose on purpose. I wanted them to face their own reflections in the mirror through the muted, painful existence of Pecola Breedlove. By creating this environment for mutual exchange of feelings and interests I do something that our community and nation has rarely granted them: I value their voice. And by confronting our lives within the context of history and reflection of the black woman experience, our collective voices are beginning to fill homes, offices, and street corners with noise.

Commentary

Mis-Education or the Development of Critical Race Consciousness: Curriculum as Heritage Knowledge

Joyce E. King

> It may be of no importance to the race to be able to boast today of many times as many "educated" members as it had in 1865. If they are of the wrong kind, the increase in numbers will be a disadvantage rather than an advantage. The only question which concerns us here is whether these "educated" persons are actually equipped to face the ordeal before them or unconsciously contribute to their own undoing by perpetuating the regime of the oppressor.
> Carter G. Woodson, *The Mis-Education of the Negro* (1933/2000)

> Our public education system has been targeted by corporate bandits that are increasingly successful at siphoning off education funding for their own profit. They are in fact destroying public education in order to grab the tax dollars that support it.
> Anne Zerrien-Lee, "Who Is Behind the Privatization of Public Education?" (2009)

In the film *Gladiator*, the African actor Djimon Honsu tells Russell Crowe, who plays the Roman general, Maximus, his fellow gladiator-captive: "You have a famous name. . . . They will have to destroy your name before they can destroy *you*." In his book *Civilization or Barbarism*, Cheikh Anta Diop (1981/1991) made a similar observation: "Imperialism, like the prehistoric hunter, first killed the being spiritually and culturally, before trying to eliminate it physically. The negation of the history and intellectual accomplishments of black Africans was cultural, mental murder, which proceeded and paved the way for their genocide here and there in the world" (p. 10). Such prescient insights suggest what more is at stake for black Americans and the society more generally than the distressing wholesale transfer of public schools to charters that is taking place under the banner of educational "reform" in post-Hurricane Katrina New Orleans.

First, Katrina precipitated not only the destruction of black lives and neighborhoods, but black education is on the frontlines of the war against public education. This is as much a "hidden race war" as the evidence of outright murders of black New Orleanians that have come to light since Katrina (Kaplan, 2009; Thompson, 2009). In other words, structural racism continues in the "guise of neoliberalism" (Giroux, 2003) and the politics of white resentment even as race is increasingly "hidden" in color-blind, post-civil rights (and post-Obama) rhetoric (Marsh, 1999, p. 5). This is the context in which the humanity of poor black people in New Orleans has been so viciously assaulted and impugned that even the city's middle-class black residents were shunned and insulted when they evacuated to other locations. For another example, my students (white women) informed our class that they had received e-mails warning them that the "Katrina rapists" had arrived in Atlanta. It is possible to foment this kind of panic and fear of black people in our society—which is akin to destroying our names—because what is taught (and not taught) in schools has predisposed us to internalize the hegemonic belief structure of race that has sustained the national mythology of black inferiority and defectivity (King, 2006).

Thus the destruction of black peoples' cultural integrity—our vilification—is linked to the neoliberal justification of the destruction of public education in order to "reform" it. David Hursh (2007) reports that "some neoliberal and neoconservative organizations have stated that their real goal is to use testing and accountability to portray public schools as failing and to push for privatizing education provided through competitive markets" (p. 501). The stated justification for the "grand experiment" in privatized education in New Orleans has been the endemic failure of the schools to educate the city's poorest children before the hurricane, indicated by persistently low levels of achievement measured by test scores. Corruption, fiscal mismanagement, and unstable, ineffective leadership at the top are identified as factors contributing to this systemic failure.

However, neither the dominant discourses of failure nor the language of reform recognizes the mis-education that suppresses black collective identity and critical race consciousness. Also suppressed, therefore, is any knowledge or memory of black people's capacity for critical, transformative, and humanizing thought that is deeply embedded in our history and culture.

Second, the alienating education Bruce Coleman and Erica DeCuir describe is particularly unsettling given the rich history of cultural and political resistance in New Orleans that is a resource for placing students at the center of empowering heritage knowledge. Dr. John Henrik Clarke (1994) equated heritage with a group's memory of their collective history. He explained that unless a group of people takes pride in their own history and values their own memories, they can never fulfill themselves completely. Further, he added that the "ultimate purpose of heritage and heritage teaching" is liberation "from the old ties of bondage" (p. 86). Also, heritage knowledge permits "a people to develop an awareness and pride in themselves so that they themselves can achieve good relationships with other people" (p. 86). Only by overcoming the effects of white supremacy ideology on our collective memories and on knowledge are critical race consciousness and good relationships in solidarity with others possible. As I have written elsewhere:

> Educators have a moral obligation to counteract alienating ideological knowledge that obstructs the right to be literate in one's own heritage and denies people the rights of "cultural citizenship." Such literacy does nothing to detract from being an American, but is fundamental for the "promotion of the well-being and preservation of particular groups." (King, 2006, p. 338)

That is to say, the possibilities for critical race consciousness and collaborative relations with others are interrelated.

This is because race-based oppression in our society that has rested on the belief in biological differences between blacks and whites, encoded in the hegemonic "alter ego" relationship between conceptual blackness (blackness in the white imaginary) and normative white-middle-class-ness, continues to define what it means to be human or civilized (Wynter, 2006). As Carter G. Woodson (1933/2000) noted in *The Mis-Education of the Negro*, black students learn that their people have contributed nothing to world developments, while white contributions are exalted. This critique was echoed by Robinson (2000) many decades later when he emphasized, "Far too many Americans of African descent believe their history starts in America with bondage and struggles forward from there to today's second-class citizenship. The cost of this obstructed view of our-

selves, of our history, is incalculable. How can we be collectively successful if we have no idea or, worse, the wrong idea of who we were and,
therefore, are?" (p. 7) Paradoxically, the opposition between black identity and white people's privileged (normative) status positions the black
freedom struggle at the forefront of the task of humanizing the entire
society. Students and teachers in New Orleans reveal that what is really
at stake for all Americans is human freedom, democracy, and justice. "If
we are ever going to be a civilized [nation]," Sothern (2005) observes,
"we are going to have to begin to work as hard for the weakest and most
maligned among us as we do for the strongest and most sympathetic. If
we don't, any of us could one day face the consequences" (p. 22).

Third, the mis-education and coming to consciousness despite the
alienating curriculum that Bruce and Erica experienced and delineate
with such passion demonstrate the urgent necessity for pedagogy that
places students at the center of their education and development, but
within a curriculum that connects black youth in meaningful ways to
their communities and heritage. Such a curriculum approach necessarily locates black people's existence on the "map of human geography"
(Clarke, 1994, p. 10). Thus it is necessary, according to Clarke, to reclaim
our identity and critical consciousness as African-descent people from the
national mythology of white supremacist racism that denies our humanity. In my work with teachers and parents, I have developed emancipatory curriculum and pedagogy to support critical race consciousness in
response to alienating representations of cultural-historical junctures: the
way slavery is taught; what we need to know about our African heritage before Arab and European enslavement; and the critical intellectual
tradition embodied in the black struggle for freedom (King, 2006). Thus
we need not just black history that includes us in uncritical "we-were-
there-too" narratives of conquest, for example. As Woodson (1933/2000)
noted, we must avoid producing the "wrong kind of educated persons"
who are not equipped to "face the ordeal" before us today, including the
role of race in the privatization of all that is public, the cradle-to-prison
pipeline, joblessness, lower graduation rates, higher dropout rates, and
the brutal attack on our communities (King, 2009). This requires educators who have a deeper appreciation of the vitality and value of black life
and culture than a society steeped in assumptions of black inferiority and
inhumanity can imagine to exist in the midst of the poverty and social
"dysfunction" that oppression produces. That is to say, we need educators
who know "it is not necessary to resemble European culture in order to
be civilized or human!" (Asante, 2007, p. 52).

Finally, if heritage knowledge is the antidote to the distortions and dis-
locations of mis-educating curriculum and pedagogy, then black parents

and educators need opportunities to develop and use culturally authentic assessments that demonstrate how such knowledge enhances students' education and socialization for academic excellence and critical race consciousness. Indeed, the voices in this chapter suggest purposes and standards for authentic education that go beyond closing the "achievement gap" and raising black students' test scores to the level of whites (and Asians, who are sometimes given "honorary white" status) (Lee, 2008). As Linda Darling Hammond (2007a) has observed, it is important to "focus on the quality of our standards and assessments" (p. E-3).

Educational policy and practice with respect to teacher preparation, or what constitutes high-quality teaching and assessment, have yet to address the complex issues of identity and belonging for African-descent youngsters—issues that are inexorably related to (mis)representations of and distorted knowledge about Africa, our African ancestry in schools *at all levels*, and the strengths of our communities. Indeed, Bruce and Erica's narratives suggest that effective teaching should be defined in terms of curriculum and pedagogy that promote deep understanding and intellectually demanding, meaningful learning for students' academic and cultural well-being. In this heightened accountability context, academic excellence is too often narrowly defined as a single test score. However, education professionals ought to be able to use the strengths of students' families and community as assets for ambitious intellectual work (Payne & Knowles, 2009) that connects with students' lives beyond school and incorporates community standards in culturally authentic assessments. Such standards and assessments would recognize how our survival as a people chronicles the triumph of humanizing moral values, empowering social relations, and justice commitments that are the opposite of the neoliberal and neoconservative policies fueling the war against public education. The black community's engagement with this tradition of struggle for human freedom that has also benefitted justice movements worldwide is needed now more than ever.

DEMANDING RIGHTS TO THE
EDUCATIONAL COMMONS

Speaking Out

If, as Joyce King argues, the curriculum should represent a critical and collective voice, then it follows that the school itself should represent a collective. But that's not what schools do, especially when driven by neoliberal experimentation. Just as the curriculum functions as a kind of sorting mechanism, discarding what is viewed as rubbish and retaining what is viewed as core, the growth of charter schools in New Orleans has reflected this same pattern. In the stories below, students convey two arguments at once: first, that schools should and must represent inclusive learning communities; and second, that current reforms serve to undermine the educational commons through selective admissions policies and deregulated charter school reform that worsens rather than resolves the segmentation of communities. Significantly, students' arguments are informed by their experiences within a segmented system as well as the shared space of Students at the Center (SAC). Jim Randels, in fact, discloses an intimate and devastating account related to one particular student's desire to learn, a desire fostered by the fact that "his thoughts and words had a space of respect in [SAC's] classroom." Through this student's experiences and the work of SAC, we may come to see the feasibility of classrooms and schools as shared spaces. This is not about platitudes, however. Rather, very specific examples and suggestions are offered regarding what needs to be done to create an educational commons, whether by engaging students in reciprocal teaching or revamping what counts as assessment. Wayne Au enters the conversation by sharing critiques of the differential effects of current policies as well as illustrations from progressive educators, schools, and grassroots organizations across the nation that aim, along with SAC, not to charter exclusionary schools but to work for change within school communities.

Honoring Community

Ashley Jones

In the summer of 2005 I had the rare privilege to see an ancient community working together to make themselves stronger. In this community, where people sit in a circle on the floor, there were expert hunters, farmers, and medicine men. Each person had a skill to share, and in the event that the medicine man was absent, people did not die because everyone was taught the healing properties of certain herbs and plants.

This ancient community was part of a play by students from Frederick Douglass and Chalmette High Schools, both schools in neighborhoods that would be severely devastated by Hurricane Katrina. Chalmette, a predominantly white high school, is in St. Bernard Parish, just across the parish line from Frederick Douglass, the all-black New Orleans public school where I was working. As part of the State of the Nation program, a project of the Douglass Community Coalition led by coalition member

Artspot Productions, these students dealt with the problem of inequities of public education, specifically starting with the New Orleans public school system.

In the six weeks that we convened to create this play, a group of black and white students, who wouldn't otherwise be affiliated with each other, became a community. I've seen them with my own eyes, learning from each other's strengths and each one growing stronger. As much as it made me happy to see this utopia of learning and understanding and community development, it was also heart crushing because in the real world—a world where the individual is more important than the group—this type of community learning would not be awaiting them at their respective schools, unless they were able to be a part of a program such as Students at the Center (SAC), which links community to school and develops youth voices and leadership.

I know of no other program that encourages students to learn through their own experiences, which means that everyone can be a teacher in his or her own way. How well you do in the class is not dependent on your grades or whether or not you can pass a test, but on how well you can connect your experiences to the current events, policies, and decisions that affect your life. SAC equips all its students with the ability to be leaders in their own schools and communities.

All of us who care about New Orleans and the surrounding parishes have the opportunity to learn from the SAC community. We can make our school system reflect true equality and community cooperation.

One of the first and most critical steps to having a public school system that works for each student is to break down the barriers that divide communities. These barriers include selective admissions schools that have the ability to design their student body based on admissions test scores or simply self-selection by students, their families, and their teachers.

Separating students who can achieve on certain levels from those who may not be able to achieve on those levels hurts and weakens *all* students. Instead of creating a system that allows students from the same neighborhood with varying degrees of knowledge to learn and help each other be better students, these selective admissions schools rip vital human resources from their own communities while discriminating against others. But these "others" are also vital human resources.

I know this because I attended McDonogh 35, a selective admissions school. Yet my relatives and friends in my own community attended George Washington Carver, Booker T. Washington, and Douglass High Schools, all of which are considered low-performing schools. Although I didn't initially understand some of my family's resentment of the high school I chose to attend, somehow I did feel like I was a part of the abandonment of not just those in my family but also those in my community. I understood that my education was somewhat better than theirs, but why? Whenever I walked into my cousin Eddie's room when he was doing homework, he would stop immediately and throw his books aside. I knew he was having trouble because his mother told me so. Even though we were cousins, for some strange reason the fact that he attended Carver and I McDonogh 35 made it hard for him to come to me for help even when I was clearly offering it.

Imagine if all of the medicine men, all of the hunters, musicians, and farmers decided to create their own communities, excluding or rarely dealing with those with other skills? They would notice that their communities would become gravely destitute as musicians realize they know nothing about hunting, the hunters can't heal the sick, and the medicine men starve to death because they don't know how to cook. The ancients understood one thing we fail to realize: You can't be a community by yourself. And even if you find a group of people who are just as smart as you, or can play an instrument just as fine as you can, there are skills that the group lacks and desperately needs.

If we are serious about creating a better New Orleans and we understand that a better school system is an important factor in that, then we know what we have to do. There is only one way to eliminate low-performing schools for good: Get rid of those schools that separate and destroy the potential of community.

Rebuilding New Orleans, Redoing Education

Christopher Burton

I attended the lowest ranked high school in the state of Louisiana. Located in the city of New Orleans, where I was born and raised, Frederick Douglass is my alma mater. It is the only high school I enrolled in, and I'm proud to have spent my four years there. Coming from the bottom school, I think that I have a legitimate say about what should be done to improve the public schools.

Being singled out as one of the brightest students in my middle school, I was strongly discouraged from attending Douglass. Out of my eighth-grade class, three of the top students, including my sister and me, went to Douglass. The rest went to the best public schools and private schools in the city. They were influenced by parents, friends, and teachers to separate themselves from other students. They were taught to see themselves as better than a low-performing student.

I started observing school life when I was singled out in elementary school. In the fourth grade my teacher thought me bright enough to try for the gifted test. Mind you, I was a nine-year-old boy whom the school board had known to be hearing impaired since kindergarten. I began speech therapy at five years old, but there was no attempt other than that to help me. I was still sort of like the kids in my class, except that I was already exceptional, having somehow been able to get kept back in kindergarten.

Once this teacher recommended me to take the test to get into gifted, I became more exceptional. I passed the test with flying colors, and some of the adults took notice. During my Individual Education Plan evaluation, these adults decided I was worth the effort to make a success. I got a gifted class, with a small number of students and an itinerant resource teacher who helped me with whatever I needed help with. With these new services coupled with speech therapy, I was able to stay out of my regular fifth-grade classroom about half of every school day. And piling one good thing upon another good thing, I started being called for over the PA system a lot. I never got called down for being bad, though. It was always because my itinerant teacher had arrived or the school nurse wanted to take me for a hearing test or the principal wanted to give me a ribbon for student of the week.

While all these good things were going on, my regular classmates made fun of me because of my big ears, my funny speech, and me being the oldest or at least the tallest boy in my grade. I don't think the students liked me much. Maybe the teachers had started using me as an example of a good student. They probably hated the fact that teachers placed me on this pedestal without ever looking at the other students they had and helping them to succeed.

My suspicion of malice came true in my fifth-grade year at an awards ceremony. Every time I walked onto the stage to receive an award, I got booed. Maybe the crowd all knew that I had cheated: I had received aid and attention that should have been directed also at the children more in need of it than me. After that night, having been booed in front of my sister and grandma and having almost cried, I developed modesty. Knowing that I was not the average student, I tried to become the average student.

It didn't work out, however. In ninth grade I tried to do nothing extracurricular, make Cs and Ds and hang out with my friends. It didn't happen that way, because I couldn't resist doing classwork and homework. It's a hard habit to break when you've been trained to do school work for eight years of your 13-year-old life. Besides that, I had a track record that said that I was not that kind of student. The counselor rode my ass behind my first four grades, three As and one C.

My years in school did not show me much disparity in opportunities given to students until I began high school. The counselor offered me every academic opportunity that she could. My gifted teacher got me a summer job being a mentor for Ralph Bunche Middle School students. And my itinerant teacher helped me manage life, school, and everything in between, having been my teacher for five years. I was definitely overprivileged in high school. I noticed that the counselor didn't try to straighten out any of the students with bad track records. The students with bad track records represented a good-sized portion of the school, Douglass being the last chance for many students expelled from other schools or formerly imprisoned. The itinerant teacher was only meant to help me at Douglass and a small number of students across the district whom the school board considered worthy of its time. The gifted teacher was only assigned the brightest students in the school: my ninth-grade year that was only one person, me.

The privileged few get all the resources, and the majority is given close to nothing. Benjamin Franklin High School, the top-ranked school in Louisiana, is in the same public school district as Douglass. The school was designed to be a school for gifted students. It is inconsequential that the majority of students in that school are white. McDonogh 35 is a high-ranking school, one of the only primarily black high-ranking schools in the state. It was designed to be a school for the high-achieving black students. If schools are able to be like Franklin and McDonogh 35, then the public schools will never be improved in New Orleans. When every last student is taken care of and able to get the attention reserved for the few, then New Orleans schools will improve. The public schools need to be *public* in the absolute sense of the word. In order to improve New Orleans schools we must break from helping *some* get a good education to helping *everyone* get a good education.

I've come back to the city and have transferred from Hampden-Sydney College in Virginia to the University of New Orleans. My reasons: (1) I couldn't handle the tuition up there; (2) there was a Confederate flag in the second-floor window of one of the dorm rooms all year; and (3) I could not sit back and watch the school system I came out of become less for the average student and more for the privileged students. I came back because charter schools to me will widen the education gap more than Benjamin Franklin or McDonogh 35 were doing before the storm. Now schools are recruiting teachers as well as students. A gifted resource teacher I know who works at Benjamin Franklin Elementary in New Orleans Public Schools has had offers, each including a salary bonus, from independent Orleans Parish School Board and Recovery School District charter schools. The problem of how to teach the students who can't get into a charter school or a selective admissions school is still not being addressed. Before I set off for college, I had been working, mainly through Students at the Center and the Frederick Douglass Community Coalition, to get resources to Douglass and give opportunities to its students. Now that I am back I will continue that struggle.

The Story of Z:
Lessons for Teachers and Educational Policy Makers

Jim Randels

In late August 2005, during the second week of school, Z tapped me on the shoulder right after class and asked if I'd talk to him outside. Z's big for his age and probably a couple years older than his classmates in my sophomore English class. He'd been struggling to make it to class every day, holding a white hand towel soaked in menthol rub over his face and working a pack of tissues to keep his nose clean. The first day he arrived with his summer cold gear I thanked him for making the effort to be in school.

I'd seen Z in the halls the previous year. He's the sort of young man who didn't always go to class. And his size and facial expression and body language might seem menacing to someone who sees him around school but doesn't really know him. But I've been a student and teacher in the public schools in New Orleans for over 30 years, so even last year when I didn't know him, I had no problem just hurrying Z along to where he was supposed to be.

So when he asked to cut into our precious 30-minute lunch break for a conversation in the hall, I was glad to join him.

"Let me file these essays before I lose them, and then I'll be right there."

When I made it outside, he was leaning against the wall in the dimly lit hallway, clutching his rag and nodding at fellow band members as they rushed to the stairwell.

"Mr. Randels, I wanted to ask if you'd teach me how to read."

Z's request calls to mind four key issues about the educational circumstances and strategies under which Students at the Center (SAC) has been working both before and after Katrina:

1. Our neighborhood high school had a population of approximately 20 percent special education students. This proportion was about the same for the 12 other neighborhood high schools in the New Orleans Public Schools. Before Katrina, our system

also had six selective admissions public high schools. The only special education students at these schools were those who were academically gifted, talented in the arts, or had an exceptionality concerning their physical abilities.

2. We work in the conditions in which we find ourselves. Those of us who work in SAC at Douglass (and other public schools) have not spent our time complaining about these educational situations. Instead, we want the public and policy makers to understand the different types of schools we have in New Orleans. And more important, we want to learn how to teach Z and his classmates as best we can. Only engaged in practice can we learn the strategies we need. In Z's case, I believe his willingness to ask for assistance after less than two weeks of time in our class comes from the fact that we engaged him in oral processes. His thoughts and words had a space of respect in our classroom. I still remember his comments about a classmate's essay about a difficult family relationship. He related a story from his own experience, asked a probing question, and offered a reassuring comment to the writer. But it's not so much what Z said that I remember; it's the expressions on the faces of his classmates who suddenly saw Z in a new way.

3. We understand students as a resource. I could not fulfill Z's request to learn to read on a personal level. He needed daily one-on-one attention. We do, however, have veteran SAC students who have trained in our classes to be resources in literacy development to our students. Rodneka Shelbia, who was a senior at Douglass, has been part of SAC since her ninth-grade year. She has trained in reciprocal teaching and other methods for helping to improve reading abilities. She and Z are also friends. Rodneka agreed to work with Z on his reading every day as part of her elective SAC course. Z was eager for this help. Then the storm came.

4. Young people such as Z are eager to learn, given the right conditions. We need to help create those conditions and find ways to assess and respect the whole student. Labeling schools such as Douglass as failures based primarily on their test scores is a disservice to the education of our students. Instead of one-size-fits-all approaches, we need ways to measure what it means for me to teach sophomore English in a class that includes about 20 percent of students who face educational challenges similar to Z's. Instead of Z's state test scores being the only way to measure his

worth and success as a student, we also need ways to measure (and to compute into the formulas that allow states to hand over public schools to private entities) Z's desire to read and the efforts that brought him to that point.

These questions are pressing as we return to a public school system in New Orleans that will now be run by the state and by foundations and universities, designed by national experts and university presidents not by teachers and parents and students who have worked hard and with pockets of success to educate the young people not allowed admission into schools the state has labeled academically acceptable. Z won't be with us in the return to New Orleans. Word is he drowned in the storm. But for the sake of the many young people like Z, I hope policy makers and national experts will listen to the lessons veteran New Orleans educators have learned from Z.

Commentary

Redesigning Urban Schools as Communities: A Grassroots Movement for Change

Wayne Au

Public schooling in the United States has always been somewhat of a double-edged sword. One edge cuts people down and creates cleavages between and within communities by fostering inequality and differentiation between students, communities, cultures, and classes. We see this sharp edge in our schools everyday as working-class students and students of color have consistently been provided with fewer educational resources and opportunities (Ladson-Billings, 2006) and have suffered subsequent institutional disparities of astronomical dropout and incarceration rates coupled with correspondingly miniscule high school graduation and college entrance rates (Sirin, 2005; Valenzuela, 2005). Conversely, the other edge of education is used to create solidarity and strike against social, cultural, and economic inequality through learning that promotes critical consciousness (Shor & Freire, 1987). Such education pushes students to understand and identify injustice as the first step in embodying Freirian "praxis"—that is, critical reflection and conscious action upon the world (Freire, 1974). Public schools, in this way, serve a dual and even contradictory function: they both reproduce social and economic inequalities and simultaneously create spaces for resistance to those very same inequalities (Apple, 1995).

The students and teachers in New Orleans stand at the sharpened tip of this sword as neoliberal forces slice up public education and promote policies that further stratify the school-going population along lines of class and race (Dingerson, 2008). Students at the Center (SAC), and the young people who have participated in the program, stand in stark contrast to these attacks, as they write defiantly in the fight to keep their communities together and thriving. In this reflection I seek to make sense of both edges of education, placing what the students and teachers see happening in New Orleans within a broader policy context, while also situating SAC as part of a broader national movement of education for social justice.

What unites the student narratives of Ashley Jones and Christopher Burton and the story of Z, as told by teacher Jim Randels, is the issue of unequally designed schools, or the disparity and unequal distribution of resources through selective enrollment and tracking in New Orleans Public Schools. Ashley talks about this in terms of how New Orleans's system of selective admissions operates to divide communities—a form of citywide, whole-school tracking. Here, select students get select access to selective schools that have selective resources. Thus, if you can pass the right admissions test or have forceful enough advocates, then you can attend a school with better educational resources. If not, then you get what you get. Such a system is a breeding ground for inequality. Similarly, in his narrative, Chris talks about his personal struggles with tracking at the school level, where as a "gifted" student he saw a significant disparity of resources. As he says, "The privileged few get all the resources, and the majority is given close to nothing." Finally, in Randels' story about Z, we see an "illiterate" student failed by New Orleans Public Schools, where the conditions and resources did not exist for Randels to either individually or systematically meet all of Z's needs, even as he did make use of SAC as a resource to begin helping Z learn how to read. Then Hurricane Katrina hit, and as Randels tells, "Word is he drowned in the storm." Perhaps Z's tragic reality can serve as a cautionary metaphor for what is happening to New Orleans Public Schools under the policy leadership of neoliberals.

The sorting of students and subsequent selective (and unequal) distribution of resources that we see happening in New Orleans today is, unfortunately, nothing new. Over 100 years ago, along with the rise of the social efficiency movement in U.S. education (Kliebard, 2004), the results of very biased standardized testing were first used to track students into different educational groups. Eerily like today's testing, people of color and the poor scored lower on those early tests, and such scores were used to justify different systems of education for different groups of students and adults (Au, 2009b). Not only do we see similar testing, test results, and use of tests to sort and rank students in contemporary times (Lipman, 2004), the policy tradition of tracking students into different levels of education lives on today in New Orleans and elsewhere, and has generally led to increased stratification by race and class among students. Such tracking-based stratification has, of course, been followed closely by the unequal distribution of educational resources between tracks, with more affluent and whiter populations being given access to a higher quality education and, by extension, greater opportunity for success in and beyond schools (Oakes, 2005).

Tracking, selective enrollments, and the maldistribution of educational resources produce the inequality so evident in public schooling in New Orleans and throughout the United States—an inequality that many have argued is one of the prime functions of the system of education (e.g., Anyon, 1997; Au, 2009b). Further, such school-based inequalities, because they correlate so closely with race- and class-based differences, generally run parallel to social and economic relations that exist outside of school systems (Anyon, 2005). One way to understand the functional inequality found in schools is to think of the system of education in the United States as part of a much larger system of differentiation, that is, a system that literally separates and severs populations from one another. Once some students are differentiated from others by testing, for instance, then they can more easily be slotted into stratified, hierarchical categories, tracked, "selected" for enrollment, and given greater access to educational resources. Research has borne this truth out: More affluent middle- and upper-class parents have consistently supported systems of tracking (Brantlinger, 2003; Oakes & Wells, 1997; Oakes, Welner, Yonezawa, & Allen, 1998) and testing (Apple, 2006; Au, 2008a), because such systems of differentiation historically have provided their children (and themselves) with increased upward mobility educationally and economically (Bernstein, 1996). Such differentiation has been racialized too, since tracking, testing, and the distribution of educational resources have generally privileged white students over students of color (Au, 2009a; Darling–Hammond, 2007b; Oakes, 2005) and, as the students' narratives make clear, sometimes generated class fractions within communities of color. While producing inequality through such systems certainly is not the *only* function of schools, the research evidence nationally, as well as what is happening on the ground in New Orleans, certainly illustrate that this process is part and parcel of hegemonic educational policy.

It is essential, therefore, to redesign schools for equity and social justice, both in New Orleans and nationally. While it is true that schools generally support the status quo of inequality, there is another edge to education—that of educating for critical consciousness and social justice (Shor & Freire, 1987). Clearly, SAC is an active part of this other edge of education, where students are encouraged to develop their own voices, to speak the critical truths of their lives, to look at their worlds with an eye toward understanding systems of power and inequality, and, most important, to see themselves as empowered members of their communities, capable of speaking out and challenging the status quo. This is one of the most powerful aspects of critical education, because the process of naming our current reality, and all of its constituent inequalities, automatically creates within us the ability to see the potential for radically new possibilities (Au, 2008b; Bernstein, 1996).

Thus I think it is vital to recognize that the young people involved in SAC are not alone, that they actually have a shared experience similar to other students, teachers, schools, and communities around the country. For instance, I would point to the work being done by Yang and Duncan-Andrade (2005) with high school students in Oakland, California. One major project these students work on, called "Doc Ur Block," asks them to take part in the cycle of critical praxis, where they identify a major problem confronting their communities (e.g., environmental racism), educate themselves on this issue, develop an action plan to effect community change, implement their action plan (including holding press conferences and presenting findings to the community), and then critically reflect on their effectiveness and learning. This project, much like SAC, creates space for student leadership in their own learning and works to concretely connect education to community needs and resources.

Doc Ur Block is simply one example. There are teachers working with students and teaching for equality and social justice all over the United States. Every year, Teachers 4 Social Justice (2009) in San Francisco holds a conference that draws well over 1,000 attendees, all of whom seek to make education politically relevant and connected to communities, and challenge inequalities in their classrooms and schools. Similarly, the Association of Raza Educators (2009), with chapters in San Diego, Los Angeles, and Oakland, California, brings educators, youth, and community activists together through critical education and community action to fight against oppression. Such gatherings not only include the sharing of critical educational classroom and community practices, but also have been directly linked to local campaigns for immigrants' rights or the struggles of local teachers to implement socially and culturally relevant curriculums. For instance, the 2008 conference culminated with a march and rally against the harsh treatment of Latinos by both San Diego police and border patrol agents. Nationally, coalitions such as the Education for Liberation Network (2009) and the Forum for Education and Democracy (2009) are convening grassroots organizers and educational leaders to work for more just schools. Increasingly, teachers, students, and parents are working together to make schools more connected to communities and to fight against systems of tracking, high-stakes testing, and the maldistribution of resources—among other pressing social and educational issues. Although the experience of students, teachers, and communities in New Orleans is unique in certain ways, the issues being confronted there, as well as the lessons being learned in the fight against the neoliberal educational experiment, are also undoubtedly important for the world.

We have a fight on our hands, and it is crucial that we bring our communities and schools together to wield education in the name of collective social justice. This work is happening with SAC, and it is part of a growing national movement proving that schools can be designed as communities of resistance and justice.

CLOSING REFLECTION

What's at Stake If We Don't Wake Up

Kristen L. Buras

The freedom dreams, pedagogic hopes, and grassroots efforts illuminated in this chapter are far from inconsequential. Just the opposite, they demonstrate how truly impoverished schools are under present reforms, and the distance we still need to go toward creating radically democratic educational spaces. By "impoverished," of course, I don't mean "culturally deficient" or "economically inefficient," which represent discourses invoked by neoconservatives and neoliberals to explain the problems in urban schools. Instead, I refer to the myopic visions of curriculum and educational reform that characterize the current era. Robin D. G. Kelley (2002) reminds us that freedom dreams—past and present—can inspire and renew, with "renewal" here constituting something very different from the mis-education, segmentation, and gentrification pursued by policy makers and urban planners whose agenda consists of privatizing rather than socializing schools and communities.

Bruce Coleman joins Erica DeCuir in emphasizing the role of historical knowledge in our capacity to envisage present-day possibilities. Relying once again on the intuitions and experiences of young people, we might look back to the mid-1800s and the ways that free children of color in New

Orleans imagined community through the critical race pedagogy and curriculum of *Société Catholique pour L'instruction des orphelins dans l'indigence*, or the Catholic Institution led by Afro-Creole writers and intellectuals in Louisiana. Drawing inspiration from the French and Haitian Revolutions and reflecting an explicit commitment to race-conscious educational advancement, teachers and students "developed a radical agenda aimed at securing civil and political rights for people of color in the Americas" (Mitchell, 2000, p. 124). Indeed, the letters of students between 12 and 17 years of age, directed to both Mexico and Haiti, where free people of color were emigrating during this period, reflect desires for black economic empowerment through cultivation and trade. Notably, however, this sense of determination was wedded to collectively empowering communities rather than undermining them through solely individualistic pursuits. For example, these young people used letter writing to envision life in Eureka—a settlement in Mexico supported by one of the school's allies—and "charted links between their own lives in Louisiana and the lives of free people of color across the Atlantic and Caribbean" (p. 130). Along the way, they dreamed of inhabiting spaces and places "where black people were in the majority" (p. 136) and shared ideals with black authors in Haiti, Guadeloupe, and Martinique on "democratic revolution, brotherhood, and equality" (p. 138). Simultaneously, they critiqued the racial oppression they experienced in New Orleans, as illustrated by one student who complained about the state legislature cutting the school's funding: "The white people have an Institution [a public school] in every district and they are all protected very well. But we, who have but a single one, cannot be protected at all" (p. 137). Through such creative, politicized ruminations, students came to a more critical understanding of "the relationship between citizenship and whiteness—and the ability of people of color to build a nation of their own" (p. 140). Consciousness of such historic Creole cosmopolitanism (see Buras & Motter, 2006) surely challenges the narrow, self-referential ethos of contemporary neoliberalism.

Sentiments such as these are echoed in the writings of Students at the Center (SAC), when Bruce underscores the cultural assets of pre-integration schools and laments the current absence of black history, or when Ashley Jones laments the "real world" where "the individual is more important than the group" and where, as Chris Burton and Wayne Au point out, schools divide communities of color through exclusive charter schools, tracking, and unequal resource distribution. Echoes may also be heard in the voices of Joyce King and Jim Randels, both of whom call for more meaningful, community-based standards for assessing what's "good" and what's "bad" in schools such as Frederick Douglass. Here the collectivist spirit of heritage knowledge and equitably resourced schools for *all* urban youth is central. These were the aspirations of free youth of color in mid-nineteenth-century New Orleans, and now, more than a century later, these same things are valued in black neighborhood schools where an educational commons is created through dedicated veteran teachers, close parental and intergenerational relations, and thriving community involvement (Buras, 2010; Morris, 1999). Imaginative and defiant voices, both past and present, can show us the way toward something more just.

Importantly, students' emancipatory visions are realizable. They invite educational spaces that reflect the work that SAC and the Frederick Douglass Community Coalition are already doing. In the interest of solidarity, Au reminds us that SAC is part of a larger set of educational movements for social justice. These movements need not look or be like the core knowledge movement, premised on rectifying so-called cultural deficits by infusing its own brand of mis-education—albeit with a multicultural nod—into the nation's schools (Buras, 2008). Nor must we embrace the desocializing tendencies of marketized education. We must, absolutely must, proceed differently and without reproducing the misrepresentation, differentiation, and dispossession that so powerfully define schooling at this moment. Too much is at stake.

Conclusion

**Schools, Cities, and Accumulation by Dispossession:
A Word on the Indisposable Instruments of Liberation**

Kristen L. Buras

ARE POOR COMMUNITIES and communities of color discardable? Are there disposable populations? Alternatively, should wealth and whiteness entitle their possessors to command the resources of the city? Demonstrably, there are those who think so. There are also those who think not, including members of Students at the Center (SAC). Whose view should shape pedagogy and policy making? Whose view will prevail? Kenneth Saltman (2007a) has argued we are living in an era of "smash-and-grab" privatization. That's surely been the way of New Orleans for quite some time. Growing up white in New Orleans, with all the privilege and power this entails, did little to challenge the sense of entitlement undergirding such material relations. If black folk were raised in a "culture of poverty" and lacked the appropriate work ethic, then weren't *they* responsible for the losses incurred? For me, a fundamental political shift in consciousness occurred when I was exposed to a different view, a different story, a different reality through grassroots educational work in the St. Thomas Housing Project, a low-income African American community just a few blocks from the wealthy and white St. Charles Avenue. Working with youth in summer camps, after-school programs, and local public elementary schools as well as assisting grandparents and elders in an affiliated senior center meant exposure to counterstories that challenged and disrupted the majoritarian narrative that informed my own worldview. These stories—really, the children, parents, aunts, uncles, and grandparents who shared them and, most poignantly, lived them—taught me about the truly oppressive ways that whiteness functioned as a form of property in New Orleans. Visiting the apartments of mothers who worked several jobs but suffered the neglect of public housing authorities who should have done repairs long ago, or accompanying seniors, who worked their entire lives under a regime of racial apartheid, to the food stamp office because they

145

couldn't afford basic necessities—let's just say these were transformative moments. Richard Delgado (2000) is right: Counterstories can indeed show us "that what we believe is ridiculous, self-serving, or cruel" and "help us understand when it is time to reallocate power" (p. 61).

Tragically, the class and race "powers that be" in New Orleans weren't listening to these stories; they were too busy circulating their own. One instance in the mid-1990s involved St. Thomas and a story intertwined with the federal HOPE VI program (Buras, 2005; Lipman, 2008). It went something like this: The St. Thomas Housing Project is full of derelicts and criminals who steal, sell drugs, and kill. It's really sad, too, because they're living on a prime piece of real estate only blocks from St. Charles Avenue and the Mississippi River. Thankfully, there's an answer to this unfortunate problem. Historic Restoration Incorporated (HRI), a real estate company based in New Orleans, can obtain federal funding to "redevelop" the area as mixed-income housing, and thereby provide both better housing and exposure to a middle-class work ethic to poor public housing residents (see Buras, 2005).

This story, of course, was problematic on many levels, not the least of which was its utter lack of connection to reality. More to the point, the St. Thomas Housing Project constituted the kind of "family" that Tyeasha Green describes earlier in this book (see "Missing Project" in Chapter 3) when writing about the Florida Housing Project where she grew up—albeit with some of the desperation that oppression generates, as she points out—but HRI disregarded this fact, with little intention of welcoming back the original low-income residents. While the initial proposal for the HOPE VI grant included 80% low-income housing units and 20% market-rate units, a very different plan emerged after the U.S. Department of Housing and Urban Development issued a $25 million grant. In short, St. Thomas was razed, hundreds of families were displaced, and the original mix of low-income and market-rate units inverted. River Garden, largely consisting of upscale rentals, condominiums, and homes, was built in its place. It's only through smash-and-grab politics that St. Thomas becomes River Garden and, more alarmingly, a blueprint for redeveloping the city as a whole (Buras, 2005, 2009a). In addition to displacing residents of the former housing project, a public elementary school down the street—one where I earlier acted as a teaching assistant—was closed and its building taken over more recently by a selective admissions charter school.

There's a lineage from River Garden in the mid-1990s *to* the creation of the Blueprint for a Better New Orleans in 2000, which the president of HRI helped generate, *to* Mayor Ray Nagin's Bring New Orleans Back Commission in 2006 (particularly the education committee, which was headed by Tulane University President Scott Cowen and advocated an all-charter school district) and Governor Kathleen Blanco's Louisiana Recovery Authority (populated by venture capitalists and shipping and oil magnates), *to* the state-run Recovery School District, its commitment to educational decentralization and marketization, and its School Facilities Master Plan (which strategically "landbanks" schools, such as Douglass, in gentrifying neighborhoods), *to* pro-charter-school organizations like New Schools for New Orleans and TeachNOLA, affiliated with the New Teacher Project and its union-busting activities (all housed free of charge at the Cowen Institute for Public Education Initiatives), *to* the public-private venture for riverfront (re)development aptly named Reinventing the Crescent, and possible plans to close Frederick Douglass High School and either sell the building to a private entity or provide it to a selective admissions charter school (see Buras, 2009a). This is the state apparatus, both ideological and material, that's responsible for the racial politics of accumulation by dispossession in the city of New Orleans. Yet, as the counterstories and critical commentaries in this book attempt to make clear, there are classrooms, schools, homes, and neighborhoods worth salvaging, even as neoliberal policy makers choose to dismiss this fact.

Along with critical race theorists and many contributors to this book, I've advanced the argument that counterstories constitute a crucial "evidentiary record" (Lawrence, 1995), one useful for understanding complex social processes and unearthing the violent effects of policies often presented as remedies rather than part of the very problems that plague us. Undoubtedly there are those who will argue otherwise, saying that a "story's just a story" or that everyone has a story or that there's no way to determine the truth value or implications of one story over another. In one infamous exchange between legal scholars Daniel Farber and Suzanna Sherry, on one hand, and Richard Delgado, on the other, the validity of critical race counterstories was called into question. Farber and Sherry (in Taylor, Gillborn, & Ladson-Billings, 2009) open with the following proclamation:

> Once upon a time, the law and literature movement taught us that stories have much to say to lawyers, and . . . that the law is itself a story. Instead of living happily ever after with that knowledge, some feminists and critical race theorists have taken the next logical step: telling stories, often about personal experiences, on the pages of the law reviews. . . . Thus far, however, little or no systemic appraisal of this movement has been offered. (p. 311)

As a result, they offer their own assessment, expressing concern regarding the accuracy and truthfulness, typicality and generalizability, and ultimate meaning of stories, especially in light of the purported absence of reasoned analysis to accompany them. They likewise question whether or not a distinct "voice of color" even exists. Thus, for example, Farber and Sherry urge that we should guard against the "pitfalls of our partiality" by putting stories in conversation with analytic arguments (p. 327). "If the story is being used as the basis for recommending policy changes," they write, "it should be typical of the experiences of those affected by the policy" (p. 329). Seemingly conceding some ground, they continue:

> On an empirical level, study of concrete situations provides an obvious source of information. . . . Even the social scientists who consider these [storytelling] techniques less reliable than more formalized statistical and experimental methods would be hard-pressed to dismiss them as useful starting points, which can then be subjected to more rigorous testing procedures.
>
> These uses of concrete examples are not necessarily tied to any ideological position, nor are they the unique domain of a particular race or gender. . . . The assumption that legal issues are best decided in the context of concrete cases, was the invention of white males.
>
> Rather, legal storytelling's most distinctive claim is that particular types of concrete examples, those drawn from the experiences of the downtrodden—have special claim on our attention. (pp. 320–321)

Ultimately, Farber and Sherry are deeply suspicious of the scholarly relevance and legitimacy of counterstories and their capacity to inform in any substantive way. As for the consequences of such stories beyond the academy and the relationship between legitimate scholarship and its material effects, they are clear:

> One frequent claim on behalf of storytelling is that stories build solidarity among the members of an oppressed group, thereby providing psychological support and strengthening community. We have no reason to question these effects, or to dismiss them as negligible. Nevertheless, we do not believe that these effects in themselves are sufficient to validate the stories *as scholarship*. (p. 321)

To summarize, oppressed groups have a right to tell their stories, but great caution should be taken in extrapolating anything meaningful from those stories, which, at worst, are dishonest or atypical and, at best, partial and lacking in scholarly rigor.

Yet as Delgado (in Taylor et al., 2009) astutely points out in his response:

> Empowered groups long ago established a host of stories, narratives, conventions, and understandings that today, through repetition, seem natural and true. Among these are criteria of judgment—the terms and categories by

which we decide which things are good, valid, worthy, and true. Today new-comers are telling their own versions, including *counterstories*, whose purpose is to reveal the . . . self-serving quality of the stories on which we have been relying to order our world. . . . Some within the mainstream have dismissed the new stories as false, manipulative, "political"—or not law. (p. 340)

In short, he explains, "stories that too forcefully call attention to injustice . . . will strike them as anecdotal, unprincipled, or unfair. They will give them pejorative labels . . . all the while overlooking that cheerful majoritarian stories . . . strike us the same way" (p. 345). Within the context of the present discussion, Delgado might put it this way: What is neoliberalism but an elaborate story—one about the supposedly indolent culture of the poor and the discipline of the unfettered market—backed by financial resources, policy making, and state power? Should we so blithely accept the truth of its claims, while dismissing the evidentiary record of its disastrous consequences for working-class communities, especially of color?

These debates imply the question, how will the counterstories of SAC be read and evaluated? What meaning and significance, or lack thereof, will be ascribed by mainstream educators and policy makers? We certainly hope that these stories will be considered with the seriousness that they deserve. As for naysayers of Farber and Sherry's stripe, we've more than adequately put these stories in conversation with current educational scholarship, and in fact, believe that these stories inform and advance such scholarship.

On the other hand, those more genuinely concerned with exactly how to transform inequitable material conditions may ask: What, then, are dispossessed communities to do? Simply tell counterstories? Here again, the Farbers and Sherrys of the world aren't even concerned with such questions—activist preoccupations allegedly reside beyond the purview of scholarship or empiricism. Yet effects "on the ground" should and do matter. For this reason, it's essential to understand that epistemic and cultural maneuvers—that is, engaging in a "war of position" to change taken-for-granted worldviews (Gramsci in Hoare & Nowell-Smith, 1971) around race and property—don't require the denial of concrete conditions and restraints, which, quite obviously, cannot be made to instantaneously crumble through story or discursive practice. In the same moment, though, it's imperative to recognize "group knowledge as the most powerful resource" that oppressed communities possess (Solinger et al., 2008, p. 8), and most importantly, cannot be dispossessed of. It is, perhaps, the indisposable instrument of liberation—an epistemic one with potentially very real material consequences and effects.

As SAC's work demonstrates, counter-storytelling is foundational to pedagogy for critical consciousness and community building. In Salaam's narrative below, he shares a compelling illustration of this generative capacity, detailing the process by which students, teachers, and community members deliberated over whether or not they should salvage the musical instruments that remained in Frederick Douglass High School after the storm. It wasn't so much the immediate decision or outcome, explains Salaam, but the nature of the dialogic process that created mutual respect and cultural bonds within the community. Such engagement, fostered through secondlining (or dancing) with brass bands and collectively circling the chairs to consider the fate of students' waterlogged flutes and trumpets, proved to be the ultimate "instrument" of transformation. It fostered a respect for both individual and collective voice, which itself can be a material force.

Through voice, students, teachers, and educational activists are able to build the solidarities on which social movements are based as well as make social justice claims through the provision of testimonials (see Solinger et al., 2008). Is it wishful thinking that counter-storytelling may function, for example, as an instrument in policy debates? Some of us think that it can expose the "gritty materiality" (Apple, 2006) or flesh-and-blood effects of policies touted as the supposed answer to some of the most pressing problems facing oppressed people. This is not to say that testimonial is the only instrument. As I and others have explored elsewhere (Apple & Buras, 2006; Kelley, 1996), it's not always easy for the subaltern to speak, nor does the subaltern always speak in straightforward or easily recognizable ways. But the subaltern does speak, sometimes by telling counter-stories, and these may trouble the claims, often *not* grounded in empirical evidence, of conservative reformers.

Significantly, the act of "speaking out" through story isn't something that characterizes the work of SAC alone. Recall the black diasporic imagination reflected by free children of color in New Orleans who conveyed their concerns and aspirations in letters to those throughout the Caribbean and Americas, or Ashley Jones's desire to produce images that put communities across the globe in control of their stories. In the spirit of subaltern cosmopolitanism, I want to widen the story circle from the "other South," as represented by SAC and dispossessed neighborhoods in New Orleans, to the Global South (see also Buras, 2009a; Buras & Motter, 2006).

Rickie Solinger, Madeline Fox, and Kayhan Irani (2008) provide examples of grassroots educational projects, from the southwestern United States to the mountains of Guatemala and the refugee camps of Darfur, that use storytelling and reveal how members of oppressed groups "claim the right to speak with dignity and knowledge and consequence in public." These educators and cultural workers from around the world understand "storytelling as a vehicle for claiming Authority or for situating the teller as Expert" (p. 7). In what is now the state of Arizona, the A:shiwi have raised their voices in defense of tribal homelands: "Commodification and diversion of a most sacrosanct element, Water, the Zuni River, is not only an assault on the ecosystem of the people, but on the ability of our distinct culture to continue to grow and flourish, and of the Earth to regenerate and sustain us. Our lands are being plundered and our resources exploited for profit" (Wemytewa & Peters in Solinger et al., p. 19). In response to this smash-and-grab operation, the Idiwanan An Chawe Theater Project was developed, which uses songs, stories, and place names to remember "ancestors who walked along the River" and "to bring Zuni language acquisition skills and fluency to its community of 10,000 citizens." In doing so, the community contends that "two precious resources, critical to A:shiwi existence [storytelling and the River], can be salvaged" (p. 20). In a similar vein, Mayan youth in Guatemala have challenged the "official" state history recorded in school textbooks by publicly reclaiming the stories of ancestors through theatrical forums. In one important scene, youth honor the resistance of those who fled to the mountains when the Guatemalan army instituted its "scorched earth" campaign, reminding all of the rebels' assertion, "Our culture is our resistance" (Thelen in Solinger et al., 2008, p. 53). In Darfur, the detailed drawings of young children attest to the brutality and genocide denied by Sudanese officials and provide a "visual vocabulary" that bolsters the work of human rights organizations engaged in documenting the crisis, including executions, forcible depopulation, and the burning of schools, hospitals, and villages. In Afghanistan as well, the art of storytelling has been of consequence, as evidenced by the Taliban's execution of *rawis* or traditional storytellers, including poets, artists, and musicians. Still, in defiance, stories have been used as a mechanism for teacher education and community development. As one example, young female teachers in Jaghori participated in a project called the Dialogue, where literary forms such as fairy tales and poems provided the means to survive, dream, heal, and rebuild Hazara culture, which has long been attacked by the majoritarian Pashtun and Tajik, and to establish the Afghan Academy project, which aims to build 20 campuses across the country and to use storytelling as a pedagogic method for ongoing community revitalization (Omar in Solinger et al., 2008).

In each of these instances, community-based storytellers, as authorities on their histories, cultures, and lives, offer narrative evidence that impugns the policies and power brokers responsible for their dispossession. Critical legal scholar Martha Minow asserts that stories can disrupt dominant forms of empiricism by introducing modes of analysis that are textured, humane, and invite the consideration of multiple and competing accounts, which can "prompt wise judgments" (Minow in Solinger et al., 2008). All of this suggests the crucial role of narratives from below in the arena of policy making, where wise judgments by the so-called experts seem few and far between.

The necessity of confronting neoliberal claims, promises, and programs is global in scale. In his book *Planet of Slums*, Mike Davis (2006) documents the disinvestment-reinvestment nexus at the heart of gentrification in U.S. cities and its confluence with the structural adjustment programs of the International Monetary Fund and World Bank that play out in the Global South. He focuses on housing markets as one instantiation. Thus, just as the HOPE VI program wreaked havoc on poor communities of color in New Orleans while advantaging more affluent families, Davis documents a pattern of eviction and "middle-class poaching" throughout the Third World, writing, "Urban segregation is . . . a ceaseless social war in which the state intervenes regularly in the name of 'progress,' 'beautification,' and even 'social justice for the poor' to redraw spatial boundaries to the advantage of landowners, foreign investors, elite homeowners, and middle-class commuters" (p. 98). Stunning illustrations include Bangalore, where demolished land is "reallocated through master planning to higher income interest groups, including corporations," and Delhi, where massive clearance was initiated "to make way for a river promenade and tourist amenities" (p. 100). Similarly, in Lagos, where the swampy area of Maroko had been peopled by a poor fishing community—one that nonetheless developed a well-known musical tradition—upper income groups gravitated to this increasingly desirable site after a bulldozing campaign left 300,000 poor inhabitants without homes. Master planning, bulldozing, and river promenades for the wealthy—these are the makings of the privatized city not simply in New Orleans, but in metropolitan areas throughout the Global South. What can be done to radically undercut the notion that there exists, to use Davis's words, "surplus humanity" (p. 201)? Rather than concluding with some grand proclamation, it seems most appropriate to close with two stories. In vivid detail, these counterstories reveal that there is no such thing as surplus or disposable humanity, but rather only a lack of humanity between urban planners and the poor communities they claim to help. As Jenna Dominique Hill explains below in reflecting on a virtually demolished family photo album that documented her coming of age in New Orleans, "I would not throw it out for anything."

CONTESTING THE POLITICS OF DISPOSABILITY THROUGH CULTURE AND PEDAGOGY

Speaking Out

Salvaging Our Culture and Our Schools

Kalamu ya Salaam

New Orleans, November 11, 2005—back home again in New Orleans.

I'm going to head out to New Orleans East to check on a storage unit where books and equipment were stored: I had over five thousand CDs. Over 4,800 of the CDs were alphabetized in steel cases, the rest were in boxes. I had a library of well over 3,000 books, pamphlets, and historic papers, plus computer and video equipment, and boxes of paraphernalia and memorabilia collected over the years. I'm pretty much resigned that the storage unit was probably flooded although I have been getting letters asking for payment of back rent and threatening a lien and forfeiture.

The first thing I notice is trash on the expressway. A couple of abandoned cars. Then the blue roofs as I passed the Treme area. Treme is the oldest continuously existing black community in the United States. Much of it was built by free people of color and enslaved blacks.

By the time I'm in the Ninth Ward it's obvious that the situation is dire. I drop down at the Downman exit, the first off-ramp after crossing the High Rise, which is the tallest structure in New Orleans and crosses the Industrial Canal, the boundary line that marks the beginning of New Orleans East.

About five blocks from Downman is where the storage unit is located. As I pull up I realize that I should have said where the storage unit "used to be" located. I don't even bother turning in to check further.

My intention was to meander around on a basic recognizance of the area. I don't feel like describing what I saw, except to say I quit driving through the East. I was beginning to cry and become totally depressed. We were here for a homecoming celebration, bringing some of our students in and trying to pull together whatever we could. I needed to be someone the young folk could lean on.

I'm a big, black, bear of a man, so the thought of me crying might seem a little unusual. This was the moment when I realized how much I love New Orleans.

She gone. I felt myself breaking down like an old blues singer moaning about that young woman he loved. It felt awful to see her like this, wasted, broke down worse than a crack addict, laying out somewhere, showing her emaciated ass. Enough. I had to get up out of there.

Welcome back, black. Look what they've done to your home. Who you mean? Katrina is not a "they." Katrina was a natural disaster. Maybe, but let me tell you that natural disaster was made worse by the politicians and the Army Corps of Engineers who were supposed to be in charge of the levees. Everything was made worse by policy experts and urban planners who did not really give a damn.

I remained haunted by all the destruction I had just seen. I slept well, but when I woke I started worrying about the future of our city.

We had a 9:00 a.m. program planned. We would start with a memorial service at St. Augustine Church in Treme. And from there second line to St. Paul's Lutheran Church in the Bywater area midway between the French quarter and Frederick Douglass High School in the Ninth Ward, which is where Students at the Center (SAC) was based.

When I arrived about a minute before 9:00, a few of the brass band members were starting to arrive. We trickled inside the church. Folk were generally moving on New Orleans time, which means we start around 9:15 and by 9:30 most of the folk will have arrived.

Baba is drumming inside the church. It's warm. The warmest Catholic church I know. I'm talking about the emotional warmth. I'm talking about how you feel welcomed. How you don't feel like you are disturbing anything if you drum or sing or even dance inside this church. How the seven principles of Kwanzaa are on the upper walls along with the religious symbols. How the pulpit is in the center of the church and how this church is a community center as well as a religious gathering spot.

Our program opened with Stephen Gladney playing an alto saxophone solo. He carried his horn with him everywhere. When they were waiting atop the old American Can building to be rescued he had his horn with him. When they were evacuated by boat and bus, he kept his horn. When they moved to Clemson, South Carolina, and now that they were back in New Orleans, my man had his horn.

At the conclusion of the service, which was essentially a time of serious sharing, we poured out into the cool but pleasant fall morning and prepared to second line. A pickup band formed around a core of Young Tuxedo Brass Band members who had been hired. Ashley is out front shooting video. I bring up the rear in the van. The band takes the long way around. People seep out of the houses. A few people are actually crying with joy.

A second line is a celebration. Post-Katrina there has not been much celebrating going on. But as the music hits, doors open and people join us.

One woman in particular I will never forget. She was the second person coming out of their house. She was this middle-aged sister with a purple umbrella. Naw, it wasn't raining. Umbrellas are part of the second line and my lady was ready. She juked—she didn't walk or run, she juked; it was a combination of dancing and running to catch up. Once she did get to where the band was, this woman gave a clinic on rump shaking. It just made you feel all kinds of good. When we got down to Colton Middle School, the band went into a dirge and that slow two-step they do to express grief. By then all kinds of people had joined in, and the thirty or so of us that had started off were now doubled in size.

I personally was bumping in the driver's seat of the van. And smiling. And feeling like, yeah, we can handle this. It's going to be alright.

And then we got to St. Paul's and in the church yard it got gooder, by which I mean two young black women took turns dancing with the grand marshal of the second line. Now being a grand marshal is no job for apprentices. You got to be able to be carrying on in fine style. My man looked to be in his sixties dancing like he was still 32, plus you know he had a store house of moves from his years of dancing in the streets.

By now, I am becoming emotional. Homesick. Critically ill. Somebody come see about me. I'm walking around laughing and joking with the students, with fellow SAC staff, with the band members whom I know, with friends who have joined us, with people who just stopped by.

Immediately after lunch we were to journey a couple of miles over to Douglass, which was walking distance. At the homecoming meeting we talked about where to go from here, what moves to make, what kind of response to mount to the ongoing abandonment. No public schools. No public hospitals. No this. No that. No. No. No.

We planned to see if there was someway we could get into Douglass. We were sitting in the back yard, next to the auditorium. Someone had climbed through a window and opened a door, so we had access to a bathroom.

The school was in relatively good shape. There had been minimal flooding in only the band room which was about three feet below street level, built to approximate an indoor amphitheater effect. No other room had flooded at the school.

We discussed what we thought might be the best way to get access to the school facility, especially given the upheaval with the school system, nothing can be taken for granted. Approximately 20 schools had been turned to charter schools. Those were the buildings that were either on the West Bank and had received no flood water or were two or three uptown East Bank buildings. No public schools were open and the state was rumored to be poised to take over most of the remaining 100 or so schools.

We had a lot of discussion about charters and decided that we didn't want to go the charter route, even though we recognized that we might be forced to do so. Sitting in a big circle, we listened to each other—high school students, teachers, staff, community activists, civil rights veterans—everyone taking a turn speaking their hearts and minds, responding to the issues before us.

And then a completely unforeseen issue came up, an issue that defines how we work and demonstrates the collective wisdom. We had about 25 students present and a number of them had been in the band. Some of them wanted to take their instruments home. The instruments were sitting there inside the band room, unused, dirty from the flood, but in the case of many of them, not damaged beyond repair. The flute and trumpet players were especially vocal about wanting to salvage their instruments.

Somebody suggested taking a vote. But Jim and I insisted that we discuss the issue and try to reach consensus rather than just take a winner-take-all vote. I explained how majority rule inevitably produces splits. As much as possible, I was strongly in favor of everyone speaking on the issue and everyone listening to each other, and from that process coming to consensus. Jim offered that by listening to each other and considering everyone's point of view we generally come to better decisions rather than forcing the issue one way or the other.

Earlier we had been talking about possibly sitting-in at the school and being prepared, if necessary, to be arrested. That's not a position to take lightly, especially when minors are involved and most especially when family and other supporters are living hundreds of miles away. Both Jim and I were keenly aware that we had guardian responsibilities vis-à-vis these young people. We knew that part of the reason that at least two thirds of the students were present is because their parents trusted us and were confident that we were caring for their children. Students came from South Carolina, Georgia, Texas, Oklahoma, and areas surrounding New Orleans.

Katrina has set off all kinds of discussions and activities in response. Some people see the possibility for organizing revolutionary activities based on the pain and anger felt by many, many New Orleanians and indeed by people all across this nation. While there is certainly an opportunity to harness all this energy, that does not mean ignoring our responsibilities to care for one another, and especially for adults to care for young people. I stand firm on that issue.

So there we sat, in a giant circle, asking each person to speak their hearts and minds on the issue of whether the students should take the instruments. Halfway around the circle the general consensus seemed to be that the instruments would probably be trashed if left in the building and that if they were salvageable then maybe the students should take them even though technically it would be theft. And then someone brought up the health issue: Who knew what was on those instruments as toxic residue from the flood waters? By the time we finished the circle, we all agreed that it might be better to leave the instruments than to take them.

The conclusion itself was not as important as the process. No one felt oppressed or put down for their view. Everyone had a turn, whether they were a 15-year-old student or 50-something visitor who was there to support organizing in New Orleans. It was a beautiful moment because when we left not only were we all in agreement but, more important, we all felt validated in the sense that our opinions were heard and considered and that we each had full input into the decision-making process.

I Would Not Throw It Out for Anything

Jenna Dominique Hill

A friend came over to my house and asked to see some of my baby pictures. I was excited, because I remembered that they had finally dried out. When I returned with the faded, mildew-covered album, she quickly left the room, covering her nose and reporting the wicked stench as literally "breathtaking." I did not care, though. I sat down to reminisce solo. Somehow I had learned to just block the smell out, and to me, the album, although very raggedy now, was worth gold. It is all that I have left of my childhood other than memories.

I remember the day the album and I remet. When the floodwaters receded and my house was no longer under the sea, my father went to retrieve some of our family's priceless goodies that we requested. Upon returning, I noticed that he had brought back my favorite picture book, along with some jewelry and other stuff. I noticed that it was soaked with muddy water and covered with mold and mildew. The pages turned differently. Some pictures were stuck together. The gold-framed cover was no longer gold, but some other color, like a mixture of grayish green or greenish black. The album was also cracked in half. Still, I decided to salvage it anyway. I set it outside so that the cool breeze would get rid of the wetness. After about a month with there being no rain, all the pages were dried, but the smell remained. I decided to take it inside anyway. The next time my father walked into my room, he thought something had died. After I told him the overwhelming smell belonged to my picture book, he could not believe that I had kept it all this time.

These pictures were my personal treasures. They were the visuals of my past. I had them when memories were just not vivid enough. As I flipped the pages, I saw my first birthday party, my first bike ride, the stage when my baby teeth were coming out, even Santa and me. I even heard voices come from the frames. I heard everyone singing, "Happy Birthday to Jenna!" I heard my dad saying, "Come on Jenna, try again," when I would fall to the ground from my bike. To me, the pages still had life, and the album, a place in my heart that will never perish. I would not throw it out for anything.

AFTERWORD

Whiteness and New Orleans: Racio-Economic Analysis and the Politics of Urban Space

Zeus Leonardo

Recently, George Lipsitz (2007) discussed the implications of pairing the study of urban spaces with race analysis. Deploying the appropriate dialectic between the "racialization of space and the spatialization of race," Lipsitz shows how space and place are products and producers of race relations. Poignantly opening his narrative with New Orleans, Lipsitz reminds us that space relations are not empty receptacles that scholars and activists fill up with racial meaning (see also Gulson & Parkes, 2009). Indeed, cities like New Orleans come with a long history of race relations, and the event of Hurricane Katrina and the subsequent rupturing of the levees are only the recent examples of neglect suffered by the largely African American 9th Ward of the city. It is tempting to analyze the disaster as "natural" turned into "social" by a government that reacted more quickly to the tsunami that devastated Asia thousands of miles away on another continent. But this would effectively reinforce the distortion that New Orleans was not already at risk as a result of racially motivated social policies, explaining away its highly segregated spatial politics between the white highlands and black lowlands. In fact, it was never a natural disaster in the sense that an objective force of nature touched down indiscriminantly on a people. The way that New Orleans was socially organized, its interaction with Katrina was utterly racial and predictable. Natural disasters are always already social disasters insofar as they involve human lives imbued with race and class histories.

As Charles Mills (1997) observes, if a society is structured this way, one could hardly be surprised at the outcomes, other than those who succumb to a certain epistemology of ignorance sanctioned by the "Racial

159

Contract," or the formal and informal agreements between whites about how to (dis)regard communities of color. The problems that such an inverted epistemology creates, transcend the assumed local origins of our New Orleans story and reach into the heart of national politics and global neoliberal restructuring, which Kristen Buras reminds us, "was from the very beginning a project to achieve the restoration of *racial* power to the *white* strata of the population." If the official story line frames Katrina as an act of nature, then this book aims to disrupt the narrative with accounts that express rage at the foreseeable injury and hope for its resolution, confirming what Apple and Buras (2006) earlier called the ability of the subaltern to speak. This is not a return to the problematic notion of a humanist agency, which we can appreciate at the individual level. The collective anger and clarity about the fateful events of 2005, and the neoliberal reforms that have followed with vengeance, strike the reader less as the celebration of agency-of-the-individual-as-usual and more the deliberate cry for solidarity.

In the spirit of speaking against what Mills calls the "epistemological contract" embedded within the Racial Contract, in this defiant volume Buras and her collaborators retell the story of New Orleans from the minoritarian perspective. As critical race educators, these organic race rebels (Kelley, 1996) reject the white spatial imagination, which "based on exclusivity and augmented exchange value, functions as a central mechanism for skewing opportunities and life chances in the United States along racial lines" (Lipsitz, 2007, p. 13). By contrast, the black spatial imagination is grounded on use value in an environment rich on network but poor on material resources, with an integrated sense of history despite living with segregated housing and schools. Students at the Center (SAC) in New Orleans, a 14-year-strong organization, has built up a counterspatial imaginary with their many books and videos. In testifying to Katrina's devastation of the already forsaken school system, SAC adds another layer to Robin Kelley's concept of "infrapolitics," or black folks' often-hidden allegories of resistance. What we receive is a portrait of a certain "creole theory" that augments the shortcomings of a class-only informed critical theory with a color-conscious analysis of the chronicle that is Katrina. Buras, Randels, and Salaam make the point that in order to understand New Orleans post-Katrina, one must appreciate the city's history pre-Katrina, which is true enough and reinforces the idea that urban spaces are not empty signifiers. By calling it "creole theory," I am not invoking the classical sense of creolization as a history of hybrid identities but appropriating the term to build a theory that blends the oppressed's racio-economic status (RES) to offset the color blindness associated with sole attention to their socioeconomic status (SES). However, I am also arguing that educators fail to appreciate the class dimensions of urban life for people of color, when they rely on a certain bourgeois race analysis that is class-blind (see Leonardo, 2009). Buras agrees when she remarks, "That the lines are racial, however, is a fundamental issue generally sidestepped in economic critiques." The partnership between white supremacy and capitalism is best explained as a double jeopardy for many African Americans. Mobilizing and privileging one analysis over the other is like paying attention to one hand as the other hand wreaks havoc.

The collection's inclusion of neo-griots, or young storytellers of color who use spoken, written, and digitally produced texts to narrate their struggles, is compatible with a creole theory that highlights intellectual disobedience. The stories told here speak to young people's epistemic insubordination and efforts to push back against the dehumanizing scripts that frame them, Ashley Jones notes, as either blameworthy for their plight and dispossession (the cult of personal responsibility) or victims without any sense of collective agency (the cult of passivity). They confirm the importance of what Patricia Hill Collins (2000) calls "controlling images" that the larger society propagates in order to subjugate a people. Taking back New Orleans means that youth reclaim the right to write themselves into history, to know themselves and decide what it is they wish to become, as Kalamu ya Salaam declares. New Orleans's neo-griots understand that both race and class oppression are responsible for their predicament and reject Chester Finn's (2008) appeal for modern paternalism to uplift them, evidenced by Jim Randels in SAC's eight principles for taking back their own education. As the critical bards of their time, these neo-griots announce the reality of racism amid pronouncements of its declining significance. As a collective act of defiance, these narratives remind the nation of its deepening educational "debt" to African Americans (Ladson-Billings, 2006). Long regarded as a national "deficit" (a "problem" in Du Bois's [1903/1989] treatise), African American children in schools represent the hope for an America unrealized, dogged by its overt disregard for them on one hand and the nagging guilt for this crime on the other.

As Buras makes clear, plans to convert the New Orleans "commons" into private commodities for white bourgeois enjoyment confirm the suspicion that whiteness and material accumulation are part of the "master plan" for the new spatial politics of the city by the sea. Currently, there is a plan to close more than 60 schools for purposes of turning disaster into profit (Klein, 2008). This description of "landbanking" is an extension of Paulo Freire's (1970/1993) critique of "banking education," where students are treated as empty receptacles to be filled with information in the latter, and black spaces are regarded as empty places to be invested in by white profiteers in the former. It is an argument for making the urban pedagogical and urbanizing pedagogy, necessitating attention to both race and class dynamics. SAC, an intensive writing program, reinforces Freire and Macedo's (1987) insistence that writing the word can never be divorced from a certain practice of freedom centered on a critical reading of the world. By this, they do not merely suggest a sophisticated worldliness but the sense that true words require an existential commitment to the basic unit of action contained in the transformative moment of literacy, where reading is not merely a decoding of the word but a remaking of the world. To recall Marx, school has merely taught students to describe the world, the point is to change it.

In certain circles, it is now well acknowledged that race is a white problem rather than a "Negro problem." When this fact is recognized, particular truths about New Orleans surface. First, white capitalism is the architect of the 9th Ward's demise and other associated casualties, not its citizens' alleged poor choices in life. In a society marred by racio-economic disparities, David Harvey's (2006) notion of "accumulation by dispossession" makes their plight a natural consequence of the structured tragedies that followed Katrina. Second, although former first lady Barbara Bush expressed her fears that Houston's good hospitality might encourage the displaced people of New Orleans to set down roots in her state, Maria Hernandez dispels that myth when she recalls (in Chapter 3) spending six days in the "stadium that housed thousands of hurricane victims, without knowing if my dad was dead or alive. We had to sneak out of the Superdome and swim past corpses and bayou animals to find him. I sliced my leg in the process of avoiding a dead woman floating. . . . There's nothing worse than walking into your 'hood and not recognizing it." These victims had already been to hell and back, and sleeping in Houston is not a good example of hospitality but sheer survival. Besides, "compassionate conservatism" does not put forth its best foot when it confuses images of home with the realities of disaster, as if the victims could not tell the difference. Finally, the white spatial imagination has partitioned this planet after its own image, often misunderstanding its own sordid creation (Mills, 1997). This fact notwithstanding, displaced people from New Orleans once again prove African Americans' ability to survive despite this nation's intent on eradicating them. This collection is testament to their living spirit and the moribund status of whiteness. As SAC reminds us, for centuries this nation has tried to wash away African Americans. Only the "watermelon tears" noted by Deborah Carey can save us now, for they bind us all to the task of liberation.

References

Alim, H. S. (2006). "The whig party don't exist in my hood: Knowledge, reality, and education in the hip hop nation." In H. S. Alim & J. Baugh (Eds.), *Talkin black talk: Language, education, and social change* (pp. 15–29). New York: Teachers College Press.

Anyon, J. (1997). *Ghetto schooling: A political economy of urban educational reform.* New York: Teachers College Press.

Anyon, J. (2005). *Radical possibilities: Public policy, urban education, and a new social movement.* New York: Routledge.

Apple, M. W. (1995). *Education and power* (2nd ed.). New York: Routledge.

Apple. M. W. (2000). *Official knowledge: Democratic education in a conservative age* (2nd ed.). New York: Routledge.

Apple, M. W. (2004). *Ideology and curriculum* (3rd ed.). New York: Routledge.

Apple, M. W. (2006). *Educating the "right" way: Markets, standards, god, and inequality* (2nd ed.). New York: RoutledgeFalmer.

Apple, M. W. (2006). "We are the new oppressed": Gender, culture, and the work of home schooling. In M. W. Apple & K. L. Buras (Eds.), *The subaltern speak: Curriculum, power, and educational struggles* (pp. 75–93). New York: Routledge.

Apple, M. W., & Beane, J. A. (Eds.) (2007). *Democratic schools: Lessons in powerful education* (2nd ed.). Portsmouth, NH: Heinemann.

Apple, M. W., & Buras, K. L. (Eds.). (2006). *The subaltern speak: Curriculum, power, and educational struggles.* New York: Routledge.

Apple, M. W., & Pedroni, T. (2005). Conservative alliance building and African American support for voucher plans. *Teachers College Record, 107*(9), 2068–2105.

Asante, M. K. (2007). *An Afrocentric manifesto: Toward an African renaissance.* Maiden, MA: Blackwell/Polity.

Association of Raza Educators. (2009). [Homepage]. Retrieved July 5, 2009, from http://www. razaeducators.org

Au, W. (2007). Epistemology of the oppressed: The dialectics of Paulo Freire's theory of knowledge. *Journal for Critical Educational Policy Studies, 5*(2), 1–13.

Au, W. (2008a). Between education and the economy: High-stakes testing and the contradictory location of the new middle class. *Journal of Education Policy, 23*(5), 501–513.

Au, W. (2008b). Devising inequality: A Bernsteinian analysis of high-stakes testing and social reproduction in education. *British Journal of Sociology of Education, 29*(6), 639–651.

Au, W. (2009a). High-stakes testing and discursive control: The triple bind for non-standard student identities. *Multicultural Perspectives, 11*(2), 65–71.

Au, W. (2009b). *Unequal by design: High-stakes testing and the standardization of inequality*. New York: Routledge.

Baker, L. (1996). *The second battle of New Orleans*. New York: HarperCollins.

Baldwin, J. (1970). A talk to teachers. In E. Hurwitz & R. Maidment (Eds.), *Criticism, conflict, and change* (pp. 82–88). New York: Dodd, Mead.

Ball, S. J. (2003). *Class strategies and the education market: The middle class and social advantage*. New York: RoutledgeFalmer.

Bernstein, B. B. (1996). *Pedagogy, symbolic control, and identity: Theory, research, critique*. London: Taylor & Francis.

Boal, A. (1985). *Theatre of the oppressed*. New York: Theatre Communications Group.

Bourdieu, P. (1984). *Distinction*. Cambridge, MA: Harvard University Press.

Brantlinger, E. (2003). *Dividing classes: How the middle class negotiates and rationalizes school advantage*. New York: RoutledgeFarmer.

Brenner, N., & Theodore, N. (2002). Cities and the geographies of "actually existing neoliberalism." *Antipode, 34*(3), 349–379.

Breunlin, R. (n.d.). The legacy of the Free Southern Theater in New Orleans: Interviews with Karen-Kaia Livers and Chakula Cha Jua. *Chicken Bones: A Journal for Literary and Artistic African-American Themes*. Retrieved November 17, 2009, from http://www.nathanielturner.com/legacyfreesouttheater.htm

Bring New Orleans Back Commission. (2006). Rebuilding and transforming: A plan for world-class public education in New Orleans. New Orleans, LA: Author.

Browder, A. T. (1989). *From the Browder file: 22 essays on the African American experience*. Washington, DC: Institute of Karmic Guidance.

Brown, R. N. (2008). *Black girlhood celebration: Toward a hip-hop feminist pedagogy*. New York: Peter Lang.

Buras, K. L. (2005). Katrina's early landfall: Exclusionary politics behind the restoration of New Orleans. *Z Magazine, 18*(12), 26–31.

Buras, K. L. (2007). Benign neglect? Drowning yellow buses, racism, and disinvestment in the city that Bush forgot. In K. Saltman (Ed.), *Schooling and the politics of disaster* (pp. 103–122). New York: Routledge.

Buras, K. L. (2008). *Rightist multiculturalism: Core lessons on neoconservative school reform*. New York: Routledge.

Buras, K. L. (2009a). *Schooling, race, and urban space: Where the market meets grassroots resistance*. Manuscript in preparation.

Buras, K. L. (2009b). "We have to tell our story": Neo-Griots, racial resistance, and schooling in the other South. *Race, Ethnicity and Education, 12*(4).

Buras, K. L. (2010). "We're not going nowhere": Urban space, race, and the struggle for Civil Rights Elementary School. Submitted to *Teachers College Record*.

Buras, K. L., & Apple, M. W. (2005). School choice, neoliberal promises, and unpromising evidence. *Educational Policy, 19*(3), 550–564.

Buras, K. L., & Apple, M. W. (2006). The subaltern speak: Curriculum, power, and educational struggles (introduction). In M. W. Apple & K. L. Buras (Eds.), *The subaltern speak: Curriculum, power, and educational struggles* (pp. 1–39). New York: Routledge.

Buras, K. L., & Motter, P. (2006). Toward a subaltern cosmopolitan multiculturalism. In M. W. Apple & K. L. Buras (Eds.), *The subaltern speak: Curriculum, power, and educational struggles* (pp. 243–269). New York: Routledge.

Buras, K. L., & Vukelich, D. (cohosts). (2006). *Post-Katrina New Orleans* [Radio broadcast]. Madison, WI: WORT Radio Station.

Burch, P. (2008). *Hidden markets.* New York: Routledge.

Bush, G. W. (2005, September 15). We will do what it takes. Available: http://www.cnn.com/2005/POLITICS/09/15/bush.transcript

Callebs, S. (2009, August 25). *After the storm: Education in NOLA* [Video]. Retrieved November 16, 2009, from http://ac360.blogs.cnn.com/2009/08/25/video-after-the-storm-education-in-nola/

Calmore, J. (1995). Critical race theory, Archie Shepp, and fire music: Securing an authentic intellectual life in a multicultural world. In K. Crenshaw, N. Gotanda, G. Peller, & K. Thomas (Eds.), *Critical race theory: The key writings that formed the movement* (pp. 315–329). New York: New Press.

Center for Community Change. (2006). *Dismantling a community.* New Orleans, LA: Author.

Chen, J. J. (2006). Struggling for recognition: The state, oppositional movements, and curricular change. In M. W. Apple & K. L. Buras (Eds.), *The subaltern speak: Curriculum, power, and educational struggles* (pp. 197–216). New York: Routledge.

Clarke, J. H. (1994). *Christopher Columbus and the African holocaust: Slavery and the rise of European capitalism.* Brooklyn, NY: A & B Publishers Group.

Collins, P. H. (2000). *Black feminist thought: Knowledge, consciousness, and the politics of empowerment* (2nd ed). New York: Routledge.

Common Ground. (2006). *New Orleans in numbers: Pre- and post-Hurricane Katrina snapshot.* New Orleans, LA: Author.

Cowen Institute. (2008). *The state of public education in New Orleans* [2008 report]. New Orleans, LA: Cowen Institute for Public Education Initiatives.

Crocco, M. S. (Ed.). (2007). *Teaching* The Levees: *A curriculum for democratic dialogue and civic engagement.* New York: Teachers College Press.

Crossroads Project. (2006). *Students at the Center* [Video]. New Orleans, LA: Author.

DaLuz, Z. (2008, May 13). *Letter to Paul Pastorek.* Retrieved July 15, 2008 from http://www.savefrederickdouglass.com

The Damned. (1973/1990). *Lessons from the damned: Class struggle and the black community.* Ojai, CA: Times Change Press.

Darling-Hammond, L. (2007a, October 14, 2007). High-quality standards, a curriculum based on critical thinking can enlighten our students. *San Francisco Chronicle*, p. E3. Retrieved November 17, 2009 from http://www.sfgate.com/cgi-bin/article.cgi?f=/c/a/2007/10/14/MN9GSOEUC.DTL

Darling-Hammond, L. (2007b). Race, inequality, and educational accountability: The irony of "No Child Left Behind." *Race Ethnicity and Education, 10*(3), 245–260.

Davis, M. (2006). *Planet of slums.* New York: Verso.

Delgado, R. (2000). Storytelling for oppositionalists and others: A plea for narrative. In R. Delgado & J. Stefancic (Eds.), *Critical race theory: The cutting edge* (pp. 60–70). Philadelphia: Temple University Press.

Desdunes, R. L. (1973). *Our people and our history: Fifty Creole portraits* (D. O. Mc-Cants, Ed. & Trans.). Baton Rouge: Louisiana State University Press. (Original work published 1911)

DeVore, D. E., & Logsdon, J. (1991). *Crescent City schools: Public education in New Orleans, 1841–1991.* Lafayette, LA: Center for Louisiana Studies at the University of Southwestern Louisiana.

Dingerson, L. (2008). Unlovely: How the market is failing the children of New Orleans. In L. Dingerson, B. Miner, B. Peterson, & S. Walters (Eds.), *Keeping the promise? The debate over charter schools* (pp. 17–34). Milwaukee, WI: Rethinking Schools.

Dingerson, L., Miner, B., Peterson, B., & Walters, S. (Eds.). (2008). *Keeping the promise? The debate over charter schools.* Milwaukee, WI: Rethinking Schools.

Diop, C. A. (1991). *Civilization or barbarism? An authentic anthropology* (Y.-L. M. Ngemi, Trans.; H. J. Salemson & M de Jager, Eds.). Brooklyn, NY: Lawrence Hill. (Original work published 1981)

Dixon, B. A. (2009, June 17). Teachers file racial discrimination suit against Obama administration's school "turnaround" plan. *Truthout.* Retrieved November 17, 2009, from http://www.truthout.org/061709EDA

Dixson, A. D., & Rousseau, C. K. (2006). *Critical race theory in education: All God's children got a song.* New York: Routledge.

Dolby, N., & Rizvi, F. (Eds.). (2007). *Youth moves: Identities and education in global perspective.* New York: Taylor & Francis.

Du Bois, W. E. B. (1989). *The souls of black folk.* New York: Penguin Books. (Original work published 1903)

Duncan-Andrade, J. (2006). Urban youth, media literacy, and increased critical civic participation. In S. Ginwright, P. Noguera, & J. Cammarota (Eds.), *Beyond resistance! Youth activism and community change* (pp. 149–169). New York: Routledge.

Education for Liberation Network. (2009). [Homepage]. Retrieved July 5, 2009, from http://www. edliberation.org

El–Amine, Z., & Glazer, L. (2008). "Evolution" or destruction? A look at Washington, D.C. In L. Dingerson, B. Miner, B. Peterson, & S. Walters (Eds.), *Keeping the promise? The debate over charter schools* (pp. 53–66). Milwaukee, WI: Rethinking Schools.

Finn, C., & Kanstoroom, M. (2008). Foreword. In D. Whitman, *Sweating the small staff: Inner-city youth and the new paternalism* (pp. ix–xvii). Washington, DC: Thomas B. Fordham Institute.

Fireside, H. (2004). *Separate and unequal: Homer Plessy and the Supreme Court decision that legalized racism.* New York: Carroll & Graf.

Fisher, M. T. (2003). Open mics and open minds: Spoken word poetry in African Diaspora Participatory Literacy Communities. *Harvard Educational Review, 73*(3), 362–389.

Fisher, M. T. (2004). The song is unfinished: The new literate and the literary and their institutions. *Written Communication, 21*(3), 290–312.

Fisher, M. T. (2005). From the coffee house to the school house: The promise and potential of spoken word poetry in school contexts. *English Education, 37*(2), 115–131.

Fisher, M. T. (2006). Earning "dual degrees": Black bookstores as alternative knowledge spaces. *Anthropology and Education Quarterly, 37*(1), 83–99.

Fisher, M. T. (2007a). "Every city has soldiers": The role of intergenerational relationships in Participatory Literacy Communities. *Research in the Teaching of English, 42*(2), 139–162.

Fisher, M. T. (2007b). *Writing in rhythm: Spoken word poetry in urban classrooms.* New York: Teachers College Press.

Fisher, M. T. (2008). Catching butterflies. *English Education, 40*(2), 94–100.

Fisher, M. T. (2009). *Black literate lives: Historical and contemporary perspectives.* New York: Routledge.

Fisher, M. T., Purcell, S. S., & May, R. (2009). Process, product, and playmaking. *English Education, 41*(4), 337–355.

Fisher, M. T., & Ubiles, J. R. (2009, April). *Worthy witnessing: Collaborative research in urban classrooms.* Paper presented at the annual meeting of the American Educational Research Association, San Diego, CA.

Forum for Education and Democracy. (2009). [Homepage]. Retrieved August 1, 2009, from http://www. forumforeducation.org

Frederick Douglass Community Coalition. (2008, May 20). Meeting minutes. Retrieved August 1, 2009, from http://www.savefrederickdouglass.com

Free Southern Theater. (1963). *Free Southern Theater collection.* New Orleans, LA: The Amistad Research Center.

Freire, P. (1974). *Pedagogy of the oppressed* (M. B. Ramos, Trans.). New York: Seabury Press. (Original work published 1970)

Freire, P. (1993). *Pedagogy of the oppressed.* New York: Continuum.

Freire, P. (1998). *Pedagogy of freedom: Ethics, democracy, and civic courage.* New York: Rowman & Littlefield.

Freire, P., & Macedo, D. (1987). *Literacy: Reading the word and the world.* Westport, CT: Bergin & Garvey.

Fullilove, M. T. (2005). *Root shock: How tearing up city neighborhoods hurts America, and what we can do about it.* New York: One World Books.

Gandin, L. A. (2006). Creating real alternatives to neoliberal policies in education: The Citizen School Project. In M. W. Apple & K. L. Buras, *The subaltern speak: Curriculum, power, and educational struggles* (pp. 217–241). New York: Routledge.

Gillborn, D. (2008). *Racism and education: Coincidence or conspiracy?* New York: Routledge.

Ginwright, S., Noguera, P., & Cammarota, J. (Eds.). (2006). *Beyond resistance! Youth activism and community change.* New York: Routledge.

Giroux, H. A. (2003). Spectacles of race and pedagogies of denial: Anti-black racist pedagogy under the reign of neoliberalism. *Communication Education, 52*(3), 191–211.

Giroux, H. A. (2006). *Stormy weather: Katrina and the politics of disposability.* Boulder, CO: Paradigm Publishers.

Goodman, A. (2006, June 20). All New Orleans Public School teachers fired: Millions in federal aid channeled to private charter schools. *Democracy Now.* Retrieved November 17, 2009, from http://www.democracynow.org/2006/6/20/all_new_orleans_public_school_teachers

Gould, S. J. (1996). *The mismeasure of man.* New York: W. W. Norton.

Greater New Orleans Community Data Center. (2008, March 28). *Census population estimates 2000–2008 for New Orleans MSA.* Retrieved November 18, 2009, from http://www.gnocdc.org/census_pop_estimates.html

Greenlee, A., Hudspeth, N., Lipman, P., Smith, D. A., & Smith, J. (2008). *Research Paper Series, Paper #1: Examining CPS' plan to close, consolidate, turn-around 18 schools* (Data and Democracy Project: Investing in Neighborhoods). Chicago: Collaborative for Equity and Justice in Education and Nathalie P. Voorhees Center for Neighborhood and Community Improvement, University of Illinois-Chicago.

Grossman, R., & Leroux, C. (2006, January 29). The unmaking of a ghetto. *Chicago Tribune Magazine,* pp. 11–16, 26–29.

Gulson, K., & Parkes, R. (2009). In the shadows of the mission: Education policy, urban space, and the "colonial present" in Sydney. *Race Ethnicity and Education, 12*(3), 267–280.

Hackworth, J. (2007). *The neoliberal city: Governance, ideology, and development in American urbanism.* Ithaca: Cornell University Press.

Hall, G. M. (1992). *Africans in colonial Louisiana: The development of Afro-Creole culture in the eighteenth century.* Baton Rouge: Louisiana State University Press.

Hall, K. L., & Karsten, P. (2008). *Magic mirror: Law in American history* (2nd ed.). New York: Oxford University Press.

Hammer, D. (2008, March 8). HUD rebuked over Katrina response: U.N. panel sees race disparity in housing. *Times–Picayune.* Available: www.nola.com

Harris, C. I. (1995). Whiteness as property. In K. Crenshaw, N. Gotanda, G. Peller, & K. Thomas (Eds.), *Critical race theory: The key writings that formed the movement* (pp. 276–291). New York: New Press.

Harvey, D. (2001). *Spaces of capital: Towards a critical geography.* London: Routledge.

Harvey, D. (2006). *Spaces of global capitalism: Towards a theory of uneven geographical development.* New York: Verso.

Haymes, S. N. (1995). *Race, culture and the city.* Albany: SUNY Press.

Hernstein, R. J., & Murray, C. (1996). *The bell curve: Intelligence and class structure in American life.* New York: Simon & Schuster.

Hill, M. L. (2009). *Beats, rhymes, and classroom life: Hip-hop pedagogy and the politics of identity.* New York: Teachers College Press.

Hill, P. T. (Ed.). (2002). *Choice with equity.* Stanford, CA: Hoover Institution Press.

Hirsch, E. D., Jr. (1987). *Cultural literacy: What every American needs to know.* New York: Vintage Books.

Hirsch, E. D., Jr. (1996). *The schools we need and why we don't have them.* New York: Doubleday.

Hoare, Q., & Nowell Smith, G. (Eds.). (1971). *Selections from the prison notebooks of Antonio Gramsci.* New York: International Publishers.

Hughes, L. (1994). *The collected poems of Langston Hughes* (A. Rampersad & D. Roessel, Eds.). New York: Knopf.

Hursh, D. (2007). Assessing No Child Left Behind and the rise of neoliberalism policies. *American Educational Research Journal, 44*(3), 493–518.

Hurston, Z. N. (2006). *Their eyes were watching god.* New York: HarperCollins. (Original work published 1937)

Imbroscio, D. (2008). "United and actuated by some common impulse of passion": Challenging the dispersal consensus in American housing policy research. *Journal of Urban Affairs, 30*(2), 111–130.

James, C. L. R. (1963). *The black Jacobins: Toussaint L'Ouverture and the San Domingo Revolution.* New York: Vintage Books.

Johnson, K. R. (1998). Race, the immigration laws, and domestic race relations: A "magic mirror" into the heart of darkness. *Indiana Law Journal, 73,* 1111–1159.

Kaplan, E. (2009, September 21). Vigilantes free to roam? *The Nation.* Retrieved November 12, 2009, from http://www.thenation.com/doc/20090921/kaplan

Kelley, R. D. G. (1993). "We are not what we seem": Rethinking black working-class opposition in the Jim Crow South. *Journal of American History, 80*(1), 75–112.

Kelley, R. D. G. (1996). *Race rebels: Culture, politics, and the black working class.* New York: Free Press.

Kelley, R. D. G. (2002). *Freedom dreams: The black radical imagination.* Boston: Beacon Press.

Kilbert, D., & Vallas, P. (2008, August). School facilities master plan for Orleans Parish. New Orleans: New Orleans Public Schools and Recovery School District.

Kincheloe, J. L., Steinberg, S. R., & Gresson, A. D. (1997). *Measured lies: The bell curve examined.* New York: Palgrave Macmillan.

King, J. E. (2006). "If justice is our objective": Diaspora literacy, heritage knowledge, and the praxis of critical studyin' for human freedom. In A. Ball (Ed.). *With more deliberate speed: Achieving equity and excellence in education—Realizing the full potential of* Brown v. Board of Education (pp. 337–360). New York: Ballenger.

King, J. E. (2009). Epilogue: Black education post-Katrina. And "all us we" are not saved. In L. C. Tillman, (Ed.). *The Sage handbook of African American education* (pp. 499–510). Thousand Oaks, CA: Sage.

Kinloch, V. (2007a). The white-ification of the hood: Power, politics, and youth performing narratives of community. *Language Arts Journal, 85*(1), 61–68.

Kinloch, V. (2007b). Youth representations of community, art, and struggle in Harlem. *New Directions for Adult and Continuing Education, 116,* 37–49.

Klein, N. (2008). *The shock doctrine: The rise of disaster capitalism.* New York: Picador.

Kliebard, H. M. (2004). *The struggle for the American curriculum, 1893–1958* (3rd ed.). New York: RoutledgeFalmer.

LaDuke, W. (2002). *The Winona LaDuke reader: A collection of essential writings.* Osceola, WI: Voyageur Press.

Ladson-Billings, G. (2006). From the achievement gap to the education debt: Understanding achievement in U.S. schools. *Educational Researcher, 35*(7), 3–12.

Ladson-Billings, G. (2009). *The dreamkeepers: Successful teachers of African American students* (2nd ed.). San Francisco: Jossey–Bass.

Ladson-Billings, G., & Tate, W. (1995). Toward a critical race theory of education. *Teachers College Record, 97*(1), 47–68.

Lauder, H., & Hughes, D. (1999). *Trading in futures: Why markets in education don't work.* Philadelphia: Open University Press.

Lawrence, C. (1995). The word and the river: Pedagogy as scholarship as struggle. In K. Crenshaw, N. Gotanda, G. Peller, & K. Thomas (Eds.), *Critical race theory: The key writings that formed the movement* (pp. 336–351). New York: New Press.

Lee, S. (2008). The ideological blackening of Hmong American youth. In L. Weis (Ed.), *The way class works: Readings on school, family, and the classroom* (pp. 304–314). New York: Routledge.

Leonardo, Z. (2009). *Race, whiteness, and education*. New York: Routledge.

Leonardo, Z., & Hunter, M. (2009). Race, class, and imagining the urban. In Z. Leonardo, *Race, whiteness, and education* (pp. 143–165). New York: Routledge.

Lieberman, R. C. (2006). "The storm didn't discriminate": Katrina and the politics of color blindness. *Du Bois Review, 3*(1), 7–22.

Lipman, P. (1998). *Race, class and power in school restructuring*. Albany: State University of New York Press.

Lipman, P. (2004). *High-stakes education: Inequailty, globalization, and urban school reform*. New York: RoutledgeFalmer.

Lipman, P. (2008). Mixed-income schools and housing: Advancing the neoliberal urban agenda. *Journal of Education Policy, 23*(2), 119–134.

Lipman, P., & Haines, N. (2007). From education accountability to privatization and African American exclusion—Chicago's "Renaissance 2010." *Educational Policy, 21*(3), 471–502.

Lipsitz, G. (2007). The racialization of space and the spatialization of race: Theorizing the hidden architecture of landscape. *Landscape Journal, 26*(1), 10–23,

Marsh, S. (1999). *God's long summer: Stories of faith and civil rights*. Princeton, NJ: Princeton University Press.

Maurrasse, D. J. (2006). *Listening to Harlem: Gentrification, community, and business*. New York: Routledge.

Maxwell, L. A. (2007, December 13). Foundations donate millions to help New Orleans schools' recovery. *Education Week*. Available from http://www.edweek.org

McElroy, E. J. (2007, January 30). *Statement to friends of public education*. Washington, DC: American Federation of Teachers.

McIntosh, P. (1989). White privilege: Unpacking the invisible knapsack. *Peace and Freedom* (July/August), 10–12.

Michna, C. (2009, September). Stories at the center: Story circles, educational organizing, and the fate of neighborhood public schools in New Orleans. *American Quarterly, 61*(3), 529–555.

Middleton, E. J. (1984). *History of the Louisiana Education Association*. Washington, DC: National Education Association.

Mills, C. (1997). *The racial contract*. Ithaca: Cornell University Press.

Mitchell, M. N. (2000). "A good and delicious country": Free children of color and how they learned to imagine the Atlantic world in nineteenth-century Louisiana. *History of Education Quarterly, 40*(2), 123–144.

Moller, J. (2008, September 24). LaBruzzo sterilization idea at odds with welfare numbers. *Times-Picayune*. Available from http://www.nola.com

Morris, J. E. (1999). A pillar of strength: An African American school's communal bonds with families and community since *Brown. Urban Education, 33*(5), 584–605.

Morrison, T. (1988). *Beloved*. New York: Penguin Books.

Morrison, T. (1993). *The bluest eye*. New York: Random House.

Myers, L. (2007, January 31). *Did Iraq contractor fleece American taxpayers?* Retrieved November 19, 2009, from http://www.msnbc.msn.com/id/16909438

Nagin, C. R., Fielkow, A., & Cummings, S. (2008, February 27). *Reinventing the Crescent: Six miles of riverfront development* [entire plan]. Retrieved December 1, 2009, from http://www.reinventingthecrescent.org/files/documents/Book_Full_001.pdf

Ndimande, B. S. (2009). "It is a catch-22 situation": The challenge of race in post-apartheid South African desegregated schools. *International Critical Childhood Policy Studies, 2*(1), 123–129.

Neo-Griot Productions, & Students at the Center (2002). *Baby love* [Video]. New Orleans, LA: Author.

New Schools for New Orleans. (2007, August). *New Orleans parents' guide to public schools*. New Orleans, LA: Author.

New Schools for New Orleans. (2008). [Homepage]. Retrieved Novmeber 17, 2009, from http://newschoolsforneworleans.org/

Oakes, J. (2005). *Keeping track: How schools structure inequality* (2nd ed.). New Haven, CT: Yale University Press.

Oakes, J., & Wells, A. S. (1997). Detracking: The social construction of ability, cultural politics, and resistance to reform. *Teachers College Record, 98*(3), 482–510.

Oakes, J., Welner, K., Yonezawa, S., & Allen, R. L. (1998). Norms and politics of equity–minded change: Researching the "zone of mediation." In M. Fullan (Ed.), *International handbook of educational change* (pp. 953–975). Norwell, MA: Kluer Academic.

Omi, M., & Winant, H. (1994). *Racial formation in the United States: From the 1960s to the 1990s*. New York: Routledge.

Our Voice Staff and Writers. (1999). November edition. *Our Voice, 2*(1), 1–12.

Pastorek, P. (2008, May 19). Letter to Ze' daLuz. Retrieved July 15, 2008 from http://www.savefrederickdouglass.com

Payne, C., & Knowles, T. (2009). Promise and peril: Charter schools, urban school reform, and the Obama administration. *Harvard Educational Review, 79*(2), 227–239.

Pedroni, T. (2007). *Market movements: African American involvement in school voucher reform*. New York: Routledge.

Perry, T. D. (1975). *History of the American Teachers Association*. Washington, DC: National Education Association.

Power, S., Edwards, A., Whitty, G., & Wigfall, V. (2003). *Education and the middle class*. Buckingham, England: Open University Press.

Randels, J., & Carriere, E. (2002). Lower 9, don't it sound fine? In C. Benson & S. Christian (Eds.), *Writing to make a difference: Classroom projects for community change* (pp. 157–173). New York: Teachers College Press.

Ravitch, D., & Viteritti, J. P. (Eds.). (1997). *New schools for a new century: The redesign of urban education*. New Haven, CT: Yale University Press.

Recovery School District & Orleans Parish School Board. (2008, May). *School facilities master plan for Orleans Parish* [website]. Retrieved May 21, 2008, from www.sfmpop.org

Reinventing the Crescent. (2008a). Economic impact presentation. Retrieved May 1, 2008, http://www.neworiverfront.com/documents/EconomicImpact_002.pdf

Reinventing the Crescent. (2008b). [Homepage]. Retrieved December 1, 2008, http://www.reinventingthecrescent.org/about/

Ritea, S. (2006a, January 18). Nagin's schools panel issues reforms. *Times-Picayune*, p. B1. Available from http://www.nola.com

Ritea, S. (2006b, January 20). Public schools are near capacity. *Times-Picayune*. Available from http://www.nola.com

Ritea, S. (2006c, January 31). Lawsuit precedes news of school openings. *Times-Picayune*, p. B1 Available from http://www.nola.com

Ritea, S. (2006d, August 1). The dream team. *Times-Picayune*, pp. A1, A7. Available from http://www.nola.com

Ritea, S. (2006e, August 12). Public schools compete for kids, *Times-Picayune*, pp. A1, A10. Available from http://www.nola.com

Ritea, S. (2006f, September 6). Five charter school openings delayed. *Times-Picayune*. Available from http://www.nola.com

Ritea, S. (2006g, October 9). Problems plague N.O. school recovery. *Times-Picayune*. Available from http://www.nola.com

Robelen, E. W. (2007, November 12). New teachers are New Orleans norm. *Education Week*. Available from http://www.edweek.org

Robinson, R. (2000). *The debt: What America owes to blacks*. New York: Dutton.

Roediger, D. R. (1991). *The wages of whiteness: Race and the making of the American working class*. New York: Verso.

Salaam, K. Y. (1979). Notes from a Banana Republic. *Black Books Bulletin*, 7(3), 14–17.

Saltman, K. J. (2007a). *Capitalizing on disaster: Taking and breaking public schools*. Boulder, CO: Paradigm.

Saltman, K. J. (Ed.). (2007b). *Schooling and the politics of disaster*. New York: Routledge.

Save Frederick Douglass. (2008). [Homepage]. Retrieved July 15, 2008, from http://www.savefrederickdouglass.com

Scott, J. T. (Ed.). (2005). *School choice and diversity: What the evidence says*. New York: Teachers College Press.

Shor, I., & Freire, P. (1987). *A pedagogy for liberation: Dialogues on transforming education*. South Hadley, MA: Bergin & Garvey.

Shujaa, M. J. (1994). *Too much schooling, too little education*. Trenton, NJ: Africa World Press.

Sirin, S. R. (2005). Socioeconomic status and student achievement: A meta-analytic review of research. *Review of Educational Research*, 75(3), 417–453.

Smith, N. (2002). New globalism, new urbanism: Gentrification as global urban strategy. *Antipode*, 34(3), 427–450.

Solinger, R., Fox, M., & Irani, K. (Eds.). (2008). *Telling stories to change the world: Global voices on the power of narrative to build community and make social justice claims*. New York: Routledge.

Solórzano, D., & Yosso, T. J. (2002). Critical race methodology: Counter-storytelling as an analytical framework for education research. *Qualitative Inquiry*, 8(1), 23–44.

Sothern, B. (2005, January). Left to die: How New Orleans abandoned its citizens in a flooded jail and a flawed system. *The Nation, 282*(1), 18–22.

Stovall, D., & Smith, J. (2008). "Coming home" to new homes and new schools: Critical race theory and the new politics of containment. *Journal of Education Policy, 23*(2), 135–152.

Students at the Center. (1999). *Resistance: Writings in honor of Louisiana's heroic 1811 slave revolt.* New Orleans: Author.

Students at the Center. (2001). *Writing not drowning.* New Orleans: Author.

Students at the Center. (2005). *The long ride: A collection of student writings for the New Orleans Civil Rights Park.* New Orleans: Author.

Students at the Center. (2007a). *Katrina and me.* New Orleans, LA: Author.

Students at the Center. (2007b). *Writing with light* [Video]. New Orleans, LA: Author.

Students at the Center. (2008, April 18). Vallas claims no community involvement. Retrieved November 30, 2009, from http://blogs.edweek.org/edweek/nola_voices/2008/04/

Tate, W. F. (1997). Critical race theory and education: History, theory, and implications. *Review of Research in Education, 22*, 195–247.

Taylor, E., Gillborn, D., & Ladson-Billings, G. (Eds.). (2009). *Foundations of critical race theory in education.* New York: Routledge.

Teachers 4 Social Justice. (2009). [Homepage]. Retrieved July 5, 2009, from http://t4sj.org/templates/system/default.asp?id=39669

Thompson, A. C. (2009, January 5). Katrina's hidden race war. The Nation. Retrieved November 30, 2009, from http://www.thenation.com/doc/20090105/thompson

Thrasher, A. (1995). *On to New Orleans: Louisiana's heroic 1811 slave revolt.* Racine, WI: Ludlow Press.

Times–Picayune. (2007a, December 13). Protesters block HUD offices downtown. *Times-Picayune.* Available from http://www.nola.com

Times–Picayune. (2007b, December 19). Live updates on demolition vote from council chambers. *Times-Picayune.* Available from http://www.nola.com

Times–Picayune. (2008, February 28). Read Thursday's statement by UN human rights officials. *Times-Picayune.* Available: www.nola.com

Tuzzolo, E., & Hewitt, D. T. (2007). Rebuilding inequity: The re-emergence of the school-to-prison pipeline in New Orleans. *The High School Journal, 90*(2), 59–68.

United Teachers of New Orleans, Louisiana Federation of Teachers, & American Federation of Teachers. (2006, November). *"National model" or flawed approach?: The post-Katrina New Orleans Public Schools.* New Orleans, LA: Author.

United Teachers of New Orleans, Louisiana Federation of Teachers, & American Federation of Teachers. (2007a, June). *No experience necessary: How the New Orleans school takeover experiment devalues experienced teachers.* New Orleans, LA: Author.

United Teachers of New Orleans, Louisiana Federation of Teachers, & American Federation of Teachers. (2007b, October). *Reading, writing, and reality check: An early assessment of student achievement in post-Katrina New Orleans.* New Orleans, LA: Author.

US Human Rights Network. (2006, July). *Hurricane Katrina and violations of International Covenant on Civil and Political Rights Article 6 (right to life) and Article 26 (prohibition against discrimination): A response to the Third Periodic Report of the United States of America.* Atlanta, GA: Author.

US Human Rights Network. (n.d.). *United Nations Guiding Principles on Internal Displacement.* Atlanta, GA: Author.

Valenzuela, A. (Ed.). (2005). *Leaving children behind: How "Texas style" accountability fails Latino youth.* New York: State University of New York Press.

Vallas, P. G. (2008, April 14). *Recovery school district status report.* New Orleans, LA: Recovery School District.

Walker, A. (2003). *In search of our mothers' gardens: Womanist prose.* New York: Houghton Mifflin Harcourt. (Original work published 1984)

Walker, V. S. (1996). *Their highest potential.* Chapel Hill: University of North Carolina Press.

Walker, V. S. (2000). Valued segregated schools in the south, 1935–1969: A review of common themes and characteristics. *Review of Educational Research, 70*(3), 253–285.

Walker, V. S. (2001). African American teachers in segregated schools in the south, 1940–1969. *American Educational Research Journal, 38*(4), 751–780.

Walker, V. S. (2005). Organized resistance and black educator's quest for school equality. *Teachers College Record, 107*(3), 355–388.

Walker, V. S. (2009a). Second-class integration: A historical perspective for a contemporary agenda. *Harvard Educational Review, 79*(2), 269–284.

Walker, V. S. (2009b). *Hello professor: A black principal and professional leadership in the segregated south.* Chapel Hill: University of North Carolina Press.

Walker, V. S. (in preparation). *The death of memory: Black educators, their organizations, and the quest for justice.* Division of Educational Studies, Emory University.

Walker, V. S., & Tompkins, R. H. (2004). Caring in the past: The case of a southern segregated African American school. In V. S. Walker & J. R. Snarey (Eds.), *Race-ing moral formation: African American perspectives on care and justice* (pp. 72–92). New York: Teachers College Press.

Waller, M. (2008, September 23). LaBruzzo considering plan to pay poor women $1,000 to have tubes tied. *Times-Picayune.* Available: www.nola.com

Walton, T., & Cast. (1999). 1811 slave revolt performance working script. In Students at the Center, *Resistance: Writings in honor of Louisiana's heroic 1811 slave revolt* (pp. 43–50). New Orleans, LA: Students at the Center.

Weaving the Web Collaborators. (2003, October 1). *Weaving the web of community* [project report]. New Orleans, LA: Author.

Weber, R. (2002). Extracting value from the city: Neoliberalism and urban redevelopment. *Antipode, 34*(3), 519–540.

Welfare Warriors. (2007, March). *New Orleans: 18 months after Katrina.* Retrieved November 18, 2009, from http://www.welfarewarriors.org/mwv_archive/w07/neworleansposter.pdf

Wells, A. S. (2002). *Where charter school policy fails: The problems of accountability and equity.* New York: Teachers College Press.

Wells-Barnett, I. B. (2009). *The red record.* Gloucester: Dodo Press. (Original work published 1895)

Whitman, D. (2008). *Sweating the small stuff: Inner-city schools and the new paternalism*. Washington, DC: Thomas B. Fordham Institute.

Wilson, D. (2007). *Cities and race: America's new black ghetto*. New York: Routledge.

Wilson, D., Wouters, J., & Grammenos, D. (2004). Successful protect-community discourse: Spatiality and politics in Chicago's Pilsen neighborhood. *Environment and Planning, 36*(7), 1173–1190.

Wilson, J. Q. (1996). The rediscovery of character: Private virtue and public policy. In M. Gerson (Ed.), *The essential neoconservative reader* (pp. 291–304). New York: Addison–Wesley.

Wing, A. K. (2006). From wrongs to rights: Hurricane Katrina from a global perspective. In D. D. Troutt (Ed.), *After the storm: Black intellectuals explore the meaning of Hurricane Katrina* (pp. 127–145). New York: New Press.

Woodson, C. G. (2000). *The mis-education of the Negro*. Chicago, Illinois: African American Images. (Original work published 1933)

Wynter, S. (2006). On how we mistook the map for the territory and re-imprisoned ourselves in our unbearable wrongness of being, of désêtre. In L. Gordon & J. A. Gordon (Eds.), *Not only the master's tools: African-American studies in theory and practice* (pp. 107–169). Boulder, CO: Paradigm.

Yang, K. W., & Duncan-Andrade, J. (2005). Doc ur block. *Education for Liberation Network*. Retrieved June 26, 2009, from www.edliberation.org/resources/records/doc-ur-block

Yosso, T. J. (2006). *Critical race counterstories along the Chicana/Chicano educational pipeline*. New York: Routledge.

Zerrien-Lee, A. (2009, August 18). "Who is behind the privatization of public education?" Retrieved November 18, 2009, from http://www.laprogressive.com/2009/08/18/who-is-behind-the-privatization-of-public-education/

About the Contributors

Michael W. Apple is John Bascom Professor of Curriculum and Instruction and Educational Policy Studies at the University of Wisconsin–Madison and Professor of Educational Policy Studies at the Institute of Education, University of London. He is the author of numerous best-selling books, including *Ideology and Curriculum, Official Knowledge,* and *Educating the "Right" Way.*

Wayne Au is an assistant professor in the Department of Secondary Education, California State University–Fullerton and editor for the progressive education journal *Rethinking Schools*. He is the author of *Unequal by Design: High-Stakes Testing and the Standardization of Inequality* and editor of *Rethinking Multicultural Education: Teaching for Racial and Cultural Justice.*

Kristen L. Buras was born and raised in New Orleans, and is assistant professor of multicultural urban education and reform in the Division of Educational Studies at Emory University. She is coeditor of *The Subaltern Speak* and author of *Rightist Multiculturalism*. Her forthcoming book is *Schooling, Race, and Urban Space: Where the Market Meets Grassroots Resistance.* She serves on the editorial board of *International Studies in Sociology of Education.*

Christopher Burton is a writer, musician, actor, activist, and teacher. He graduated from Frederick Douglass High School and has continued his work with Students at the Center as a staff member. He attends the University of New Orleans, where he is majoring in secondary education with a minor in music. He plans to teach English and social studies in New Orleans.

Deborah Carey attended Frederick Douglass High School and is majoring in political science at Dillard University. Her involvement with Students at the Center inspired activism in New Orleans and internationally, including an internship for 10,000 Girls, a young women's cooperative in Senegal, West Africa. She plans to teach English or pursue international social justice work.

Bruce Coleman attended Frederick Douglass High School and is a graduate of Students at the Center in New Orleans. He was also a writer, staff member, and editor for the teen newspaper *Our Voice*. Coleman served in the U.S. military and is a disabled veteran living in Houston. His passions include writing poetry, and he aspires to publish a book of his writings.

Erica DeCuir graduated from McDonogh #35 High School in New Orleans and is a former student and teacher with Students at the Center. She holds a master's degree in social studies education from Columbia University and is an Urban Graduate Research Fellow completing her doctorate in the College of Education at Georgia State University.

Adrienne D. Dixson is an associate professor in the School of Teaching and Learning at The Ohio State University, where she teaches courses in critical race theory and urban education. Her co-edited book *Critical Race Theory in Education* received the 2006 Critics Choice Award from AERA. In 2009 Dixson was granted an Early Career Research Award from AERA.

Maisha T. Fisher is an associate professor of language, literacy, and culture in the Division of Educational Studies at Emory University. She is the author of *Writing in Rhythm: Spoken Word Poetry in Urban Classrooms* and *Black Literate Lives: Historical and Contemporary Perspectives*. Her recent research examines girls in the school-to-prison pipeline. Fisher received an Early Career Research Award from AERA in 2008.

Tyeasha Green attended Frederick Douglass High School in New Orleans and is thankful that Students at the Center fostered her talent for writing. She is majoring in nursing at Southern University of New Orleans. Upon graduation, her plan is to become a nurse and give back to the community that made her who she is today.

Maria Hernandez has worked with Students at the Center since 2003, when she was a tenth-grade student at Frederick Douglass High School. She traveled with her mother from Tulsa, Oklahoma, in October 2005 to Clemson, South Carolina, to participate in the first SAC strategic planning session after Katrina. Her family moved back to New Orleans in May 2009.

Jenna Dominique Hill graduated as valedictorian from Eleanor Mc-Main Secondary School in New Orleans. She is a biology premed student at Xavier University of Louisiana. She plans to attend medical school and become a doctor.

Katrena Jackson-Ndang is a veteran educator in New Orleans, where she taught at Alfred Lawless High School, worked with Students at the Center at Eleanor McMain Secondary School, and served as executive board member of United Teachers of New Orleans and vice president of Louisiana Federation of Teachers. She is also a member of the Frederick Douglass Community Coalition.

Ashley Jones is a filmmaker and a senior member of Students at the Center. She entered the program during her sophomore year at McDonogh #35 High School and continued throughout her undergraduate years. She holds a master's degree from Bread Loaf Graduate School of English and is working on a master's degree in Film and English at Savannah College of Art and Design. She continues to work closely with SAC.

Robin D. G. Kelley is a professor of American studies and ethnicity at the University of Southern California. He is the author of the prize-winning books *Hammer and Hoe: Alabama Communists During the Great Depression; Race Rebels: Culture, Politics, and the Black Working Class; Yo' Mama's Dis-Funktional!: Fighting the Culture Wars in Urban America*; and *Freedom Dreams: The Black Radical Imagination*.

Joyce E. King holds the Benjamin E. Mays Chair of Urban Teaching, Learning, and Leadership in the College of Education at Georgia State University. Her publications include *Black Education: A Transformative Research and Action Agenda for the New Century* and *Preparing Teachers for Diversity*. She served as Associate Vice Chancellor for Academic Affairs and Diversity Programs at the University of New Orleans from 1994 to 1998.

Zeus Leonardo is an associate professor of education at the University of California–Berkeley. He is the author of *Ideology, Discourse, and School Reform* as well as *Race, Whiteness, and Education*. He is editor of *Critical Pedagogy and Race* and coeditor of *Charting New Terrains of Chicano(a)/Latino(a) Education*. He is currently working on the *Handbook of Cultural Politics and Education*.

Pauline Lipman is a professor of educational policy studies at the University of Illinois–Chicago. Her research focuses on race and class inequality, globalization, and intersections of education, housing, and urban development. Her forthcoming book is *The New Political Economy of Urban Education: Neoliberalism, Race, and the Right to the City*. She is active in social movements, including Chicago Teachers for Social Justice.

Jim Randels is a graduate of and parent and teacher in New Orleans Public Schools. He taught at Frederick Douglass High School before and after the state takeover and currently teaches at McMain and McDonogh #35 High Schools. He is the executive vice president of United Teachers of New Orleans (AFT Local 527) and has authored over $5 million in grants to assist public education in New Orleans.

Kalamu ya Salaam is a writer and producer who co-directs Students at the Center, including its digital media work through Neo-Griot Productions. He is editor of *360 Degrees: A Revolution of Black Poets* and author of *The Magic of JuJu: An Appreciation of the Black Arts Movement*. Salaam founded the NOMMO Literary Society and has received awards nationally and internationally for his poetry, playwriting, and radio production.

Vinnessia Shelbia attended Frederick Douglass High School and is a graduate of Students at the Center. She is currently a full-time student at Delgado Community College in New Orleans, where she is majoring in nursing.

Damien Theodore graduated from Frederick Douglass High School. He is majoring in elementary education and serves as student government senator for the College of Education and Human Development, University of New Orleans. He is president of Alpha Phi Alpha fraternity, vice president of the Progressive Black Student Union, and committee member of Student Persistence and Recovery Initiatives.

Kirsten Theodore participated in Students at the Center programs from her elementary school years through her graduation from Frederick Douglass High School in 2007. She currently attends college in Pittsburgh, Pennsylvania and lives with her older sister, also a Douglass graduate and former SAC member.

Gabrielle Turner graduated from McDonogh #35 High School, earned a degree in communications arts from the University of New Orleans, and completed a master of arts in teaching at Emory University. She has served as lead literacy mentor for numerous programs and produced nationally aired radio commentaries and video documentaries. She teaches English language arts to seventh graders in New Orleans.

Vanessa Siddle Walker is an educational historian and professor in the Division of Educational Studies at Emory University. Her research explores the segregated schooling of black children in the South, including school climates and black teacher advocacy. She has received numerous awards, including the AERA Early Career Award and the prestigious Grawemeyer Prize for Education for *Their Highest Potential*.

Demetria White graduated from Eleanor McMain Secondary School in 2007. She works part-time for Students at the Center as a resource teacher in English and writing classes at Sarah T. Reed High School. She is a pharmacy major and cheerleader at Xavier University in New Orleans.

Index